Additional

"There are many books on preaching John, but Lewis offers something different: John read thoroughly and intentionally through the lens of the preacher. The goal of this approach is not simply to improve sermons on John, but rather to allow a guided encounter with the theological world of the Gospel of John to reshape how we understand the very work of preaching."

Gail R. O'Day
Wake Forest University School of Divinity

"Growing up as a young fundamentalist, I memorized a lot of verses from the Gospel of John. And I was sure I knew what those verses meant. I got older and began to question a lot of what I had been taught, especially when I began to preach from John and was forced to read the text—the whole text—closely. What I needed back then was exactly what Karoline Lewis has provided in her new commentary: an honest, intelligent engagement with the Fourth Gospel. If you want commentary on others' commentary on John, go elsewhere. But if you want thoughtful, thorough, and practical help in grappling with the content and meaning of John's gospel for people today, be sure this commentary is open on your desk. I learned a lot and had several long-standing questions answered."

Brian D. McLaren
Author and Speaker

JOHN

JOHN

FORTRESS BIBLICAL
PREACHING COMMENTARIES

KAROLINE M. LEWIS

Fortress Press
Minneapolis

JOHN

Fortress Biblical Preaching Commentaries

Cover design: Laurie Ingram

Library of Congress Cataloging-in-Publication Data

Print ISBN: 978-0-8006-9924-6

eBook ISBN: 978-1-4514-3095-0

The paper used in this publication meets the minimum requirements of American National Standard for Information Sciences — Permanence of Paper for Printed Library Materials, ANSI Z329.48-1984.

Manufactured in the U.S.A.

This book was produced using PressBooks.com, and PDF rendering was done by PrinceXML.

CONTENTS

Series Foreword

A preacher who seeks to be creative, exegetically up to date, hermeneutically alert, theologically responsible, and in-touch with the moment is always on the hunt for fresh resources. Traditional books on preaching a book of the Bible often look at broad themes of the text with little explicit advice about preaching individual passages. Lectionary resources often offer exegetical and homiletical insights about a pericope with little attention given to broader themes and structures of the book from which the lection is taken. *Fortress Biblical Preaching Commentaries* provide the preacher with resources that draw together the strengths of these two approaches into a single text aid, useful for the moment of preparation halfway between full scale exegesis and a finished sermon.

The authors of this series are biblical scholars who offer expositions of the text rooted in detailed study and expressed in straightforward, readable ways. The commentators take a practical approach by identifying (1) what the text invited people in the ancient world to believe about God and the world and (2) what the text encouraged people to do in response. Along the way, the interpreters make use of such things as historical and cultural reconstruction, literary and rhetorical analysis, word studies, and other methods that help us recover how a text was intended to function in antiquity. At the same time, the commentaries offer help in moving from then to now, from what a text meant (in the past) to what a text means (in the present), by helping a minister identify issues, raise questions, and pose possibilities for preaching while stopping short of placing a complete sermon in the preacher's hands. The preacher, then, should be in a position to set in motion a conversation with the text (and other voices from the past and present) to help the congregation figure out what we today can believe and do.

The commentators in this series seek to help preachers and students make connections between the various lections from a given book throughout the lectionary cycle and liturgical year in their sermons and studies. Readers, preachers, and their parishioners will have a deeper appreciation of the book's unique interpretation of the Christ event and how that influences their approach to living the Christian faith in today's world. The most life-giving preaching is nearly always local in character with a minister rooted in a particular congregation, culture, and context encouraging listeners to think specifically about how the text might relate to the life of the congregation and to the surrounding community and world. *Fortress Biblical Preaching Commentaries* are set forth in the hope that each volume will be a provocative voice in such conversations.

Acknowledgements

My initial gratitude for this invitation to contribute to the *Fortress Biblical Preaching Commentary Series* goes to David Lott, with whom conversations about this book first began. Having worked with him as my editor for New Proclamation, I knew immediately that I wanted to be a part of any project he had in mind.

I am grateful to Fortress Press for the past projects of which I have been honored to be a part, including *New Proclamation* and the *Lutheran Study Bible*. Fortress Press continues to create meaningful resources for the church, to imagine inventive possibilities for engaging God's people with God's word, and to invest in new voices for biblical scholarship and preaching. In particular, I want to thank Will Bergkamp for the additional conversations about the vision of this series and Lisa Gruenisen for her individual tending and editing of my volume on John.

In the perplexing circumstances and uncertain future of theological education, Luther Seminary granted me a sabbatical to work on this project. I am very aware of the monies, time, and commitment that such an award implies. I could not have completed this book without Luther's decision to invest in the academic future of its faculty. For this space and occasion for deliberate focus, creativity, and scholarship I am extraordinarily grateful.

I am indebted to my teachers Craig Koester and Robert Kysar for instilling an initial interest in this peculiar Gospel, seemingly always outside the realm of normalcy and expectancy, but yet so critical to the theological imagination of those listening to our sermons. For six years, five times a year, Gracia Grindal and I used John 18:1-13a as our primary text for inviting our students into the rhetorical impact of the Bible for preaching, and each time we were stunned that we heard something new. Teaching with her helped me realize the power and presence of the Word made flesh. Where my love of John became exceedingly clear was in my studies with and advising from Gail O'Day. Her interpretation of John inspired me, moved me, changed me, and made me realize that the incarnation is everything. This is no small issue, because the incarnation is central for preaching and for how we are called to be in God's world.

No writing project results or should develop on its own. Anyone who has heard me talk about, teach, or preach John over the last six years will hear themselves in this commentary, at least I hope so. My conversation partners for this project are not only scholars but also colleagues, students, pastors, and the people in the pews. I have witnessed to John's story of Jesus time and time again and in the process been witnessed to with remarkable insights about this most amazing story. From all of you I continue to learn about John's unique testimony. Thank you.

Thank you to my husband, Mark Orvick, who picks up the pieces at home when I go deep underground in my writing and maintains a sense of peace in the midst of what should be chaos. And finally, thank you to my sons, Sig and Stellan, whose love for me and depth of understanding of this crazy mother of theirs never ceases to amaze me, "You need to work on your book, mommy." From them I have experienced the abundant love to which the Fourth Gospel testifies. Their love and the joy beyond measure that they give me are indeed grace upon grace. To them I dedicate this book.

Preface

For parishioners and preachers to have a deeper appreciation of John's unique interpretation of the Christ-event and how that influences their approach to living the Christian faith in today's world is the primary goal of this volume on preaching John. Little matters in what follows if those who peruse these pages will not discover anew how John's story of Jesus shapes and gives worth to being a disciple for the sake of the world God loves. In other words, the intent of this commentary is to invite the reader into an encounter with the Jesus of John's Gospel that might result in seeking out ways to witness to how an experience of the Jesus of John actually matters. Or it may very well be that, after reading this book, one will find encouragement in believing, even a renewed sense of what it means to follow Jesus. To paraphrase John 20:31, the following words are written so that you may be sustained and nurtured in your faith that Jesus is the Messiah, the Son of God, and that through believing you may have abundant life now and forever in his name.

With the above commitment in mind, my approach with this commentary was to replicate that which I hope might happen in the reading of both this book and the Gospel of John. The reader will not find in the pages that follow multiple references to various scholars weighing in on a passage. Rather, I took seriously the encounter with the text, with only the text (and the Greek text) in front of me. Yes, I had years of research, knowledge, and study of the Gospel of John to accompany me in my reading and insights. This academic background is certainly brought to bear in the following discussion and is that which is expected in a commentary on a biblical book for preaching. At the same time, careful, attentive, and creative reading of texts yields multiple insights for many, regardless of expertise. This commentary is by no means an exhaustive treatment of the Gospel of John. To assert such a claim would be an affront to its very core that, in Jesus, God embodies abundant life. This is a commentary for this time and place and purpose, what struck me when encountering the text and being encountered by it and all for the sake of preaching its timely witness into communities of faith.

As a result, my wish is that the reader will sense an invitation to play, creativity, and imagination when it comes to interpreting biblical texts, and this Gospel story, for the pulpit and pew. Too much of our preaching is beholden to denominational commitments and obliged to theological constraints that preference dogma and getting the right answer over an event of the Word. There is no other Gospel than John that most desires for its readers only to abide in its testimony about Jesus.

The commentary takes seriously that which is outlined in the Introduction and the Prologue, particularly the central themes at stake for the Fourth Gospel. The essential exegetical approach of this commentary is to have these themes ever present and to listen for them in every text. If there is a key to preaching John, the Prologue is it. It should be the preacher's fallback when understanding and interpreting the last Gospel seems elusive. The Prologue is the discourse on the Gospel. It is the interpretation of the primary sign, the incarnation, lest we misunderstand the revelation of God in Jesus articulated in the rest of the chapters.

One of the significant contributions of this volume on John and the series as a whole is its commitment to commentary on the entirety of the text and not only those pericopes assigned by the lectionary. This has a practical implication in that preachers are afforded trusted exegesis on the four Gospels, Acts, and the letters of Paul for teaching and preaching. More important, however, is a homiletical implication, that preaching any part demands an awareness of the whole, regardless of the biblical writing. There are parts of John, and therefore parts of this commentary, that would be easily avoided so as to read only the discussions on lectionary texts. This series, and this commentary, insists that to do so is at the peril of the preacher and faithful preaching of the biblical writing in question.

One final assumption will help readers traverse the logic of this commentary. My exegesis and interpretive suggestions are grounded in taking seriously the nature of biblical texts—that they are written for the ear and not for the eye. They are encapsulated for memory but are written to make their stories memorable. The Gospel of John is not unique in this regard. This is the nature of biblical texts, which sought to capture in writing an oral, communal, and situational experience for the sake of encouragement and conversion. The mutually interpretive relationships between passages in the Gospel of John are not my musings, but John's appeal that we make these connections. For the Fourth Evangelist, this has a twofold function. First, it is the necessary and desired result of oral communication, which is based on resonance and allusion. No part can be interpreted, understood, or preached in isolation. Second, it seeks to replicate an experience of abiding in the Word. Little outside this Gospel is necessary to understand who Jesus is and what God intends in the incarnation. While external references are advantageous at times, the primary referent for making sense of any portion of this Gospel is the Gospel itself.

This second function is profoundly theological and is almost worth suggesting a third function for John's narrative impulse. The self-referential quality of the Fourth Gospel reiterates its primary theological wish and claim, that to abide in the Word means being in relationship with the Word. Beyond having an actual encounter with Jesus, the Gospel of John assumes that its witness is your next best bet. In other words, once you enter into this Gospel, because this is about our God who entered into our humanity, it will never want to let you go. The reader of this commentary might anticipate and be prepared for this kind of relationship with what seems only to be words on a page. Not so when it comes to John. After all, this is about the Word made flesh.

Index of Passages from the Book of John in the Revised Common Lectionary

*[ ] indicates Roman Catholic and Anglican Church Lectionary

12:1–11	Holy Monday: A, B, C	164
12:12–16 (Alt, palms)	Palm/Passion Sunday: B	168
12:20–33	Lent 5: B	169
12:20–36	Holy Tuesday: A, B, C	169
13:1–17, 31b–35	Holy Thursday: A, B, C	177
13:21–32	Holy Wednesday: A, B, C	181
13:31–35	Easter 5: C	183
14:1–14	Easter 5: A	186
14:8–17, (25–27)	Pentecost: C	188
14:15–21	Easter 6: A	190
14:23–29 (Alt.)	Easter 6: C	194
15:1–8	Easter 5: B	196
15:9–17	Easter 6: B	198
15:26–27; 16:4b–15	Pentecost: B	201
16:12–15	Trinity Sunday: C	204
17:1–11	Easter 7: A	208
17:6–19	Easter 7: B	210
17:20–26	Easter 7: C	212
18:1–19:42	Good Friday: A, B, C	215
18:33–37	Reign of Christ [34]: B	224
19:38–42 (Alt.)	Holy Saturday: A, B, C	231
20:1–18 (Alt.)	Easter Sunday: A, B, C	237
20:19–23 (Alt.)	Pentecost: A	243
20:19–31	Easter 2: A, B, C	243
21:1–19	Easter 3: C	254

Introduction

From the beginning of biblical interpretation and homiletical thought, the Gospel of John has had its share of troubles when it comes to preaching. The perceived challenges in the interpretation of John and a misunderstanding of its homiletical inclinations are due to a number of factors that are helpful to discuss at the front end of this commentary. One of the goals of this commentary will be to offer a counterproposal to the perception of the Fourth Gospel as difficult to preach. It actually longs to be preached and has a fervent conversional urge.

Several issues have contributed to the aversions to preaching the Fourth Gospel, but perhaps the primary fault, from which all others eventually stem, lies at the feet of Clement of Alexandria, "Last of all John, perceiving that the external facts had been made plain in the gospel, being urged by his friends and inspired by the Spirit, composed a spiritual gospel" (Eusebius *Ecclesiastical History* 6.14.7). John as the "spiritual" Gospel firmly established its fourth-tier status, a worthy supplement to the Synoptic Gospels but not at the same level of historicity. Much of scholarship on John over the past two thousand years has been determined by this description, including authorship, dating, and theology. As a result, long before any lectionary ever existed, John was seen as ancillary, in part because spiritual meant less historical. There are two problems with this supposition. First, a number of "facts" related to the historical Jesus are mined from the Fourth Gospel and not the Synoptic Gospels. For example, the supposition that Jesus' ministry was three years in length is made possible by John, whose Jesus travels to Jerusalem for Passover three times. There is a selective nature by which John is used to answer historical questions about Jesus' ministry. Second, this conjecture then understands the Synoptics as primarily histories, which they are not. They are no more interested in a historical account of Jesus than John is committed to a spiritual description of Jesus. The Gospels are gospels, the good news of Jesus Christ. When Mark, usually understood to be the first Gospel written, begins his story of Jesus, it is not by describing his account as a history or even biography of Jesus, both of which were available genres in Greco-Roman literature in the first century, but rather, "the beginning of the good news of Jesus Christ (Mark 1:1). Mark draws on what was already good news, the presence of God. The prophet Isaiah (40:9-11; 52:7-10) provides the language of *euangelion*. These passages are in Second Isaiah, prophecy directed to the exiled Israelites. Despite all evidence

1

to the contrary, God is indeed present. The sentinel returns from the front with the good news that God reigns, God is here. For a Jewish existence after the destruction of Jerusalem and the temple (70 c.e.) this theological crisis resurfaces: where is God? Mark's answer is a most surprising location, in the suffering and death of Jesus on the cross. The Gospels are witnesses to the promise of God's presence among God's people, now in the person and ministry of Jesus Christ.

This "less historical" slant toward the Fourth Gospel has also led to the argument in scholarship for its later dating. That is, a more spiritual Gospel implies a higher christological presentation, which then necessitates time to develop. Therefore, John must have been written considerably later than the Synoptic Gospels; perhaps it is even a second-century document. There are two problems with this assertion. First, the discovery of the Dead Sea Scrolls suggests that the writers of the Gospels had multiple sources at their disposal for constructing their narratives. In other words, John's sources could easily have been contemporaneous with the sources the Synoptic Gospels had in front of them. Moreover, the Dead Sea Scrolls determined that there was not just one Judaism but multiple "Judaisms" in the first century. This claim suggests not only that the Jesus movement had more success as a result, but that there was no uniform understanding of Judaism, no absolute representative Judaism. The second problem with the later dating of John and a supposed "high" Christology is that it has perpetuated a distant Jesus. A high Christology is equated with a diffident, mystical Jesus, one far less "humanlike" than what we find in Matthew, Mark, and Luke. There are two related issues that accompany this perception. First, the attraction of John to heterodox movements such as Gnosticism and Docetism due to John's christological portrait has made John suspect. If it appeals to heretics, this cannot be good. The view of Jesus as barely human has made the Jesus of John virtually incomprehensible, unapproachable, unavoidably distant. The second issue is related to the first. As a result of this opinion of John's Jesus, interpretation has ignored where and how the Fourth Gospel actually offers an opposite view of Jesus, a very human Jesus. John's Jesus is not a faraway, barely graspable Messiah, but a relational, deeply intimate Christ. After all, this is the story of the incarnation. It is surprising how the principal promise of the Fourth Gospel as the Word made flesh has been overshadowed by one trajectory in its interpretation thereby marginalizing its primary theological claim.

John's dissimilarity with the Synoptic Gospels, rather than perceived as a gift to discussions on and about Christology, has made it too different to know what or how to preach. The early church's process of canonization gives evidence of and witness to our current challenges when it comes to preaching the four Gospels. Before any official canonical list of the New Testament, there were multiple canonical lists proposed, some with only one Gospel, even a harmonization of all four. In the end, the criterion of universality won out. That is, the church saw that four were better than one and that difference was better than uniformity. Yet the advent of biblical scholarship, the historical-critical method, and the arguments for the inerrancy of Scripture resulted in erasing the particularities of the Gospels for the sake of historicity, orthodoxy, and denominationalism even among the Synoptic Gospels. The development of biblical scholarship in the twentieth century gave rise to concerns about particular hermeneutical goals and methods. While biblical interpretation has progressed from an emphasis on the discovery of meaning behind the text to attention to how the text works and how the text means, the dominant principle of hermeneutics operative in current liturgical and homiletical practices is still a latent pledge to doctrine, and doctrine is hard to argue in the midst of difference.

The principal witness to an upholding of accepted dogma, for good or for ill, is the Revised Common Lectionary itself. John does not have its own year, for all of the reasons stated above. Inspiration for the principal tenets of the church comes primarily from the Synoptic Gospels. At the same time, even a brief glance at the use of the Fourth Gospel in the Revised Common Lectionary reveals a reliance on John for some of the more significant beliefs of the Christian faith, particularly the passion and resurrection of Christ. An additional difficulty when it comes to preaching John is its unique and massive stories. A pressing challenge in preaching John is that so much of its material is distinctive to its Gospel. As a result, the preacher has less exposure to these texts than those encountered in Matthew, Mark, and Luke. Less exposure means less comfort, familiarity, and assurance. The neglect of John in the pulpit is as much an issue from preachers whose own insecurities lead to a dissociation and dislike of certain texts. In other words, to what extent should preachers admit their own complicity in John's current homiletical state? What we do not know, we are reluctant to preach. The same can be said for the dearth of preaching on the Old Testament lessons.

Admittedly, John's inimitable stories are also lengthy sections of text. John does not lend itself well to pericope preaching. That alone should tell us something about our homiletical inclinations. If we perceive small texts to be self-contained sermons in and of themselves that reveals our own propensity to disavow a lesson's literary context. The Fourth Gospel's sizeable stories are not a lectionary nuisance but a theological commitment. There is something being said theologically if who Jesus is cannot be grasped in brief and manageable passages. The preacher is compelled to engage not only what is being said but to imagine that what a text means has something to do with its literary and narrative features.

DATE, AUDIENCE, AND AUTHORSHIP

One of the most prevalent assumptions about the Fourth Gospel is that because of its so-called high Christology, it should be dated later than its counterparts, sometimes even into the beginning of the second century. John's alternative portrait of Jesus is a perspective that needed time to develop. Yet there is no reason to date John any later than, say, Matthew or Luke (if we assume they both had Mark as a source), anywhere between 75 and 90. It is also worthwhile to note the correlate assumption about the Synoptic Gospels in this argument. To argue that John's Gospel represents a particularly high Christology is equally reductionistic of the Synoptic Gospels. It also raises the question, what do we mean by "high" Christology, and how and why does time determine it? Moreover, the Synoptic Gospels also have their own operative Christologies and should not be relegated to a lower status, whatever that might mean. John's christological portrait is not high; it is just different. This commentary will assume this as difference only, not higher development, and will pay attention to the differences. Thus, there will be nominal comparison of John to the Synoptics, not for the sake of John's betterment but to underscore the uniqueness of each of the Gospel stories. This is again for the sake of preaching. We are better biblical preachers when we listen carefully and attentively to the particularities of the entirety of the biblical witness. When we neglect these nuances, we risk overlooking where preaching really happens, in the various shades and tones of the portrait being presented.

Whether John had the Synoptic Gospels as sources for his writing has also been a matter of significant debate, with little consensus among scholars. That John relied on the Synoptics is not necessarily an advantageous determination when it comes to preaching, but a comparison of the four remains helpful. That is, like each of the other Gospels, John has his own interpretation of the Jesus-event to which he is committed and that he wishes to convey. Much of the material in John has no parallels in the other three, so clearly John was working with either written or oral sources to which he was privy, but the material was selected because the stories spoke to a particular situation. For the preacher, the more important question is not where these stories came from but how they distinctively represent, in a different voice, a portrait of Jesus and how they illustrate larger theological themes of this Gospel.

A good deal of Gospel scholarship over the years has directed attention to the alleged audiences of each book. The best we can do in these circumstances is conjecture based on what we have in front of us. In other words, we are getting only one side of the story. How each author organizes the stories, themes, theology, and interpretation of Jesus is for the sake of individual struggle but also for those who would hear it. As a result, questions of authorship are directly connected to the perceived audience. Our conclusions about audience are typically broad generalizations. Matthew seems to be writing to a Jewish audience; Luke, to a gentile audience; Mark—who really knows? Then we get John. But the question of audience for the Gospel of John cannot be relegated to some sweeping or unsupported statements. The reason for this concern is because John's Gospel has repeatedly justified anti-Semitic beliefs and behavior due to Jesus' strong words to the "Jews" throughout the narrative.

While we will take up these issues more explicitly in the discussion of chapters 7–8 below, it is important to note here several basic problems with this assumption. First, Jesus was a Jew, the audience of the Gospel are Jews. Jesus is not implicating himself or his own people. Second, there has been much debate over how to translate *hoi ioudaioi* in John, as Jews or Jewish leaders. The general consensus at the writing of this book is that, for the most part, when Jesus references or speaks to "the Jews," the intended referent is the Jewish leaders. Jesus, a perceived authority in Jewish law and Scripture, is essentially in dialogue with his colleagues. Third, when the Dead Sea Scrolls were discovered, it became apparent that there was no standard Judaism at the time of Jesus, nor in the first century in general. There were many expressions of the Jewish faith, much like our many denominations of the Christian faith today.

What this means for the audience for this Gospel is that the author of John seems to be speaking into, or for the sake of, an intra-Jewish debate. There were Jews who came to believe in Jesus who were then in conflict with those who did not. The most salient evidence of such a reading is the references in the narrative to *aposynagōgos*, being put out of the synagogue (9:22; 12:42; 16:2). In John 9, when the Pharisees determine that the blind man has loyalties to Jesus, he is thrown out, presumably from the synagogue and from his community. His parents fear the same for themselves and backpedal their response about knowledge of their son (9:20-21). In the Farewell Discourse, Jesus will specifically tell his disciples that they will be put out of the synagogue. In other words, John is writing for a community that had been ostracized for belief in Jesus and now needed to hear what Jesus means in no uncertain terms. The absolutism of this Gospel, "I am the way and the truth and the life. No one comes to the father except through me" is an example of this kind of sectarian language, representative of a community that sees itself as most certainly outsiders, but then in a position of having to justify to themselves and to others their choice to follow and believe in Jesus. So as not to perpetuate John's misuse and misinterpretation, preachers should alter the translations read aloud in worship from "Jews" to "Jewish leaders."

We know more about the author of John by the discussion of audience than through any other means of conjecture. Like Matthew, Mark, and Luke, we have no substantiation to support a determined author for John. While many commentators have argued for the author of the Fourth Gospel as the Beloved Disciple, and therefore, John, the son of Zebedee, there is simply no extant proof of this claim. The primary evidence for this argument is 21:24, "This is the disciple who is testifying to these things and has written them, and we know that his testimony is true." The commentary in chapter 10 on this verse will suggest that its function has more to do with reiterating key themes in the Gospel than to amass proof of authorship. Furthermore, as the commentary in chapter 8 on the foot washing and the Farewell Discourse will show, the Beloved Disciple as a character in the story, even as representative of the reader or hearer of the Gospel, is a far more compelling read of the disciple whom Jesus loved than whether or not he wrote the Fourth Gospel.

OUTLINE, STRUCTURE, AND LITERARY PATTERNS

Much of Johannine scholarship has argued that the final version we have in our canon is the result of a redactionary process over time. While this line of reasoning is certainly viable, it is, in the end, not very valuable when it comes to interpreting the Gospel of John for preaching. This commentary takes the existing version on its own terms and works with what we have, regardless of its compilation history. There is little benefit in investigating layers of redactional activity when it comes to preaching. Moreover, these kinds of approaches tend to be an easy way out so as to explain and then dismiss difficulties in transitions or texts that seem out of place.

One of the most compelling reasons to accept an intact and cohesive literary text is its overall structure and repeated literary patterns. Typically, John's Gospel is divided into two larger parts, chapters 1–12, referred to as the "Book of Signs," and chapters 13–21, the "Book of Glory." This makes a lot of sense and is helpful for the preacher on several levels. First, the Book of Signs indicates the section of the Gospel that concentrates on Jesus' public ministry. His last public act is the raising of Lazarus in chapter 11. Chapter 12 functions as a sort of bridge chapter into the last half of the Gospel, which essentially narrates Jesus' last day with his disciples, the crucifixion, and the resurrection appearances. There is a natural break between chapters 12 and 13 where the narrative pace slows down considerably. This is especially true when we remember that the first half of the Gospel takes place over three years. This realization heightens the significance of the break between chapters 12 and 13. If the first half of the Gospel has been a span of three years, imagine the difference in tone and feeling if now chapters 13–20 take place in a span of only three days.

Given the larger two-part framework above, a more detailed outline of the story could be something like below, but it is important to notice the relatively large sections. These are massive texts, taking up entire chapters (the numbering of which was, of course, added later). John is difficult to break down into small sections of texts. Moreover, as we will discuss below, each passage builds on and foreshadows other portions of the Gospel. This has plagued the preaching of John because it appears that, for every small section, you have to preach the entire Gospel. This is, in part, true but should be so for all biblical preaching. Having a general sense of the location of stories in the larger framework of John is essential. One of the goals of this commentary, however, is to highlight the Gospel's major themes in each smaller section that then can be connected to other locations in the narrative where these themes receive further development.

1:1-18   The Prologue
1:19-51 The Calling of the Disciples
2   The Wedding at Cana and the Temple Incident
3   Nicodemus
4   The Samaritan Woman at the Well/Healing of Official's Son
5   Healing of the Man Ill for Thirty-eight Years
6   Feeding of the Five Thousand
7–8   Conflict with the Jewish Authorities
9   Healing of the Man Blind from Birth/Shepherd Discourses
11   The Raising of Lazarus
12   Discourse on Glory
13   The Foot Washing
14–16   The Farewell Discourse

A major literary feature of John's Gospel is a repeated pattern that has to do with the seven signs narrated in the story. In the Gospel of John, the miraculous deeds of Jesus are designated not as miracles but as signs. There is a decisive difference in these two terms, not only in how they are then understood but in what they assume theologically for the fourth evangelist. The recurring structure of these signs is that Jesus performs a sign, followed by a dialogue of sorts, and then a discourse in which Jesus explains or interprets his act for the audience. The interpretation or explanation of the sign, the discourse from Jesus, is essential for making sense of what Jesus has just done. Signs in and of themselves are not the central idea. They exist not for their own merit or worth but because they point to something, something beyond themselves. We might imagine our need to interpret road signs or directional signs. It is not the sign alone but the direction it takes you that provides meaning.

While the first example of this pattern does not occur until chapter 5, we address this pattern in the Introduction because it illustrates an overarching theme that is critical for interpreting John. For persons interpreting texts for preaching, the fact that Jesus over and over interprets his own actions should invite intentional reflection. How does Jesus do this? What are his own methods of interpretation? Can they be helpful for our interpretation of texts for a particular moment in time? There is something inherently homiletical in this pattern that undergirds this Gospel. Something is being shown to us, as preachers, or revealed to us (a sign), that is followed by dialogue, with ourselves, with the text, with commentators, with our parishioners, with contexts outside of our own. To engage then how Jesus makes sense of what he does, the discourse, draws us back into the text. This assumes a pattern of biblical preaching that much of biblical preaching does not demonstrate these days. Biblical preaching should be a sermon based on the Bible. But too many preachers, once finding their point, their theme, their nugget of truth, abandon the biblical text in favor of story after story after story, supposedly illustrating the text but instead revealing a distrust that the biblical text has worthwhile stories on its own. The homiletical commitment of John's Gospel reminds us to return to the story that the text itself wishes to tell.

THEOLOGICAL THEMES

The main theological themes reiterated throughout John are all found in the Prologue to the Gospel. As a result, an entire chapter of this book is dedicated to the commentary on 1:1–18 which will provide an extensive analysis of these verses as they encapsulate what is at stake theologically for the Fourth Gospel. At this juncture, however, these themes are summarized, because this list of theological themes provides a taxonomy by which to interpret any passage in the Gospel. The preacher can ask to what extent a particular passage is representative or demonstrative of one or more of these themes, thereby connecting an individual passage to other portions of the Gospel.

When buried in the luxury of *reading* Bibles and commentaries we tend to forget that the books of the Bible were written to be heard and not read. They are "residually oral" or "textualized orality."[1] They are deeply acoustical, even musical, using every possible rhetorical device at their disposal to create resonance and reverberation for the sake of memory. Repetition, echoes, foreshadowing, images, and melodies are meant to create mutual interpretative relationships for association and meaning. Assonance, puns, alliteration, and other rhetorical techniques are intended to generate an effect. In our haste and love for the thesaurus, our writing and preaching tend to eliminate these kinds of repetitions and correlations. Paying attention to the oral and aural nature of biblical texts will make us better preachers, not only in making connections between passages, but also in writing for the ear. As a homiletical exercise, preachers might consider having their first "readings" of the lectionary texts for that Sunday be hearings. Have someone read John's stories to you. What do you *hear* that you never *read*?

The Prologue sets out eight major theological themes that are then revisited and unpacked throughout the course of the narrative. The first theme is the connection of Jesus to the creative activity of God, indicated by the Gospel's opening phrase, "in the beginning." Jesus' activity as the Word made flesh will be representative of God not simply doing something new in Jesus but that God is about recreating God's very self. One lens through which to view Jesus' ministry is through the concept of new creation, rebirth, and how Jesus' signs and words give witness to this primary characteristic of God.

A second theme is the origin of Jesus, which is connected to his relationship with God, and his identity. Questions of Jesus' origin, relationship with God, and identity are intertwined throughout the story. Jesus comes from God but is, of course, God made flesh among us and reveals what a relationship

1. Waler Ong, "Text and Interpretation: Mark and After," *Semeia* 39 (1987): 7-26.

with God might be like. To recognize one is to affirm belief in another. The question of Jesus' origin is of particular interest when it comes to interpreting the distinct portraits of Jesus presented by the four Gospels. That is, what difference does it make that Matthew traces Jesus' origins back to Abraham? Or Luke back to Adam? What is each communicating about who Jesus is with a specific genealogical span?

A third theme is that the primary role of the Word made flesh is to reveal God. The revelation of God in Jesus is not just of aspects of God's character but of the very heart of who God is. No one has ever seen God (1:18), but in Jesus, not only will God be seen, but the entire sensorium of sight, sound, feeling, taste, and hearing will now be possible in experiencing and knowing God. A fourth theme is then introduced by this truth, that the Fourth Gospel will give simultaneous evidence of and witness to the fact that God revealed in Jesus is at the same time holding the human and divine together. There can never be a choice of one over the other because this is the primary claim of the incarnation. The incarnation is not just that God became *human*, but also that *God* became human. There can be no partial, half humanity, no "sort of" incarnation. God has fully committed God's self to everything that it means to be human, and the human Jesus reveals the full divinity of God.

A fifth major theme at work in the Fourth Gospel is that of contrast between light and darkness. Light and darkness are synonymous with belief and unbelief, respectively. References to light and darkness are not simply details of setting but expose the true nature of those who encounter Jesus in the Gospel. Jesus is the light of the world, who magnifies the darkness that symbolizes unbelief. Any reference to light and darkness in the Gospel speaks to this issue in some way, even indirectly. In addition, the presence and purpose of light and darkness are rooted in God as creator. That the light shines in the darkness (1:5) is another way to state that the Word became flesh. At the same time, when Jesus as the light exposes those who do not believe, judgment happens in that moment of disclosure. The fourth evangelist states clearly that God does not come in Jesus to judge the world, but one's response to God in Jesus, belief or unbelief, is a judgment that is self-determined.

A sixth theological theme for the Fourth Gospel is that of witness. Perhaps the primary category of discipleship is that of witness. Discipleship will demand being a witness of and for Jesus. This requires certain attributes that are demonstrated first by John the Baptist, then by characters in the Gospel who have an encounter with Jesus, and then by Jesus himself, with even God and the Holy Spirit engaged in the activity of witnessing. As a result, what it means to be a disciple in John has a unique frame of reference and vocation that should be attended to when preaching on discipleship.

What it means to be in relationship with God by describing it and creating experiences of it is the seventh theological theme. To be called children of God (1:12) in this Gospel is not a metaphorical or sentimental claim. To be children of God is actually a literal promise for the fourth evangelist. God, as the parent, provides everything necessary for a child to be nurtured and supported, from food and water, to shelter and safety, to intimacy and belonging. The primary term by which the fourth evangelist will describe this relationship is *menō*, "to abide." The term *menō* is used over forty times in the narrative. While it is translated a number of different ways, "abide, remain, stay, continue, dwell" it is the same word over and over again. This repetition not only reiterates this theme of abiding, that to abide in Jesus is what it means to believe in Jesus, but it also keeps the reader, the listener, in the text. The repetition creates the experience of abiding. Sermons on John will do the same.

The last theme indicated in the Prologue and essential for interpreting and preaching the Fourth Gospel is that of abundance. In Jesus, we receive grace upon grace, an abundance of grace. The word "grace" is used only four times in the Gospel of John and only in the Prologue (1:14, 16, 17). While scholarship suggests that this is due to John's use of an extant hymn for the Prologue, this is not a reason to conclude that the author could not have used the term throughout the Gospel. The absence of the term "grace" after the conclusion of the Prologue indicates a theological and homiletical appeal. That is, the rest of the Gospel story, rather than tell the reader *about* grace, shows the reader what grace looks like, tastes like, smells like, sounds like, and feels like. When the Word becomes flesh, grace is then incarnated. It is no coincidence that the first act of Jesus in his public ministry is that of changing water into wine. While the miracle itself is certainly noteworthy, the transformation of water into wine is, in the end, not the point. The primary revelation in this first sign of Jesus in the Fourth Gospel is that this is what abundant grace looks like and tastes like—an excess of the best wine when you least expect it.

The changing of water into wine is not simply demonstrative of the theological claim of abundance but communicates a homiletical invitation. That is, preaching John insists that sermons will not describe, explain, or argue for the grace of God but will create *experiences* of God's grace. When Mary encounters the resurrected Jesus in the garden, she does not return to the disciples and offer a doctrinal summary, such as our utterances on Easter Sunday "Christ the Lord is risen! Alleluia!" Rather, she personalizes it. She embodies and gives voice to her belief in such a way that communicates what a response to a sermon on

John would be, "I have seen the Lord!" When the Greeks ask, "Sir, we would see Jesus" (12:21), they too articulate this essential theological theme for the Fourth Gospel. If an encounter with Jesus, or an encounter with any portion of this Gospel, does not elicit a reaction like that of Mary or the Greeks, then the sermon has not preached the fullness of the Gospel of John. This Gospel is deeply experiential, hands on, incarnated, and embodied. Not to take seriously this radical claim will reduce sermons on John to simple platitudes about Jesus.

John 20:30–31 articulates the primary function of the Fourth Gospel and therefore what a sermon on John should do. These words are written so that you may "come to believe" or "continue to believe." John does not claim that these words are written to give you information about Jesus. Something is supposed to happen to you. There is an important textual variant in this verse that is represented in different English translations. There is equal manuscript evidence to suggest that *pisteuō* can be an aorist subjunctive or a present subjunctive in a *hina* clause. If it is the former, the meaning is something along the lines of, "you were not a believer in Jesus before hearing this story. But now that you have, you will start believing," the aorist tense indicating a single occurrence; that is, this Gospel has in mind potential converts. There is also reliable manuscript evidence to suggest the use of the present subjunctive, the present tense signifying ongoing, linear action. In other words, these words are written so that you may be sustained or nurtured in your believing, with the audience being that of current believers. Either version can be sustained by the Gospel itself. While the Gospel is clearly written for a Jewish community that has chosen to identify itself as believing in Jesus it invites those who have yet to believe into an encounter with God that might result in belief. Either way, John imagines, anticipates, and expects that by hearing this story of Jesus, the reader will be affected in some way. The preacher should imagine, anticipate, and expect that every sermon on John would do the same.

1

The Prologue

A Summary of the Fourth Gospel (John 1:1-18)

The first eighteen verses of the Gospel of John are typically referred to as the Prologue. The Prologue sets out the major themes of the Gospel and is the lens through which to read the entire book. This chapter will also suggest that the Prologue provides a homiletical strategy for the preacher or a theology of preaching that reveals how this Gospel wants to and should be preached.

JOHN 1:1-5
THE LIGHT SHINES IN THE DARKNESS

The first verse is deceptively complex. "In the beginning" should stir up biblical resonances. In the Septuagint, these are the very same words that open the book of Genesis. These are not simply apt words by which to start a book, but set out one of the eight theological themes central to the Gospel. What follows is going to have something to do with creation. God is about creating, about life, about abundant life. God is a life-giver at every turn in this story. And, as it turns out, so is Jesus, thereby reiterating his identity as the incarnated God. The threefold claim in the rest of the verse, "in the beginning was the Word, and the Word was with God, and the Word was God" (all verse translations are NRSV unless otherwise noted) reveals where Jesus came from, his inherent relationship with God, and his identity as God. As noted in the Introduction, these interwoven issues when it comes to Jesus are central to this Gospel. The preacher will look for how a passage is addressing where Jesus came from with the correct answer being from God, how the passage describes Jesus' relationship with God which is profoundly intimate and true also between the believer and God, and what the passage has to say regarding the true identity of who Jesus is—he is God

13

in the world. There is an inseparability between each of these aspects about Jesus that is yet another way to describe what incarnation means. Distinctive to the conceptualization of what denotes being human is origin, relationship, and identity. Imagine the many ways in which we understand who we are on a daily basis through these categories. Moreover, for the audience of this Gospel, concerns about these categories would have been acutely felt given its situation. These were believers who had lost their ancestry, possibly every relationship they had, and their Jewish identity. John 1:1 offers three words of comfort: first, that their concerns are normal, justified, and central to being human. Second, permission to rethink and reorient these essential aspects that demark being human through the revelation of God in Jesus. Third, that Jesus himself will face these same concerns.

While there are a number theories as to the source of the term "the Word," the Gospel itself proposes that this is God's word revealed and spoken in the world in a new way. The connections to Genesis suggest that this is God's creative, redeeming, and sanctifying word that has now become flesh. It is likely no narrative accident that Jesus talks more in the Gospel of John than the other Gospels. Furthermore, the sign, dialogue, discourse pattern suggests that words are critical for revelation. Jesus' words that interprets a sign he performs actually reveal what he has done more than the sign itself. Conversations and dialogue are the moments of developing recognition of who Jesus is and they are also intrinsic to relationship. After the Prologue, Jesus as "the Word" will not be used again because God's word has become flesh.

The next verses (1:2–4) secure Jesus' role as in the beginning with God. At the same time, disclosed are not only Jesus' origins but also his primary role as creator with God. At the heart of Jesus' presence in the world is the manifestation of God's creative activity. Jesus in the Fourth Gospel is about creation, new birth, and new life. "In him was life" (1:4). For those who encounter Jesus, salvation and eternal life have everything to do with new and abundant life.

In fact, God as Creator in Genesis serves as bookends for the entire Gospel. In 20:22, John's Pentecost story, Jesus appears to the disciples as they huddle behind locked doors. He "breathes on them" the Holy Spirit (NRSV). This translation is unfortunate because the verb used is the very same verb that is used in Genesis 2:7, *emphysaō*, "Then the Lord God formed man from the dust of the ground, and breathed into his nostrils the breath of life; and the man became a living being." God's life-giving, creative activity surrounds this Gospel and suggests that every sermon should envisage the same effect.

Verse 5 has been a topic of ongoing debate for scholars with regard to pinpointing the moment of the incarnation. Is it here, or in 1:14, "the Word became flesh"? An appealing argument that it is here (1:5) is that the presence of John in the next verses make more sense. Otherwise, to what or whom would John be witnessing? Regardless of the exact moment of the "Word made flesh," there is something important imagining that the incarnation of God is first presented as light shining in darkness, with the darkness unable to overcome it and suggests that our preaching this Gospel will always have something to do with shining light in darkness. That the incarnation is first described as light in darkness once again calls upon the creation story in Genesis. Light and darkness in this Gospel will symbolize the two realms of relationship with Jesus. To be in the light is to be in relationship with Jesus, synonyms being "believing," "knowing," and "abiding." The darkness represents that lack of relationship, an inability or refusal to believe that Jesus is God in the flesh. The Word became flesh is primarily a relational claim, not a confessional or doctrinal claim. As a result, this should infuse a homiletic for preaching John. Every passage in this Gospel reveals some aspect of the relationship with God and Jesus that Jesus' presence now in the world makes possible.

The verb "overcome" in "the darkness did not overcome it" can be translated "grasp" or "seize," and has connotations of "understanding" or "comprehending." While the word is not the same, there is a foreshadowing of Jesus' statement in 16:33, "I have overcome the world." A quick review of the science of light in terms of our ability to see underscores the theological claim that is being made. It only takes the slightest bit of light for our optical system to adjust and see in the dark. When there is no light present at all, our eyes will never become accustomed to the darkness. There is hope in this claim, that the smallest source of light might create the possibility of belief. For the community to whom this Gospel is addressed, this hope was essential.

JOHN 1:6-8 (CF. 1:15)
WITNESSING TO THE LIGHT

A rather abrupt transition from the Word made flesh to "there was a man sent from God, whose name was John" has made many a scholar run to redactional theories. Admittedly, these verses are a rather strange interlude in what seems to be a cosmic birth story. What is John doing here anyway? Commentators have regularly explained away John's presence as a later interpolation that does not belong in such a majestic, hymnic, and poetic narration of Jesus' origins and identity. The presence of John here, however, points to another major theme of this Gospel—holding together, simultaneously, at every moment, the divine and the human. Contrary to popular assumption, the Gospel of John is every bit as interested in Jesus' humanity as it is in Jesus' divinity. While this Gospel is the clear source for dogmatic arguments and confessional responses for the sheer divinity of Jesus, to interpret this Gospel as only interested in Jesus' divinity is to ignore its very human and relational claims about God, Jesus, and relationship. John is interjected as an important reminder of this truth.

The uniqueness of John's character in the Fourth Gospel has everything to do with the theological theme of witness. The noun form alone is used fourteen times in the Gospel. The figure whom we know as John the Baptist from the Synoptic Gospels is never called the Baptist in the Fourth Gospel, but is the witness. He will be the one to testify or witness to the light and will show us what testimony and witness look like later in the first chapter. John's role as witness is confirmed in verse 15 and looks forward to the elemental expression of testimony in the Gospel of John, "Here is the Lamb of God who takes away the sin of the world!" (1:29)

John 1:9-13
On Being Children of God in the World

The next section in the Prologue introduces the concept of the world. The world in the Gospel of John is the object of God's love yet also represents the primary source of opposition to God's love revealed in Jesus Christ. God loves the world (3:16), but many in the world will resist and reject this expression of God's love. That God loves the world is immediately demonstrated in Jesus' mission to the Samaritans in chapter 4. For God so loved the world is not simply a nice idea but demands a real presentation of what that love will look like. God's love for the world will take on a very real, incarnational, embodied reality in Jesus' encounter with the Samaritan woman at the well. Moreover, God's love will be extended through the witness of the woman at the well to the entire town of Sychar. In other words, to articulate in the story of the woman at the well God's love for the world this early in the Gospel suggests that God relies on God's witnesses, disciples, believers, to make this possible. To be a disciple in the Gospel of John is to be an extension of, or act out, God's love. Discipleship is an incarnated reality, just as the Word made flesh. It is not an abstract existence of following, or confession, but suggests that discipleship is the presence of the Word made flesh in the world when Jesus returns to the Father.

The other important topic introduced in these verses is "children of God." Christianity has had a tendency to sentimentalize this promise usually through conceptions of and arguments for baptism. For the Gospel of John, however, to be a child of God is a literal claim. This Gospel imagines that every single aspect of the parent–child relationship is operative in our relationship with God. Everything a child needs from a parent, for survival, protection, to be sustained and nurtured, to grow and mature— this is what God provides.

The rest of the Gospel will demonstrate how God provides for God's children. In addition, to be a child of God is to come from God, as did Jesus. Jesus will reveal this to Nicodemus, who will misunderstand the radicalness of what Jesus is saying. Yet this is exactly what this Gospel wants to claim—that the believer, like Jesus, comes from God, is birthed by God, is given life by God and no one else. As a result, water and spirit for Nicodemus do not have to refer to baptism, but to birth itself. In the Farewell Discourse, the Spirit will be who accompanies the disciples in Jesus' absence, the source of ongoing truth and the means of growth in relationship. The Spirit is the very breath of God, the promise of God's presence but also a promise of growth, maturity, and understanding in relationship with God. Jesus will breathe the Spirit into the disciples after the resurrection and they will become living beings (20:33; cf. Gen. 2:7).

John 1:14-18
The Word Becomes Flesh

The Fourth Gospel is replete with well-known one-liners, and 1:14 is certainly one of them. "The Word became flesh" states most clearly and specifically this primary promise of the Gospel of John. This primordial Word, which was in the beginning with God, a partner in creation, in relationship with God and who is God, has now become human. While the NRSV translates the verse, "and lived among us" the verb here is *skēnoō*, "to tent" or "to tabernacle." Most readers of the Gospel of John will be familiar with the translation "and dwelt among us." John is clearly situating this new activity of God in the characteristic of God made manifest in the wilderness wanderings. God dwells with God's people. The verb can also be translated, "took up residence" and thus, Eugene Peterson's *The Message*, "moved into the neighborhood." This characteristic of God appears only here in John and in the book of Revelation (7:15; 12:12; 13:6; 21:3).

This is as much a declaration about the Word as it is about who God is, what God is about, and to what and whom God is committed. The fourth evangelist understands that God's promise to be with God's people wherever they go has now taken on a different representation in Jesus. The dwelling of

God is a deeply intimate and personal claim and draws on God's commitment to God's people. In addition to a theological statement about the character of God, that God is now once again dwelling with God's people in Jesus also assumes the continuity of God. That the Word made flesh engages in activity once witnessed of God points to continuity but also reinforces Jesus as the presence of God, if he engages in the same kinds of activity as God has and as God does.

That the Word became flesh and dwelt among us also suggests that the concept of dwelling has taken on a different meaning in the presence of Jesus as God in the world. Before, God went wherever God's people went. God was with them continually. In the Word made flesh and dwelling among us, now God not only goes where God's people go, but is who they are. That is, God now dwells with us by taking on our form, our humanity. This "different" dwelling of God will find expression in the abiding relationship between the believer and God that will be described throughout the Gospel. In other words, there will be a radical intensification of the dwelling of God as not simply where God's people are, but *who* God's people are. Reading forward in the narrative, we will discover just how close this dwelling is, a relationship so deeply intimate as to make some uncomfortable. God is not just close, but dwells beside us and in us, sharing everything God has because of God's love for us.

What "glory" means in verse 14 needs to be situated in the larger framework of John. The moment of glory will be the crucifixion, resurrection, and ascension, but none of this is possible without first the glory of the incarnation, which is described as light shining in the darkness (1:5). The term "glory" has a number of different intimations but, significantly for John's Gospel, has the sense of "brightness, radiance, splendor," particularly of God. There is a proleptic claim here, looking toward 1:18 that no one has ever seen God. God's glory, surprisingly, astonishingly, is seen in the incarnation. Grace and truth are paired here and again in 1:17, suggesting that there is something at stake by interpreting both concepts side by side. Later in the Gospel, Jesus will identify himself as the truth (14:6).

"From his fullness" (1:16) has the sense of the "sum total," "complete," and can also connote "superabundance." In the context of the Fourth Gospel, Jesus' fullness will be the full expression of God's presence in the world as well as the extent to which God's presence in Jesus is the fullest expression of everything God provides for those in relationship with God. As noted in the Introduction, the word "grace" is used only four times in the Gospel of John (1:14, 16, 17) and only in the Prologue. While a number of commentators argue that the reason for this omission is John's use of a pre-exiting hymn for the Prologue, a more convincing theological case suggests that the absence of the term after the

Prologue underscores the embodiment of grace itself. Once the Word becomes flesh, grace is incarnated in the rest of the Gospel. That is, the entirety of the Gospel will show what grace looks like, tastes like, smells like, sounds like, and feels like. As a result, the first public act of Jesus' ministry in the Gospel of John is a miracle of abundance. It is not just that Jesus is able to turn water into wine, which in and of itself would be worthy of wonder. It is the abundance of wine that is key for interpreting the sign. Jesus' ministry as the Word made flesh will be about demonstrating how God's grace is experienced when it dwells among us.

This has important theological significance for understanding and interpreting the Gospel of John. For John, God in becoming flesh in Jesus has committed God's self not only to revealing what God's grace looks like, but that God wants to know it and feel it as well. While the source of our experiences of grace is most certainly God, we do not take the incarnation seriously if we think God is unaffected by such action. The fact that God decided to become human cannot, by definition, be a one-sided pledge. To be human means mutuality, reciprocity, and affectation.

To assert this fundamental reality about the human reality and condition is an important counter to interpretations of John's Gospel that are preoccupied with the divine Jesus, omnipotent, surreal, and seemingly untouchable. Thus, the Docetic heresy found its legitimation in the Fourth Gospel. While the church officially offered a counterattack to the Docetists with the Apostles' Creed, the history of interpretation and the function of the Fourth Gospel in the church reveal the latent perception that this Gospel and this Jesus barely touch the ground.

That the word "grace" appears only in the Prologue not only presents significant theological implications but homiletical propositions as well. That after the Prologue grace is then shown and not explained means that sermons on the Fourth Gospel should do the same. To preach a sermon on the Gospel of John that seeks only to tell the congregation *about* God's grace is antithetical to the Gospel's theological and homiletical inclinations. Additional narrative evidence for this working homiletic is Mary's report to the disciples after her encounter with the resurrected Jesus in the garden. She does not go to Jesus' believers and offer a statement of fact, "Christ is risen! He is risen indeed! Alleluia! but rather, "I have seen the Lord!" Her announcement about Jesus' revelation to her is personal and gives witness to her own experience.

Verse 17 marks the fourth occurrence of the word "grace" in the Prologue and the second time the term is paired with truth. This pairing indicates an important theological assumption for the rest of the Gospel. After the Prologue, both grace and truth will be incarnated in the Word made flesh, Jesus. The concept of truth in the Fourth Gospel has little to do with an absolute that can somehow be verified by substantiation. Truth is not fact in that it is a proposition able to be proven outside of itself. Rather, truth denotes relationship. For Jesus, to state that he is the truth (14:6) reveals that truth has been redefined as the person of Jesus Christ, yet the one who is the Word made flesh. That Jesus now is embodied truth and that truth represents relationship are made most clear at the very end of Jesus' trial before Pilate. Pilate asks Jesus, "So you are a king?" Jesus answers him, "You say that I am a king. For this I was born, and for this I came into the world, to testify to the truth. Everyone who belongs to the truth listens to my voice" (18:37). To testify to the truth refers back to the witness of John, who points to Jesus and says, "Look! It's the lamb of God!" (1:36) Truth is not a proposition but the revealing of the presence of God in Jesus. In other words, to testify to the truth is not to compile enough evidence to make a case but to recognize that the case has already been made, according to the witness of John, the Holy Spirit (15:26), and even God. Pilate's final response to Jesus in the trial scene indicates his inability to see that Jesus himself is the truth. His interrogative "what," not "who," intimates that truth for him remains a product of proof and not relationship with God and Jesus.

Verse 18 concludes and yet encapsulates the Prologue, specifically verse 1. It is a recapitulation of the first verse, so that the entirety of the Prologue is framed by the three critical themes of the origin of Jesus, Jesus' relationship with God, and the identity of Jesus. In summary, verse 18 answers again the question of who Jesus is, what Jesus' relationship with God is like, and where Jesus comes from.

A comparison of translations for 1:18 exposes the theological difficulties with each of these three theological themes. Recognizing these challenges with which translators and interpreters of the Fourth Gospel have struggled over the centuries of interpretation gives yet more reason for the accompanying homiletical difficulty with John. In other words, a persistent issue that has influenced perceptions of the preaching of the Gospel of John is the profound complexity of its central theological tenets. The fundamental theses on which this story of Jesus are grounded are to blame for its perceived impediments when it comes to preaching. Moreover, as these themes permeate the Gospel, there is no getting around any of them in any passage encountered. The preacher must come to terms with these three essential premises, not only for the sake of faithful interpretation of the whole but also for the sake of regard and respect for the Fourth Gospel's unrivaled presentation of Jesus.

The only portion of accord for translators in verse 18 is the first sentence of the verse, "No one has ever seen God." After this fundamental truth, any agreement between translations quickly disintegrates. The conformity with the opening phrase is a theological and scriptural given. To see God is to incur the fate of death (Exod. 33:18; Isa. 6:5). The presence of Jesus means that we will now be able to see God and invites imagination of what this possibility entails. The emphasis on sight may be taken both literally and figuratively. Quite literally, of course, to see God is to die, so there is a promise made here that sight will now be possible. At the same time, that no one has ever seen God points to a preoccupation with the senses. To see God will not just be limited to the sense of sight but suggests that an experience of God in this Gospel is beyond constructs that have to do only with knowledge. The revelation of God in Jesus will be a fully embodied and sensorial experience. This opening phrase in 1:18 hints at the fact that God revealing God's self in this Gospel will take on a different kind of meaning and experience than we have known before.

The next section of verse 18 is one full sentence that should be demarcated into three separate statements that correspond to the three claims of verse 1. The first clause, "It is God, the only son" is the first statement of the sentence and restates the identity of Jesus made clear in the last clause of verse 1. The declaration of Jesus' identity is complicated by a translation issue and by a text-critical issue. The translation issue centers on *monogenēs*, rendered in different versions as "the unique," "the one and only," and "the only begotten." The identity of Jesus is once again God, as stated in verse 1, "and the Word was God," but it is further clarified that the Word made flesh is a unique God, a one and only revealing or representation of God, calling attention to the limits of the incarnation but also to the distinctiveness of who Jesus is. The text-critical issue is the word "son" included in some translations. The earliest and most reliable manuscripts of the Gospel of John do not include the term "son." It is added later, most likely by scribes in hopes of taming or making more sense of John's radical claim. While it is true that Jesus is God's son and that the Father–Son relationship will become front and center after the Prologue when the Word has become flesh that is not the focus here. Jesus is God revealing God's self in a new and profoundly different way. Translations have sought to domesticate this central theological claim, yet the Prologue will not let us go without another prompt that the answer to the question of Jesus' identity is always, for this Gospel, the promise that Jesus is God and fully divine.

The next two clauses in this final sentence of the Prologue reiterate Jesus' origin, another major theme of the Gospel of John. From where does Jesus come? will surface as a critical inquiry throughout the narrative, in part because it provides another way to answer the question of Jesus' identity. The location of Jesus as the unique and one and only God as "close to the Father's heart" (NRSV) communicates that relationship and origin and identity are, in fact, intimately connected and reciprocal.

The term translated as "heart," "side," and "bosom" is indeed *kolpos*, "bosom." The fourth evangelist certainly knew the Greek word for "heart," *kardia*, but did not use it. The same is true for "side." Rather, John situates Jesus, the unique God, soon to be designated as God's son, as having his home at the bosom of the Father. The choice of "side" and "heart" over "bosom" suggests an essential difficulty with the concept that Jesus, as God's unique expression of God and God's son, dwells at the bosom of the father. Margaret Miles, in her study of the breast as a religious symbol in art (*A Complex Delight: The Secularization of the Breast, 1350–1750* [Berkeley: University of California Press, 2008]), argues that before 1750 a primary image for salvation was the infant Jesus nursing at the exposed breast of Mary. The believer, in viewing this picture, was invited to imagine being in Jesus' position and, in this way, experience the salvific act of God as nurturer. The year 1750, however, marks two critical events in the history of humanity that forever altered this image as a possible depiction of God's love for God's people. These two events include the advent of medical anatomy and pornography. When the female body moves from being a source of nourishment and life to becoming a detached object of study and desire, there is no longer the possibility of visualizing God in this way, and viewing the breast as a religious symbol becomes impossible. As a result, the primary representation of salvation in art after the introductions of anatomy and pornography is the crucifixion.

Translations of John 1:18 published after 1750 represent this remarkable shift in the perception of the female body. To depict Jesus nursing at the bosom or breast of God would then appear sexual. To eschew this image in favor of a more socially acceptable portrayal is problematic on several levels. First, the meaning conveyed in this picture of Jesus at the bosom of God is extraordinary tenderness. One would be hard-pressed to secure a description of relationship more intimate than the nursing of a child. The rest of the Gospel depends on this description of Jesus' relationship with the father. Who God is for the believer as a child of God is the parent, the mother, who provides everything necessary for sustenance of life. God is a life-sustainer in the Fourth Gospel, and this is not a metaphorical platitude. God, quite literally, will reveal that *everything* we need for life, right here and right now, God will give, over and over again. An essential lens through which to view Jesus' ministry in the Gospel of John is how Jesus' signs and words articulate the theological truth that God is our source for all things necessary to provide, nurture, and maintain life. As a result, a primary hermeneutical approach for the Fourth Gospel means tending to the life-giving expression of God in every aspect of Jesus' ministry. To be a child of God will ring false without the very literal manifestation of what it actually means to be a child. This Gospel stakes everything on the incarnation. If, at any time, the Word made flesh is simply a euphemism meant only to offer support or encouragement, then the entirety of John's theological argument crumbles.

Second, at stake in this image is not only who Jesus is as the Word made flesh, as the unique and one and only God, but who we are as believers. The only other time in the Gospel of John that the word "bosom" is used is in 13:23, the first introduction to the disciple whom Jesus loves. It is, at the very least, odd that this beloved disciple is never mentioned before this point in the story. Why is that? If Jesus loves this disciple so much, where has he been? The beloved disciple's introduction and placement in the story indicate that his function and meaning are more important than his identity. While scholars still devote significant effort to determining who the beloved disciple was, the more important question, narratively and theologically, is *why* the beloved disciple. The fact that the term "bosom" occurs only in 1:18 and 13:23 affirms the premise of the Gospel that every claim about the relationship between God and Jesus is at the same time a claim about the relationship between the believer and God/Jesus. To describe the relationship between Jesus and God has little meaning if the believer is not able to imagine that same relationship personally and experientially with God and Jesus.

John 1:18 foreshadows 13:23 and the abiding intimacy that Jesus will define in the Farewell Discourse between himself, God, and the believer. None of what Jesus says to his disciples in his departing words will make sense without the foundational premise that the relationship that Jesus has with the Father is the relationship into which every believer is invited here and now but also promised since Jesus will prepare abiding places for us (14:2). Where does Jesus come from? This is also where he is going (14:2). Jesus will return to abide with his Father, at the bosom of God. This Gospel assumes a theological full circle: incarnation, crucifixion, resurrection, and ascension.

The last clause of verse 18 seeks to describe what the Word made flesh does. Once again, the discrepancy in translations indicates challenges in the Greek text. There is an essential function for the Word made flesh that offers a counterpoint to the opening sentence of verse 18, "No one has ever seen God." God becoming human will mean that now it is possible to see God. Moreover, it will be possible to taste, smell, feel, and hear God. A comparison of versions offers several possibilities when it comes to interpreting the term *exagō*, including "declare," "reveal," and "make known." While all of these translations may find legitimacy in the rest of the story, they cannot be limited to levels of simple manifestation or cognition. The verb *exagō* is a compound verb, combining the prefix *ex*, which means "out" with the verb *agō* which means "to bring or to lead." In other words, the principal purpose of the Word made flesh is to bring God out, to lead God out, so that an experience of God is possible. It makes no sense for the Word to become flesh if God is not able to be experienced, and on every level of what it means to be human.

For the preacher, every sermon on the Gospel of John will seek to bring God out, to lead God out, so that a true and real encounter with God is possible. Mary's words to the disciples after Jesus' revelation to her in the garden, "I have seen the Lord," mean nothing without the fundamental premise of 1:18. Her confession gives witness to a live and embodied engagement with the risen Christ. To that end, every encounter with Jesus in this Gospel foreshadows Mary's meeting with the supposed gardener, anticipating that to meet Jesus is to have an intimate and personal experience of and with God.

Biblical exegesis for preaching should take a cue from *exagō* as it functions in 1:18. While biblical scholarship has claimed this word for its intellectual discipline, "exegesis," for the Fourth Gospel it has everything to do with relationship. For preaching the Fourth Gospel, therefore, the preacher would do well not to start at the place of historical, critical, exegetical method but at the place of encounter with Christ as felt in the hearing of John's witness, thereby creating an experience of Christ rather than a report of research gleaned from an office or library.

CONNECTIONS TO THE LECTIONARY

The lectionary appoints the Prologue of John's Gospel primarily in the Advent/Christmas season. There is good reason for this decision as the "beginning" of Jesus' ministry and the beginning of the church year. However, to limit the Prologue simply to beginnings overlooks the very earthy and human tone of the first eighteen verses of John. This is Christmas, according to the Fourth Gospel. It is a cosmic Christmas story that invites preaching a Christmas sermon in which the complexities of what exactly happened when God decided to become flesh are given attention. This is John's birth story. Assigned for Christmas 2, Years A, B, and C is 1:(1-9), 10-18. While John 1:1-9 is optional, the entirety of the Prologue should be preached for the reasons argued in the commentary above. The latter part of the Prologue makes little sense without the premises set out in the opening verses. John 1:1-14 is the lection for Christmas Day in Years A, B, and C. Again, the entirety of the Prologue needs to be read on this Sunday, particularly so that the congregation hears the restatement of the incarnation in 1:18. A preacher might also consider preaching on the Prologue of John at some other point in the church year. The themes in the Prologue outlined above lend themselves to multiple expressions of discipleship, the identity of Christ, the character of God, and even salvation. For Advent 3 in Year B, 1:6-8 is coupled with 1:19-28 for a lection on John the Baptist. As Mark's portrait of John comes only a week earlier in Year B (Mark1:1-8), the Fourth Gospel's presentation of John who is not the Baptist but the Witness would provide an interesting comparison so as to understand the function of this important figure in the Gospels. John, for the fourth evangelist, has such a different role, and that difference is worth exploring in the imagination of how the four Gospel writers set up and introduce Jesus' ministry. Furthermore, these side-by-side portraits of John would serve the additional purpose of helping our congregations be better readers of the Bible, to recognize its distinctions not for the sake of shock value but because the differing perspectives of these four diverse confessions of faith reflect the variety of expression in our own lives of faith.

2

The Calling of the Disciples, the First Sign, and the Temple Incident (John 1:19—2:25)

The calling of Jesus' first disciples, the wedding at Cana, and the temple incident are grouped together in this chapter for the purpose of facilitating connections between key themes in these inaugural events for Jesus' public ministry. All three incidents articulate aspects of discipleship, point to Jesus' true identity, and embody the fundamental theological tenets outlined in the Prologue.

John 1:19-36
John the Witness

John 1:19 marks the transition in the Fourth Gospel to Jesus' public ministry with an expansion of the role of John. For the fourth evangelist, John is not John the Baptist but John the Witness, who will give testimony to the coming of the Word in the world. His identity is confirmed by the questioning of the priests and the Levites sent by the Pharisees. Interesting in this dialogue is John's response, a negative "I AM" to the revelation of Jesus as "I AM" later in the narrative (1:21). We are meant to hear a resonance between these two, which then emphasizes Jesus' own identity. In sorting out John's identity, Jesus' own identity is underscored. John's opposite assertion, "I AM not" also highlights the striking dichotomies that permeate this Gospel. There is and only can be one Messiah, one "I AM," and one God. There is an important theological declaration in this juxtaposition. Here is a Jewish group, most likely expelled from its community, which is now alleging that the one God in which they all believe, the one Yahweh, is now revealing God's self in Jesus. This radical claim of monotheism stands behind John's interrogation.

Verse 29 demonstrates the pivotal action of discipleship in the Fourth Gospel. At the heart of what it means to be a disciple is to be a witness, to give testimony. As Jesus approaches John, John announces, "Behold, the Lamb of God who takes away the sin of the world!" The principal act of discipleship is to point to Christ and say "look, there he is," so that others might see him. This is the premise of 1:18, no one has ever seen God, and the request of the Greeks, "Sir, we would see Jesus" (12:21). A Gospel about an incarnated God insists that the reader experience Jesus with every sense—sight, taste, smell, hearing, and touch. Operational at this moment are both hearing and sight, which will be held together frequently throughout the Gospel, in particular in the healing of the blind man and the Shepherd Discourse.

The designation of Jesus as Lamb of God is significant. We will discover at Jesus' crucifixion an alteration in chronology of the time and day of Jesus' actual death from that of Matthew, Mark, and Luke. In John, Jesus dies not on the day of Passover but on the day of preparation for Passover. His time of death would be approximately the period when the Passover lambs would be slaughtered for the prescribed Passover meal. Interpreting this passage for preaching will bring forward the meaning and significance of Passover (Exodus 12–13). In its larger theological context, the Festival of Passover celebrates God's deliverance of Israel from Egypt. The Israelites were spared from the divine plague sent to kill all the firstborn of Egypt with the blood of the lamb being smeared on the doorposts so that the homes of the Israelites would be secure. There is great theological weight, then, in that Jesus is God's firstborn. Passover signifies protection, lineage, deliverance, and God's promise of relationship. God's covenant with Abraham is reworked in this Gospel's most famous verse, "for God so loved the world" (3:16).

This is the first time that the word "sin" is used in the Gospel of John and in the singular (1:36). It will not appear in the noun form again until much later in the Gospel (8:3, 21, 24, 34, 46; 9:34, 41; 15:22, 24; 16:8, 9; 19:11; 20:23). The concept of sin has a very distinct theological meaning for the fourth evangelist. Sin is not a moral category, a way to designate unlawful or iniquitous behavior; sin functions as a synonym for not being in relationship with God. The essential theological thrust of this Gospel is to make one a believer or to sustain belief (20:30-31). Belief in God is not an ascent to certain faith claims, an intellectual decision, or a creed of sound doctrine; rather, belief in God means being in a relationship with God. It is an active, living, dynamic reality, not a static, dogmatic confession. In the Gospel of John, the word "belief" is never a noun but always a verb. This grammatical use signifies that believing in Jesus, believing in Jesus as the Word made flesh, as the incarnation of the one and only God, is not about knowledge but about relationship, the intimate relationship first revealed in 1:18.

The Lamb of God who takes away the sin of the world, therefore, takes away any separation from God and makes it possible for all to be in the same kind of relationship with God that Jesus has with the Father. This would have been an extraordinary promise for the audience of this Gospel, who were indeed separated from their God by being put out of the synagogue. While the chronological pinpoint of Jesus' death corresponds to that of the Passover lambs, the significance of the term "Lamb of God" who takes away the sin of the world does not have to be located solely in the crucifixion. Jesus' presence as God, as the revelation of God, is that which creates the possibility of relationship with God. The death of Jesus is not the moment of "atonement," so to speak. It is the life of Jesus that makes that relationship possible.

For the fourth evangelist, the crucifixion has a very different role and one that will seem counterintuitive to dominant interpretations of Jesus' death. Jesus' death in the Gospel of John has two functions. First, that which is human must die. The crucifixion is the death of the human Jesus, the incarnated God. It is not in and of itself the "moment of salvation" for John. Rather, the salvific moment is when God became flesh. Yet to isolate atonement to a place and space and event in time is also to misinterpret this Gospel. Salvation is not a once-in-a-lifetime occurrence but the ongoing reality, here and in the future, of being in relationship with God. Salvation in the Fourth Gospel is a linear concept. Second, the function of the crucifixion is to show that not even death will separate this relationship once established. The primary proof of this assumption is the presence and positioning of the resurrection of Lazarus. This final sign in the Fourth Gospel will be fully discussed in chapter 7. The raising of Lazarus promises that the death of Jesus will not be the end.

Verses 30-31 reveal how integral John the Witness is to the Prologue of the Gospel. John testifies to who Jesus is and reasserts Jesus' origins. While it seems that Jesus comes after John, John testifies that, in fact, Jesus is before John because in the beginning was the Word. John realizes his place fully, that his sole role in this story is to witness to Jesus, to reveal Jesus to the world. To witness is to say "behold," so that Jesus might indeed be made manifest to others. John also testifies to having witnessed Jesus' baptism, another reason why John is not the baptizer in the Fourth Gospel. He himself does not baptize Jesus but sees it happen and, in this way, witnesses not only the baptism but the first revelation of the Spirit in the Gospel. The baptism of Jesus in John emphasizes not John's role but God's in the entirety of who Jesus is and what Jesus will do. When it comes to preaching Jesus' baptism, John's account suggests that to be baptized is to be baptized by God. The act of baptism by God is the giving of the Spirit, according to John, who abides with the baptized. While there are a number of interpretations and practices of baptism in our churches, those that assert God's direct activity in this ritual will find resonance in John's version of Jesus' baptism. For the Fourth Gospel, it is another means by which to show the presence and power of God in and with Jesus and later with believers in the giving of the Spirit (20:22).

This is the first time in the Gospel that the Spirit is mentioned and the first time that the term *menō* is used. That they appear for the first time together is critical for understanding and preaching the pneumatology of the Fourth Gospel. While many translations will render *menō* as "remain" "and it remained on him," "he on whom you see the Spirit descend and remain" the term is "abide," as noted before, used over forty times in the Gospel of John. It is the essential means by which to name the relationship between Jesus and God, between Jesus and his disciples, between the believer and God. The connection between the Spirit and *menō* points to the fact that baptism is yet another way to depict what it means to be in relationship with God.

CONNECTIONS TO THE LECTIONARY

In the lectionary, 1:19-28 is yoked with 1:6-8 in Year B, Advent 3, so as to focus on the character of John the Baptist and his identity. The unique presentation of John as witness in the Fourth Gospel stands in contrast to the other Gospels, and a sermon might ask what is at stake for the fourth evangelist to argue for John's identity not as Elijah or as a prophet but as witness. John 1:29-42 is the lection offered for Epiphany 2 in Year A. The first half of this passage narrates Jesus' baptism according to John, which is quite a different experience from that of Matthew's version of the week before (Matt. 3:13-17). Preaching on the initial portion of this lection might call attention to the diverse theologies of baptism at work in these two stories. Critical for the Fourth Gospel is that John witnesses Jesus' baptism but does not himself baptize Jesus. A preacher could ask what it means to be the witnesses to the baptisms in our church services. The second half of this passage turns attention to John's primary role as witness in the Gospel of John. A sermon on this passage could explore how witness is a characteristic of discipleship, particularly the Fourth Gospel's understanding of what witness looks like, which John embodies in these verses. The concept of witness is an important category by which to understand our Christian identity, and John's Gospel offers a unique model in John of what witness might mean in our everyday lives.

John 1:35-51
The Calling of the Disciples

In 1:35 John points again to Jesus and says, "Behold the Lamb of God who takes away the sin of the world," this time with two of his disciples present. The response of the disciples to John's statement is to follow Jesus. Why do they follow Jesus? What is it that they see and hear that their response is to follow Jesus without question? This discipleship moment foreshadows the reaction of the Samaritans to the invitation from the woman at the well. Her testimony, like John's, is enough to elicit a response to go to Jesus and experience Jesus for one's self.

Jesus' very first words in the Gospel of John are to these potential disciples, "What are you looking for?" Jesus will ask the soldiers who come to arrest him in chapter 18 (18:4, 7) and Mary in the garden (20:15) the very same question, though altered in an important way, "who are you looking for?" Holding all three of these occurrences of this phrase together points to a main issue for this Gospel, that Jesus is not a *what* but a *who* and *who* indicates relationship. The question also calls attention to the importance of hearing and seeing that will be demonstrated most clearly in the healing of the man blind from birth.

The disciples' answer to Jesus' question is odd at best, not an answer but another question. The response to Jesus further emphasizes that what will be recognized in Jesus, or what it means to be a disciple of Jesus, has little to do with correct understanding or identification of his titles, but rather to be in relationship with Jesus. The disciples ask Jesus, "Where are you staying?" better translated, "Where are you abiding?" because the verb again is *menō*. For the disciples to find *what* they are looking for, their parameters need to be recalculated. They will find the *what* and the *who* in the experience of abiding with Jesus.

Jesus' invitation to "come and see" foreshadows the invitation of the Samaritan woman at the well to her townspeople. Jesus models what it means to witness, to be a disciple. It starts with an invitation to come and see for yourself who Jesus is. The disciples come and see and abide. The Samaritan woman at the well will act out this very scenario for the sake of her townspeople to have their own encounter with Jesus.

The final section of chapter 1 relates the calling of the disciples. The two central themes in the call narrative are following and finding, and they look toward several key events in the story to come. In the previous verses, after hearing John's witness to Jesus, two of John's disciples literally follow Jesus. Now, in this next portion of the calling of the disciples, to follow Jesus becomes the pivotal means by which to understand discipleship. After the renaming of Peter, Jesus' first words to Peter are "follow me." These will also be Jesus' final words to Peter in chapter 21. It is essential to bring forward the last conversation between Jesus and Peter for interpreting this first conversation. To follow Jesus will certainly require a literal following. It will be following Jesus for three years during his ministry, witnessing his signs, and listening to his words. In the end, however, Jesus will call on his disciples to follow him by taking on his ministry when he returns to the Father. This will include death, as Jesus prophesies Peter's inevitable death for the sake of following Jesus (21:18-19). It will also include, however, the seemingly impossible invitation to be the Good Shepherd when Jesus cannot be. In other words, discipleship, for this Gospel, means being the "I AM" in the world when Jesus returns to the Father. This may seem overstated but it is a summation of what will transpire between Jesus and his disciples, particularly in the Farewell Discourse. There, Jesus will reiterate the close relationship that the disciples and Jesus have in the most intimate terms that communicate this closeness, abiding. "I abide in you and you abide in me" (15:4). Moreover, Jesus will breathe into the disciples the Spirit, the Paraclete, so that they are literally possessed with God's breath (20:22). To be the "I AM" for the sake the world God loves, to carry on Jesus ministry, to do "greater works than these" (14:12) will be possible only because of this intimacy.

Another theme important for understanding the Fourth Gospel's presentation of discipleship is the idea of finding or being found. Andrew, a disciple of John and brother of Simon Peter, *finds* his brother after his encounter with Jesus and shares with him that they have "found" the Messiah. Importantly, the first "finding" in this discipleship narrative is not by Jesus but by his first disciples, "Philip found Nathanael" (1:45). This becomes another way that the close relationship between Jesus and his disciples is underscored. Jesus' disciples act out "finding" and "being found" before Jesus does, thereby emphasizing the mutuality of Jesus and his disciples. Philip will find Nathaniel and use the same words as Andrew of having found the Messiah, "we have found him about whom Moses in the law and also the prophets wrote" (1:45) The verb tense used by Philip in verse 45 is critical because it is in the perfect tense. Finding

Jesus is not a singular occurrence, but having found him will mean an ongoing relationship. While the actual verb is not used in chapter 4, Jesus will "find" the Samaritan woman at the well and Jesus finds (same verb) the formerly blind man after he has been cast out of the synagogue (9:35), making him a disciple.

Verse 45 is one of two references to Joseph as the father of Jesus, here and again in 6:42, and both occur against a backdrop of allusions to Moses—in 1:45, "Jesus son of Joseph from Nazareth;" in 6:42, "Is not this Jesus, the son of Joseph, whose father and mother we know? How can he now say, 'I have come down from heaven'?" In both instances, the question of where Jesus comes from is key. While Jesus is on earth as the Word made flesh, his humanity will be reiterated in a number of ways. The combination of "son of Joseph, from Nazareth" recalls the truth about Jesus stated in 1:1 and reframed at the end of the Prologue in 1:18. The identity of Jesus is a critical theme for this Gospel. The reader knows that, yes, Jesus is God's son, but Jesus is also this unique revelation of God, God in the flesh, the incarnated Logos. The origin of Jesus is also at stake for this Gospel as introduced in the Prologue. Where Jesus comes from will be questioned over and over again, with the correct answer being not "from Nazareth" but from the beginning with God. The assertion that Jesus is from Nazareth will return again during the arrest scene, when Jesus asks the soldiers who have come to capture him, "Whom are you looking for"? The answer, "Jesus of Nazareth," is only part of the truth, just as it is here. As the story unfolds, the question will be whether or not potential believers are able to see that Jesus is both from Nazareth and from God. The fourth evangelist cannot let either truth go because at stake is the fundamental theological declaration of this Gospel: Jesus is the "I AM" in the flesh. To choose one, or to see only one, in favor of the other threatens this essential argument.

Philip's invitation to Nathaniel, "come and see," are the very same words that Jesus said to the first disciples, and that the Samaritan woman will say to her townspeople. Invitation is vital for discipleship. When Nathaniel encounters Jesus, another category of relationship is then introduced for this Gospel, the idea of "knowing." Knowing is synonymous with being in relationship with Jesus. Nathaniel's confession in verse 49 looks forward to Thomas's confession of 20:29. There, Thomas states the whole truth about Jesus, that Jesus is both Lord and God, that Jesus is both human and divine. Nathaniel states only the partial truth. Nathaniel will return to the narrative in the last resurrection appearance, "Gathered there together were Simon Peter, Thomas called the Twin, Nathanael of Cana in Galilee, the sons of Zebedee, and two others of his disciples" (21:2). Jesus' response to Nathaniel intimates Nathaniel's recognition of only part of the truth about Jesus. The reference to "greater things than these" is indeed the promise that what will be revealed is not only Jesus as God's son but Jesus as the very presence of God.

A first glance at 1:51 will conclude that it is a rather strange verse to interpret let alone to preach. The title "Son of Man" is known from the Synoptic Gospels as a title for Jesus connected in particular to his suffering. The first use of the title in John is in the context of the traversing of heaven and earth. As a result, the Fourth Gospel reimagines this title for Jesus as one that signals the act of the incarnation, or that represents what the incarnation means, that God became flesh. The title, here at the end of chapter 2, before the beginning of Jesus' ministry, recalls and is a restatement of 1:14, and the "Word became flesh." The disciples will not witness the heavens opening at Jesus' baptism with the Spirit descending on Jesus as narrated in Matthew, Mark, and Luke. Rather, they will be witnesses to the heavens opening and God's very self coming down to dwell on earth.

CONNECTIONS TO THE LECTIONARY

The overlap between the lectionary pericopes of 1:29-42 and 1:43-51 suggests that a preacher might want to adjust the boundaries of these lessons to 1:29-34 and 1:35-51. John 1:43-51 is the assigned text for Epiphany 2 in Year B, yet 1:35 marks a shift in emphasis to John as witness and the calling of the disciples. As argued above, John embodies one of the primary features of discipleship in the Gospel of John, witnessing, which is then implicitly communicated to Jesus' first disciples. It is John's words "Look!" that then cause the disciples to follow Jesus. Jesus does not first call his own disciples, which places significant emphasis on the importance of witness. John 1:43 brings Jesus into the act of finding disciples, but this is only after John has made possible Jesus' first followers, which led to their abiding with Jesus. To witness is to point, to say "Look!" so that abiding with Jesus becomes possible. John's role anticipates Philip's, who finds Nathanael. Neither Jesus nor the disciples are on their own when it comes to finding disciples. The preacher could invite the congregation to imagine the ways in which they are invited into this activity of John and Jesus, essential for making true "for God so loved the world" (3:16; cf. 10:16). John 1:35-51 is a fitting text for the season of Epiphany not only because of what Jesus reveals about himself but also because discipleship is about the revealing of Jesus. A preacher might encourage the congregation to imagine their important role in making Jesus known and how Jesus relies on them to make himself manifest to the world.

JOHN 2:1-11
THE FIRST SIGN: THE WEDDING AT CANA

An interesting exercise so as to appreciate the particular portrait of Jesus painted in each of the four Gospels is to notice Jesus' first act in his public ministry. In Matthew, it is the Sermon on the Mount; in Mark, an exorcism; in Luke, a disturbing sermon in his hometown of Nazareth sets up the major theme of rejection and elicits the desire to throw him off a cliff. In John, it is none of the above, but the changing of water into wine which is only found in the Gospel of John. This is Jesus' first of seven signs in the course of his public ministry:

Wedding at Cana (2:1-11)
Healing of Official's Son (4:43-54)
Healing of Man Ill for Thirty-Eight Years (5:1-18)
Feeding of the Five Thousand (6:5-14)
Walking on Water (6:16-24)
Healing of the Man Blind from Birth (9:1-7)
Raising of Lazarus (11:41-44)

In the Gospel of John, the miracles of Jesus are never called "miracles," but rather "signs" because by themselves they have little significance apart from the awe of the miraculous. They are signs because they point to something about Jesus, a critical revelation of Jesus that he himself usually explains after performing the sign. As discussed briefly in the Introduction, this Gospel outlines the structural pattern of sign, dialogue, discourse. Jesus performs a sign, followed by a dialogue in which the observers of the sign try to make sense of what happened, ending with Jesus' own interpretation of the sign. The meaning of the sign is incomplete, even misunderstood, without Jesus' elucidation.

This pattern occurs most obviously in chapters 5, 6, and 9. The pattern is altered, however, for this first sign and for the last sign, the raising of Lazarus. For the raising of Lazarus in chapter 11 the dialogue and discourse occur before the sign so that it will not be misinterpreted because it is indeed misconstrued by Martha. When Jesus asks Martha, "Do you believe in the resurrection?" She responds with, "Yes, I believe in the resurrection *on the last day*." This is an incorrect interpretation of the raising of Lazarus. The raising of Lazarus indeed anticipates the end-time resurrection but also points to life possible with Jesus now.

There is a similar pattern here with the first sign. There is no dialogue or discourse following the sign, because these have occurred in the Prologue before the sign has taken place. The commentary on the Prologue above discussed the importance of the concept of grace for this Gospel and that the term "grace" is never used outside of the Prologue. As a result, the first sign that Jesus' performs is a sign of grace upon grace. It is a "miracle" of abundance.

The details are crucial for the meaning of the sign. "On the third day" anticipates Jesus' words to the Jewish authorities at the cleansing of the temple (2:19). As such, "the third day" signals resurrection, new and abundant life, lending a feeling of anticipation to the scene. Jesus, his disciples, and his mother are attending a wedding in Cana of Galilee. Weddings in ancient Palestine lasted approximately a week, with an abundance of wine expected until the end of the celebration. Jesus is a guest. It is in his role as invitee and not host that Jesus first reveals what grace upon grace looks like. This is an unexpected setting for a first miracle, particularly because of Jesus' role as one invited and not as the one throwing the party. The setting of a wedding should also elicit some creative homiletical thought. The celebration is not a religious festival or a nondescript banquet but a wedding. Why a wedding? What do weddings intimate that would add to the sense of meaning of this passage? First, weddings are normal events of human life. Jesus introduces the presence of God into the day-to-dayness of being human. Second, weddings are a celebration of relationship, albeit sometimes strained ones in antiquity. They still held the promise of new life and festivity. Third, the setting of the wedding also anticipates the location of Jacob's well as the place where Jesus meets the Samaritan woman. The well is a site of relationship but also the fulfillment of God's promise to Abraham; so also the wedding at Cana carries similar overtones.

It is at this initial sign that we are first introduced to Jesus' mother. She is never called "Mary" in the Fourth Gospel, always the "mother of Jesus." She appears only twice in the entire story as a present character—here and at the foot of the cross with the beloved disciple. The mother of Jesus is here at the start of Jesus' ministry and at the end of his life. She is a witness to Jesus' first revelation of his glory (2:11) and his last. She *abides* with Jesus, witnessing his life and his death, and thereby is representative of this chief characteristic of God and of

Jesus. To be in relationship is to abide. She is denoted by her relationship, her essential role in Jesus' life, not by her name.

The fact that the mother of Jesus brackets Jesus' dwelling on earth is no minor literary feature. It is a significant rhetorical device that communicates a theological statement. As noted above, that she is never referred to by name emphasizes the mother–son relationship and calls attention to her specific meaning and function in the Fourth Gospel. The Prologue introduced the question of Jesus' origin, which then the rest of the Gospel unpacks, and which the persons who encounter Jesus must answer. Jesus is from the beginning, from the beginning with God. As a result, there can be no traditional birth story in the Gospel of John, since Jesus comes from the Father. The mother of Jesus takes on a different function therefore, that of the parental figure while Jesus lives on earth. Jesus comes from the Father and will return to the Father at his ascension, but during his earthly ministry his mother symbolizes the abundant life indicated in 1:18. It is no accident that John describes the relationship that Jesus has with the Father, and then accordingly, the relationship that believers will have with the Father because of Jesus, as the sustenance suggested by the image of the breast. Everything that a child needs to survive and live and thrive comes from nursing at mother's breast. That provision is not only food but water, nurture, shelter, protection, and bonding.

There is an implied shared parenthood between the Father and the mother of Jesus that holds together one of the major claims of the Fourth Gospel, that the divinity and humanity of Jesus can never be compartmentalized or separated. The mother of Jesus is the nurturing force when he is the Word made flesh. There is something remarkably poignant about this role for Jesus' mother in a Gospel that has traditionally been viewed as portraying an "otherworldly" Jesus. Jesus' humanity is not only understood as the Word become flesh, but is also underscored by his assumed dependence on his parents. Just as he has needed and will need his Father, now, during his three years of ministry, he needs his mother. That is, another means by which this Gospel will describe the human/divine identity of Jesus is by the poles of dependence and independence.

The presence of the mother of Jesus and her unique position suggests that one of the primary aspects of having a relationship with Jesus and, therefore, with the Father, will be dependence. A central characteristic of discipleship is dependence on Jesus. It is not often that we are given the opportunity to conceive of discipleship in these kinds of categories of need, reliance, and dependence. Too often, our interpretation of discipleship maintains a certain level of independence and fortitude, of apostleship and mission, of flailing and failure. Discipleship in the Gospel of John is cast primarily in classifications of relationship, and preaching discipleship according to John will explore what this means for our parishioners.

Jesus' push into public ministry is not his baptism or his testing in the wilderness but the coaxing of his mother. There is a sense here that the mother of Jesus is the one who is encouraging Jesus to be who he is, as if she is saying to him, as a mother would say to her kindergartner getting on the bus for the first time, "Come on, you can do it. Get on the bus! You are going to have a great day!" She demonstrates trust in Jesus. She sees something in her son. And it takes her initiative to move Jesus into his ministry. The unfortunate occurrence of running out of wine at a wedding would mark a major hospitality blunder. It is she who approaches her son Jesus and says to him, "they ran out of wine." It is worth wondering why she goes to Jesus about this—does she see something in him that no other can? A preacher might ask, what did she see in that moment? What had she seen in her life with him thus far? What had Jesus revealed to her up to that point that would cause her to believe that such a miracle was possible from him? How did she know that this was the time for revelation, the event of epiphany? A preacher should not overlook the humor in this dialogue. Jesus responds as if to say, "well, mom, that's not my problem. They should have hired a better wedding planner."

The reference to the hour is crucial here. The moment of the hour is the passion, resurrection, and ascension all wrapped up into one with the arrest and the trial as that which sets the hour in motion. That it is first mentioned here is significant because it is another link of this story with the scene at foot of the cross. The time of Jesus' hour will not come until his public ministry is over (13:1). The use of the term "hour" to describe the events of the end of Jesus' life is an interesting choice. It is obviously a designation of time over a description of a happening. In this regard, it is another means by which the fourth evangelist emphasizes both the uniqueness and the temporality of the incarnation and thereby, once again, the humanity of Jesus. The Word became flesh is a very real yet interim revelation of God in and for the world.

That Jesus' mother tells the servant "Do whatever he tells you" indicates her belief in Jesus, as if he is the one to solve this problem. Her words foreshadow what could happen if you do what Jesus tells you to do. The man ill for thirty-eight years will be made well because he obeyed Jesus' command, "Stand up, take your mat and walk" (5:8). The man blind since birth will be able to see because he did as Jesus said, "go, wash in the pool of Siloam" (9:7).

The details that follow are specifics of over-the-top abundance. Six jars, twenty to thirty gallons in volume, filled to the brim. A little modern day research of wine barrel capacity would yield that one hundred and eighty gallons is about a thousand bottles of wine. When the wine is brought to the steward, it turns out to be the best wine. This would be unheard of in the ancient world. As the steward notes, the wedding host would offer the good wine first when the guests were sober, but by day three or four, the cheap libations are served when guests are drunk and no one can tell the difference. The disciples believe in him but to believe in the signs themselves will not be adequate. The disciples have only partially seen Jesus' glory. Like the truth of the first sign itself, the best is yet to come.

This is a sign of abundance and a sign of promise. It is a sign of abundance that manifests what grace upon grace tastes like. It tastes like the best wine, more than you could possibly want or drink, when you least expect it. It is a sign of promise, because the best is saved for last. There is a promise of the resurrection and the life in this sign, that life with Jesus will be beyond when you think it has ended. An abundance of the best wine, at the end of the celebration, promises the abundance of grace, at the end of our physical lives, carried over into the resurrection and even more so, in the promise of the ascension.

CONNECTIONS TO THE LECTIONARY

Jesus' first sign of water into wine appears in Year C, Epiphany 2 in the lectionary. As the first act by which Jesus reveals his glory and power in the Gospel of John, it is an appropriate text for this season in the church year. It is followed by Jesus' first "sign" in the Gospel of Luke, the sermon in Nazareth (Luke 4:14-21). A preacher could compare Jesus' first acts in each of the Gospels and show how each event reveals the unique character of Jesus presented in the four Gospel narratives. If the season of Epiphany is about the manifestation of Jesus, what we see, learn, and know about Jesus takes on complexity and interest when not limited to a one-sided portrait. Perhaps it might help us to remember Jesus in a manger in the midst of miracles. The wedding at Cana is a reminder that whenever Jesus reveals his divinity, he is simultaneously revealing something about his humanity. Perhaps, in the sign that is water into wine, we will even experience something that we need to know about ourselves. What do we look for in Jesus and why? This Epiphany season might expand our ideas of what Jesus actually does reveal about himself. At the same time, the preacher could point to the specificity of this first sign in the Gospel of John in terms of what it reveals about Jesus. A sermon on Jesus' first sign could talk about all seven of Jesus' signs in John, naming what each sign shows about who Jesus is. In the case of water into wine, it is our first glimpse into what grace upon grace tastes like.

JOHN 2:13-25
THE TEMPLE INCIDENT

The first thing to notice in interpreting and preaching the temple incident in the Gospel of John is its different location in the Fourth Gospel compared to the Synoptic Gospels. Whereas in Matthew, Mark, and Luke, the temple scene follows Jesus' entry into Jerusalem, in John the episode is moved to immediately after Jesus' first sign. There are a number of significant theological meanings communicated in this transferal of a central event in the ministry of Jesus. First, it suggests that another circumstance will serve as the impetus for Jesus' arrest in the Fourth Gospel. If the temple skirmish functions in the Synoptic Gospels as the final public act whereby the authorities make the decision to arrest and kill Jesus, there will be another confrontation that will secure Jesus' fate in John. That act in the Gospel of John is the raising of Lazarus. To bring someone back from the dead will elicit the desire to end Jesus' life. Life begets death, which ironically underscores the truth of the incarnation.

Second, the shift in location calls attention to the fact that, for John, this incident will have an altogether different meaning. While this altered purpose will be discussed in greater length below, at this point it is worthwhile to press the rhetorical effect and significance of having Jesus' first sign and the temple incident side by side. Juxtaposing these two critical events in Jesus' ministry suggests levels of interpretation of each that are not necessarily observable when the episodes are construed in isolation from one another. Where and in what circumstances Jesus will offer abundance will not be in the usual places and spaces. Whereas Jerusalem signals a place of plenty, it was at a wedding in Galilee (mentioned twice) at which Jesus was a guest that the experience of abundance is first realized.

Third, it introduces the conflict between Jesus and the Jewish establishment early on in the Gospel. This is a story that has a constant tone of confrontation that will escalate as we move forward in the narrative. The establishment of conflict near the beginning of the Gospel offers a glimpse into the very real situation of the Johannine community, as a group that believed in Jesus in the face of opposition. It also suggests that the act of theology is inherently provocative. This rings true with the Fourth Gospel's main claim, which should, at its core, be challenging. The introduction of resistance and offense at this point in the story underscores the intrinsic theological difficulty on which this Gospels insists—that Jesus is from God, is with God, and is God, the Word made flesh. To narrate the ministry of Jesus without calling attention to the absurd and antagonistic aspects of this assertion would be to reduce its import and impact.

The reference to Passover in 2:13 is critical for determining the length and chronology of Jesus' ministry in the Gospel of John. Jesus will travel to Jerusalem for Passover three times throughout the course of his ministry (2:13; 6:4; and 13:1), thus providing the basis for a three-year ministry for Jesus. This is not the case for the Synoptic Gospels, in which Jesus' pilgrimage to Jerusalem for Passover, or any pilgrimage feast (Festivals of Passover, Weeks, and Booths) happens only once. The trip to Jerusalem not only secures the timeline of Jesus' ministry but also focuses the meaning of Passover and the importance of the city of Jerusalem. The Festival of Passover will be rethought and reimagined three times over the course of Jesus' ministry, and each time, of course, Jesus is in Jerusalem for the festival. As we will see, in the case of the temple incident here, Jesus immediately calls to mind a fundamental theological premise of the Festival of Passover, the presence of God.

To bring the city of Jerusalem this far forward in the narrative changes the symbolism of the city itself. It will not just be the place where Jesus will die; it is also a source of life. This adds yet another level of support for the main theological principle of this Gospel that in Jesus God is revealed. At the same time, the city of Jerusalem is not only the location of God but simultaneously represents everything that temple worship and the religious system give witness to about God. The pilgrimage festivals were not purely religious duties but represented the promise of God's steadfast love for God's people manifested in real moments of their history. For the fourth evangelist, the incarnation is another real moment in the history of God's people.

The levels of meaning of the temple incident in John are also found in the details of the how the event is told. Jesus enters the temple and finds what one would expect during a pilgrimage festival. The vital trades are in place for the necessary exchange of monies, animals, and grains for the required sacrifices. Nothing is out of order at this point. The narration happens in real time, as if the reader can see everything that Jesus sees. Jesus' command to the dove sellers differs strikingly from the accounts in Matthew, Mark, and Luke (Matt. 21:12-13; Mark 11:15-19; Luke 19:45-48). Instead of a concern for temple malpractices ("den of robbers"), Jesus orders that his Father's house not be made a marketplace. Yet, for the temple system to survive, the ordered transactions of a marketplace were essential. The temple had to function as a place of exchange for maintaining and supporting the sacrificial structures required for preserving a relationship with God. Jesus is not quibbling about maleficence or mismanagement but calls for a complete dismantling of the entire system. Underneath this critique lies also the intimation that the temple itself is not necessary. At the center of such theological statements is the fundamental question of God's location, which will be confirmed in the dialogue between Jesus and the Jewish authorities.

The authorities essentially ask for some sort of proof that Jesus has the right to do what he just did and say what he just said. They ask for signs, recalling the wedding at Cana and foreshadowing the next six signs that Jesus will perform during his public ministry. As noted in the Introduction, the signs that Jesus performs are in and of themselves not revelatory of Jesus' glory. Rather, they point to or indicate an aspect of who Jesus is that the believer needs to recognize.

Jesus' response to the request of the Jewish authorities is typically enigmatic. This will be a pattern throughout the Gospel, of Jesus providing answers to questions that do not appear to be answers at all. In every case, they are meant for the interlocutor to move ahead, forward, or more deeply toward an understanding of, and believing in, who Jesus really is. In that regard, the enigmas cannot be relegated to straightforward rhetorical devices or a puzzling Jesus. The perplexities of Jesus' answers are invitations, drawing the reader into the narrative, the dialogue, so as to figure out for oneself who Jesus is and what Jesus means. This deeper engagement also underscores the theological theme of abiding. The response of the Jewish authorities will be emblematic of the reactions to Jesus' cryptic statements. They interpret Jesus' declaration literally, that the temple of which Jesus speaks is the one Jewish temple in which they are standing. We find out, however, that the temple to which Jesus refers is not the temple in Jerusalem but the temple of his body. This reworking of the temple incident will be decisive for understanding the conversation between Jesus and the Samaritan woman about worship (4:19-24). When the women at the well inquires of Jesus where should be the proper place of worship, Mount Gerizim or Jerusalem, his answer, "neither on this mountain nor in Jerusalem," assumes this interpretation here of the temple incident. When the blind man "sees" who Jesus is, his response is to worship Jesus (9:35-38). Jesus himself is the presence of God.

In the Gospel of John, the reference to the three days is a foreshadowing of the resurrection but also the ascension. As a result, Jerusalem is at once the location of the completeness of Jesus' ministry—his incarnation, crucifixion, resurrection, and ascension—not just the place of his death. If the temple and, with it, the meaning of Passover, have to do with the location and presence of God, Jesus is essentially saying to the Jewish leaders that he is the presence of God. Where one looks for God, expects to find God, imagines God to be are all at stake for the Gospel of John. In Jesus, God is right here, right in front of you. That Jesus is the revelation of God, the one and only God (1:18), will be repeatedly reinforced with different sets of images, different characters, different directives, all pointing back to this essential truth.

The promised presence of God would also have been critical for the community to which John was writing. As noted in the Introduction, this was a Jewish group who had been thrown out of their community for their belief in Jesus. To hear that in their excommunication and exile God is present would have been exactly what they needed to hear and would serve to enact, in part, the rhetorical and theological purpose of this Gospel (20:30-31). An essential function of the Gospel of John is to sustain believers in their faith. As a result, listening for the ways in which the Gospel encourages, nurtures, and supports having faith in Jesus becomes a critical hermeneutic for each encounter and episode throughout the story. In other words, one primary interpretive lens for preaching this Gospel is to listen for the particular way in which a specific story, sign, or segment of the narrative is giving witness to how God's presence can be experienced. Each pericope articulates in some way a sense of what God's presence means and what it feels like.

JOHN 2:23-25
THE MEANING OF THE SIGNS

These last verses of chapter 2 function as transitional verses between the temple incident and the encounter with Nicodemus yet also set up issues that will be important for interpreting the encounter between Nicodemus and Jesus. Nicodemus's first statement to Jesus suggests that he and his fellow Pharisees have witnessed Jesus' signs while he was in Jerusalem. Nicodemus is perhaps the figure elected to represent the Jewish leaders in Jerusalem. He notes that it was because of witnessing Jesus performing signs that he is sent to inquire how these might be possible. That he will come at night, therefore, is a statement not just about his own disbelief but about the general unbelief of the main religious establishment. It is not that Nicodemus is simply an agent for the

Pharisees and therefore some sort of prototype or pawn. Rather, recognizing that Nicodemus exemplifies the larger group communicates the importance of one's own individual encounter with Jesus when it comes to believing in him. This will be true for the Samaritan woman's witness to her town as well. The townspeople will confess that they needed to hear for themselves from Jesus in order to come to believe that Jesus is the savior of the world. As a result, in several ways, these verses introduce both Nicodemus and the Samaritan woman at the well. She, too, will be an individual from a group, having her own encounter with Jesus. While Nicodemus asks about signs, not recognizing in the end who Jesus is, the woman finds herself encountering the very sign itself, Jesus, and Jesus reveals himself to her as such.

Connections to the Lectionary

The lectionary offers John's version of the temple incident for Lent 3 in Year B. This will be the first of three Sundays in a row from John, John 3:14-21, and John 12:20-33, which could invite a brief sermon series connecting these three texts, especially as heard in the season of Lent. The preacher should note that this incident is out of place here, as we move toward Jerusalem and Jesus' arrest, trial, and crucifixion. What is it doing here, anyway? Here is where John's distinctive presentation of the temple scene can be explored for the ways in which we will then end up interpreting the events of Holy Week. John 2:23-25 does not appear in the lectionary. To include these verses with the temple incident would call attention to the role of signs and what we see in what Jesus does. These verses ask us, what sign will convince us of Jesus' identity and power? The preacher might also let linger the final claim of chapter 2, "for he himself knew what was in everyone" (2:25). What does Jesus see in you, individually and as a community of faith, as we get closer to the cross?

3

A Tale of Two Disciples and the Second Sign (John 3–4)

Nicodemus and the Samaritan woman at the well are characters unique to the Gospel of John, and they could not be more different. Nicodemus is male, a leader of the Jews, a Pharisee, and he has a name. He comes to Jesus by night, some think so as not to expose his curiosity in Jesus lest his colleagues see fit to boot him out of the synagogue as they do the blind in chapter 9. In contrast, the woman at the well is female, is a Samaritan, and is nameless. She meets Jesus at noon, the brightest, lightest time of the day, ostensibly because of her questionable past, because of which she has been ostracized from the women who would usually accompany her. What woman in her right mind would fetch water at the hottest time of the day?

While our modern Bibles have neatly separated these two encounters with designated chapters and verses, there is little doubt that their proximity to each other invites comparison and contrast. We are meant to interpret Nicodemus and the Samaritan woman at the well together, not as separate, unrelated characters. To place these two chapters side by side elicits far more fodder for proclamation than isolated treatment. Moreover, in the lectionary they occur on two successive Sundays (Lent 2 and 3, Year A). The divergences between Nicodemus and the Samaritan are numerous and significant. Nicodemus is a man, a Pharisaic Jew, a religious leader; he has a name and approaches Jesus by night. The woman at the well is a Samaritan, a religious outsider; she is nameless and meets Jesus at noon, the brightest part of the day. The conversation with Nicodemus lasts nine verses, whereas the conversation between the Samaritan woman and Jesus lasts twenty-six.

John 3:1-21
The "Disciple" Nicodemus

The fact that Nicodemus approaches Jesus at night is not merely indicating the time of day for this encounter. We already know that light and darkness symbolize states of believing and unbelief. Many commentators suggest that Nicodemus's late-night, stealthy arrival specifies his concern not to be seen with Jesus, perhaps not wanting his fellow religious leaders to know that he has been talking to Jesus. While this may the case, a more compelling connotation is the anticipation of Nicodemus's response to Jesus. If this is a nighttime conversation, the chances are not good for positive results.

Nicodemus's first statement is one of predicted respect. He acknowledges Jesus' religious leadership, suggesting that he too might be able to learn from Jesus with the greeting, "Rabbi." Nicodemus simultaneously speaks the truth about Jesus yet reveals his misunderstanding of what it means for Jesus to be "from God." As noted above, one of the most important themes of the Gospel is where Jesus comes from. It is at the heart of the first verse in the Prologue, "In the beginning was the Word." Nicodemus states the truth that Jesus is from God, but he grounds that belief in the signs that Jesus does. In 2:23, Jesus stated that the signs that he has performed are not that on which one's belief in Jesus should be based. The structural pattern of sign, dialogue, discourse underscores that the signs are not enough and may even be misleading for believing in Jesus. While Nicodemus affirms what is most definitely true about Jesus, what he sees as true is located in an incomplete revelation of implication. While Nicodemus acknowledges the important question of Jesus' origin, he misstates again the reason for Jesus' ability to perform signs. Nicodemus concedes that God must be with Jesus, that God is present in Jesus' activities. This is, however, a partial truth because not only is God present with Jesus, Jesus is the very presence of God.

Jesus' answer is characteristically furtive. His enigmatic responses are usually misunderstood or misinterpreted but are meant to further the conversation toward fuller understanding of who Jesus is. One could see these episodes between Jesus and those who encounter him as a kind of theological trick, that Jesus is simply taunting his conversation partner when he knows full well how things will progress. A more generous reading suggests that there is something theologically important in dialogue. Revelation, understanding, possibility, and openness happen in conversation. Conversation itself is indicative of theological curiosity and not doctrinal conclusiveness. Words are important when it comes to the Word becoming flesh. In the larger context of John, these conversations are representative of what it means to abide in Jesus.

Abiding will take on numerous forms and examples and conversation is a means by which abiding takes place.

Nicodemus's clear misunderstanding of Jesus posits a literal interpretation of "born again." The Greek word *anōthen* can be translated "again, anew, from above." It is humorous that someone of Nicodemus's assumed intellect would offer such a basic and banal understanding of what Jesus means. This is perhaps one of the most well-known and misused verses in the Bible—what "born again" means. Parishioners will no doubt have had their own experiences with "born again" theology in Christianity. It would be hard to argue that this theological interpretation is incorrect since that is indeed one of the meanings of the word. Yet its one-sidedness flattens Jesus' claim as a one-dimensional possibility for salvation. What *anōthen* can imply suggests a three-dimensional reality that incorporates all three meanings. This is critical when it comes to the possible ways to understand Jesus' response to Nicodemus's misunderstanding. Too often 3:5 is interpreted through the lens of baptism alone. While the reference to water and Spirit certainly has baptismal overtones, the specific terms of water and Spirit have deep significance when one takes into account the entirety of the Gospel. Jesus is the provider of living water, to the Samaritan woman first. He will again reveal that he is the source of water, a basic need for the sustaining of life, in chapters 7–8. Water has to do with sustenance and nurture and what is essential to live.

The same is true of the mention of the Spirit. The reference to the Spirit here needs to be situated within the larger portrayal of the Spirit's activity and character according to John. John's pneumatology will be worked out significantly in the Farewell Discourse as the Paraclete. Yet the passage that should be brought to bear in the interpretation and preaching of 3:5 is the giving of the Spirit to the disciples in 20:22. The resurrected Jesus appears to the disciples as they are secluded together in fear. Jesus stands among them, says "Peace be with you," and breathes into them the Spirit. As discussed previously in this commentary, the verb in 20:22 is *emphysaō*, the same verb that is used in Genesis 2:7 for God's breathing God's very breath into *Adam*. As a result, the reference to the Spirit here in 3:5 is not just about baptism, but literally about becoming a child of God, a new creation, a new created identity, rebirth, that encompasses being born again, anew, and from above. If the preacher chooses to move in the direction of baptism, then any discussion of baptism needs to be specific to this connection to the creative activity of God and should certainly recall the particularities of Jesus' baptism in John. In other words, preach how the significance of baptism is changed by John's theological insights. What might we hear anew about baptism because of the associations the fourth evangelist envisions?

The perceived exclusivity of Jesus' words "cannot enter the kingdom of God" needs to be located in the larger understanding of the Johannine community, but more so, in the fourth evangelist's identification of what the kingdom of God means. Differentiated from its references in the Synoptic Gospels, the kingdom of God in John appears only here (3:3, 5). The only other time "kingdom" is used in the narrative is 18:36, three times, and there specifically "my kingdom": "My kingdom is not from this world. If my kingdom were from this world, my followers would be fighting to keep me from being handed over to the Jews. But as it is, my kingdom is not from here." The first person possessive to describe the kingdom suggests that when Jesus speaks of the kingdom in the Gospel of John it is another synonym for being in relationship with God. It is the abiding place for God and Jesus and the believer. Jesus' kingdom is not necessarily an alternate empire to that of Roman control but, given the reality of John's first readers, the place and space of belonging.

Verses 6-7 emphasize the dichotomy that Jesus represents, flesh and Spirit, but also recalls what it means to be a child of God (1:9-13), the claim on which this dialogue is premised. Jesus is talking about new birth, becoming a child of God, a new creation. One direction for preaching each of the encounters in the Gospel of John is to explore connections to that which has been outlined in the Prologue. The Samaritan woman at the well will be the embodied demonstration of 1:6-8. Nicodemus's encounter with Jesus exemplifies the power to become children of God (1:9-13).

Verse 8 plays with the multiple translations of *pneuma* in Greek. "Wind," "spirit," and "breath" are all possible renderings of the term, and it seems that at this point John wants us to hear all three. Why? What do the three meanings communicate to illuminate the role of the Spirit? The fickleness of the wind suggests the assurance of the source of the Spirit. As noted above, there is an intentional connection to the creative act of giving breath. These various possibilities for the purpose and function of the Spirit look ahead to the further development of the concept of the Spirit in the Farewell Discourse. A choice to focus on the meaning of the Spirit for Nicodemus would necessitate a wider discussion of the role of the Spirit in John's Gospel.

With Nicodemus's question in 3:9 the dialogue ends. Nicodemus cannot seem to move beyond the confines of his own understandings of God. He will return again in the story, in 7:50-52 and to bury Jesus (19:38-42). Assessing his status as a disciple is best left for his final occasion in the story. At the same time, preaching Nicodemus here should bring his appearances later in the Gospel to this moment. How do they help interpret the interchange between Nicodemus and Jesus? His final words in his dialogue with Jesus can be the very question from which a sermon on Nicodemus might originate, "how can these things be"? In many respects, Nicodemus's question is quintessential for John's Gospel, resaid, re-languaged, and reinterpreted throughout the narrative. Responses to Jesus' signs and sayings are essentially restating Nicodemus's question, "How can these things be?"

Jesus keeps talking—to what extent is this discourse by Jesus an overall commentary on signs in general? The audience shifts from second person singular to second person plural, thus disarming the reader by direct address. We can no longer relegate misunderstanding to the know-it-all Pharisee but must answer for ourselves Jesus' questions to Nicodemus. What follows becomes a key summary for the major themes in this Gospel that will play out in various encounters and circumstances.

3:10 points to the contrast between Nicodemus and the Samaritan woman at the well but also looks forward to the larger conflict between Jesus and the religious authorities in the Gospel. Any reliance on known constructs of God will no longer suffice when it comes to what God is up to in becoming flesh. The inability of someone in the know to recognize who Jesus is foreshadows the wide reach of God's grace, "for God so loved the world" (3:16). In verse 11 Jesus summons his witnesses, the Spirit and the Father, and reiterates the importance of testimony. That Nicodemus "does not receive their testimony" anticipates the reception of the witness of the woman at the well by her townspeople. They are able to hear her witness, but Nicodemus cannot hear the witness of Jesus. Verse 12 is another summary of a primary premise of this Gospel—that in Jesus the divine and human are held together, inseparable. The importance of the ascension for the Gospel of John is introduced here and recalls Jesus' origins (1:1) as well as the truth of 1:51. The ascension will be the true end of Jesus' witness, and this verse holds together the incarnation, "the one who descended" and the ascension, Jesus' return to the Father. Verse 14 is a reference to Numbers 21:8-9, which brings out the themes of deliverance and sight. The Israelites must look at the bronze serpent on the pole for their life to be saved. In the case of Jesus, his "lifting up" will be the crucifixion, resurrection, and ascension. Each aspect of the incarnation will expound on what life means. This verse is an invitation to watch for what eternal life means going forward in the narrative.

One of the major challenges of preaching this portion of John is that it includes perhaps the most famous verse of the Bible—John 3:16. To preach on this verse will seem like tinkering with constructs of faith so embedded and beholden that a preacher might ignore it all together. There are three strategies to preaching this verse. First, relocate it in its literary context. Why does Jesus say this here, to Nicodemus? Why does Nicodemus need to hear this from Jesus? Second, that God loves the world will be the very next encounter in the Gospel. God loves the world through Jesus' going to Samaria to find the woman at the well. Where is God's world now? What world do we need to see? Third, that God loves the world demands pressing the question of what does *loving* mean? How does God love the woman at the well? In other words, this verse may actually have new meaning if it is placed back into its narrative context, given specificity, and allowed to take on the flesh-and-blood reality into which it was first preached. Moreover, the original audience of this Gospel would hear in Jesus' words that God loves them, even them, those who have been cast out, abandoned.

Another key issue in preaching John 3:16 is to continue reading; verses 17-21 introduce the concept of judgment in the Gospel of John, not as that which comes from outside or from God but as that which is brought on oneself depending on one's response to the revelation in and of Jesus. God sent Jesus to save the world. What does this mean? No general definition of salvation will suffice. Salvation must be situated in a particular encounter and understood with the specificity that the incarnation necessitates. At a basic level, in the Gospel of John to be saved is to enter into the intimate relationship that God wants with every believer. How that salvation happens depends on the person, the encounter, and the circumstances, because of incarnation. By definition, incarnation demands particularity. Salvific moments in the Gospel of John are beholden to the individuality of the encounter. Salvation for Nicodemus is not the same as for the Samaritan woman at the well.

The root of the term "judgment" or "condemnation" is *krisis*, from which the English word *crisis* is derived. Encountering Jesus in the Gospel of John is a moment of crisis in that one must either believe or not. This claim of assumed exclusion has to be situated in the identity of the members of the Johannine community, who made the decision to follow Jesus and were expelled from their synagogue for this decision. Typically misused and misinterpreted, it may therefore be important to preach that this language is not a blanket demand for belief in Jesus. It calls attention to the very real dynamics of this community and names their plight. It is their specific problem that can be relevant for us today, not as a means by which to condemn others but in the context of how we struggle with those closest to us who do not believe. This Gospel will not provide an easy answer. Neither should we.

John 3:19-21 restates what it means that Jesus is the light of the world, that the incarnation is first known as the light shining in the darkness (1:5). In John, the concept of judgment is never more clearly stated than in 3:19, "This is the judgment, that the light has come into the world, and people loved darkness rather than light." Judgment does not come from God but is that which one incurs. Preaching this text would explore why it is that we love darkness. What does it hide? How is it safe? Why is it more appealing than light? These are the very real human dynamics that lie behind Jesus' often cryptic words. The term "deeds" has only one meaning, and that is to believe in Jesus as the Word made flesh, God incarnate. Not to believe is to be exposed, and any other works of discipleship are premised on this primary work of believing.

CONNECTIONS TO THE LECTIONARY

The story of Nicodemus has an interesting role in the lectionary, materializing four different times over the three lectionary years and for various liturgical observances. John 3:1-17 is offered as the Gospel reading for Lent 2, Year A, and Trinity Sunday, Year B. The designated lection for Holy Cross Sunday in all three lectionary years is John 3:14-17. For Lent 4, Year B, the pericope is 3:14-21. In all instances, the totality of the Nicodemus passage, that is, 3:1-21, should be included. Little about the latter part of this lection makes sense without the previous conversation between Jesus and Nicodemus. Moreover, to leave off 3:18-21 from the Nicodemus story ignores the themes of light and judgment that are clearly present in the first part of the chapter. While the preacher will certainly choose portions of this story on which to focus a sermon, the entirety of the text needs to reverberate for it to make sense. Otherwise, the preacher will spend an inordinate amount of time setting up a literary context that could very well be included in the reading. One of the extraordinary aspects about John 3:1-21 is the way in which it restates and reimagines the themes set out in the Prologue. The story of Nicodemus and his encounter with Jesus is the first embodiment of the rather abstract themes presented in the Prologue. Any sermon on Nicodemus could choose one of these themes and show how Nicodemus's character demonstrates the importance of the theme in light of an encounter with Jesus.

John 3:22–36
The Final Appearance of John the Witness

John 3:22–36 is omitted from the lectionary. At the same time, these verses should be incorporated into the texts included in the lectionary where John is featured so as to round out his character according to the Fourth Gospel. These verses seem to indicate the awareness of the fourth evangelist of other traditions related to John the Baptist. They provide another occasion for John to give witness to Jesus. His "joy" in being a witness for Jesus anticipates the joy of which Jesus will speak in the Farewell Discourse (15:11; 16:20, 21, 22, 24; 17:13). Moreover, these are John's last words as witness. That this is John's final testimony means that we are able to overhear the last words of Jesus' first witness. An important lens through which to hear John's last words is as summary and restatement. While the punctuation in 3:31 suggests that John has ceased talking at 3:30, there is no reason to assume that John's testimony concludes there. What follows is an opportunity for us to hear how John has interpreted the meaning of Jesus and to imagine the ways in which we might give witness to who Jesus is. The concepts presented in John's last testimony also look forward to the purpose of John's Gospel, 20:30–31. To be sure, there are aspects about this last portion of John 3 that seem either out of place in John or simply repetitive of the Synoptic presentations of John, particularly expressions of God's wrath. While it may be true that the fourth evangelist incorporates other known traditions of John, this concluding witness of the first witness must be situated in the presentation of John already established in this Gospel.

John 4:1–42
An Unexpected Witness

There could be no character more opposite to Nicodemus than the Samaritan woman at the well. As noted above, she contradicts Nicodemus in virtually every possible way, thereby highlighting our expectations for how we will view and interpret the conversation that follows.

4:1–6
The Setting

The opening verses of the chapter (4:1–6) set the stage for the encounter between Jesus and the woman. The first two verses are a reminder that conflict is ever present when it comes to Jesus' ministry. Jesus has been in Jerusalem for Passover, the first of three trips to Jerusalem for this pilgrimage feast. The temple incident brought to the forefront early on in this story pointed to the clash between Jesus and the dominant religious party. Now Jesus will return to Galilee before traveling again to Jerusalem in chapter 5 for an unnamed festival. It is difficult to determine exactly the issue around baptism present in these two verses, except that it points to the ways in which Jesus will become increasingly intolerable in the eyes of the Jewish leaders. He leaves Judea to start back to Galilee, evidently a journey that will necessitate going through Samaria. A casual glance at a map of ancient Palestine or a rudimentary knowledge of Palestinian geography reveals that it is not, geographically speaking, necessary to go through Samaria when traveling from Judea to Galilee. In fact, a Jew would most certainly not journey through Samaria because of the risk of coming in contact with Samaritans. As a result, Jews traveling between Judea and Galilee would cross over the Jordan River and go up the other side to Galilee.

The rift between the Jews and the Samaritans has a complex history. Considered outsiders and even idolaters by the Jews (2 Kings 17), the Samaritans nevertheless understood themselves to be descendants of the northern kingdom. The name means "keeper of the law," and the Samaritans held to the Pentateuch as their Scripture. Their place of worship was Mount Gerizim over against Jerusalem. The proper place to worship, or the primary religious center, is the issue that maintained the schism between the two groups throughout the centuries, perhaps dating as far back as the fifth century B.C.E. People in the pew will be relatively aware of other stories of Samaritans (Luke 10:35-37), but the taming of that story might have a negative effect on the preaching of the Samaritan woman at the well. A key challenge for preaching will be to inform our congregations that Samaria would be the last place, not the first place, expected for Jesus to go to show God's love for the world.

That Jesus "had to" go through Samaria is better translated "it was necessary for him" to go through Samaria. The detail is not a geographical but a theological necessity. That Jesus must travel through Samaria is stipulated by John 3:16, "For God so loved the world." The disciples, the hearers of this Gospel, need to know what and who the world is. That God loves the world will be demonstrated by Jesus' ministry in Samaria. The "world" is not a general claim about God's love, or a universal description of God's positive inclination toward new believers. Rather, the world represents the entirety of God's creation, including those who cannot imagine themselves as objects of God's love. The "world" calls to mind the creation imagery present throughout this Gospel and first established in the opening verse, "in the beginning." There is nothing in God's creation that God does not love, even the least anticipated persons.

The "world" here also has a sense of "to the ends of the earth," thus representing again the abundance of God's love. God loves even those on the margins, the peripheries, the outer boundaries of the centralized community. This would have been a critical claim for the first hearers of this Gospel, struggling with their own reality of excommunication and the question of whether God's love could still be for them and even reach them in the outskirts of community and identity.

The fact that Jesus' very next encounter in the Gospel is with the woman at the well confirms that God's love is for those on the outside of the religious center. While this would have been good news for the audience for which this Gospel was written it should also elicit possibilities for contemporary audiences, our congregations who feel unworthy of God's affection and abundant love. When and how do they sense their own outsider status and why?

Verse 5 establishes the underlying unity that existed between the Samaritans and the Jews. They both trace their lineage back to Abraham and his descendants. This is not just any well, but Jacob's well. The emphasis on this accord suggests a secondary commentary throughout the Gospel that the differences between the Johannine community, those who believe in Jesus as the Messiah, and the religious establishment may not be as pressing as most of the story that follows will narrate. In other words, the perceived differences between the Jewish groups depicted in the Gospel are not as urgent as we might make them out to be. This is not a new God at work, but a new revelation of God's self, a unique manifestation of the God of our ancestors (1:18). This is the God that has been for God's people since the call of Abraham and to whom both Jesus and the woman at the well can trace their ancestry. This attention to the idea of unity will underscore the theme of unity in the later chapters of the Gospel, when Jesus talks to the disciples about the unity between him and the Father, between him and the disciples, and between the Father and the disciples.

The site of Jacob's well has additional significance as a betrothal scene in the Old Testament Jacob and Rachel (Genesis 29), Moses and Zipporah (Exod. 2:18-22), Isaac and Rebekah (Genesis 24). The setting points to a number of possible interpretations of the encounter between Jesus and the woman at the well. First, there is an overt reference to betrothal, marriage, and relationships. This obvious allusion may feel uncomfortable to those who want to remove Jesus from any real human emotion, feelings, or affection. Surely, this very specific setting could not possibly indicate any romantic or sexual thoughts on the part of Jesus, right? But, what if it did? What would be the purpose of evoking such ideas when it comes to a portrayal of Jesus? Answering this question mandates locating this story in the larger theological framework of the Fourth Gospel. To take the incarnation seriously, to give it the fullest extent and expression, demands that no aspect of what it means to be human be overlooked. To do so would be to truncate the principal theological claim of this Gospel. At stake for the fourth evangelist is that Jesus is truly God in the flesh and every aspect of what humanity entails God now knows.

This setting also calls to mind the levels of intimacy that abound in this Gospel. Jacob's well is a site of betrothal, which recalls the wedding at Cana. The display of abundance at Cana should be anticipated in the encounter that follows. The intimate relationship with God into which the believer is invited is as close as it gets. The categories of intimacy are given full representation in the Fourth Gospel, including father and child, mother and child, husband and wife, lovers, and friends. By desiring an intimate relationship with us, God also wants to experience the full spectrum of intimacy. God is presented as Father with children, as friend, and as lover.

The verses that establish the setting for the encounter in chapter 4 end with an important detail, "it was about noon." Some translations use "the sixth hour" the standard measuring of time by the hour after six in the morning. Nicodemus came to Jesus by night. Now the woman at the well meets Jesus at the lightest and brightest part of the day, when the sun is the highest in the sky and there is the most sunlight possible. Many commentators interpret this odd time to draw water as a statement about the woman's morality. She arrives at the well at noon because she does not want to be seen by others; she's embarrassed by her questionable past or she has been ostracized to come to the well when no one else is around. Such curiosity makes little sense for this Gospel where issues concerning morals, values, and what we would equate with sin, are of little significance. For John, sin has nothing to do with past actions or present indiscretions. Sin is a synonym for lacking a relationship with God. To cast judgment on the perceived "sin" of the woman misconstrues what sin is for the Fourth Evangelist. The reference to the time of day points to the theological theme of light and darkness, with darkness representing the realm of unbelief and light, the realm of belief. The fact that the Samaritan woman meets Jesus at noon invites hopeful anticipation of this conversation. The guiding question should be, how will she do in the conversation with Jesus? This detail suggests that she may very well fare better than her counterpart in Nicodemus.

To be at the well at noon is a most inopportune time for Jesus as well. Jesus is tired, yet another reminder of his finitude. The trip between Jerusalem and Galilee would have taken about three days. Jesus is worn out. He needs water, as does she. He is vulnerable, in need, and she can be the source of his need. There is a mutuality of need present before the two ever utter words to each other.

4:7-10
THE ENCOUNTER

Verses 7-10 narrate the first words exchanged between the woman and Jesus. Jesus is sitting by the well when the Samaritan woman comes to draw water. The initial words in the conversation are spoken by Jesus and are a request to fill his need. Jesus needs water and she has what he needs, emphasizing the reciprocity in this pending relationship. Jesus needs water, and she will need his living water. Jesus needs her to be a witness, and she needs Jesus to invite her into this new identity. Jesus' first words also draw attention to Jesus' humanity. He is dependent on her, modeling the mutual dependence on which relationship and discipleship is based. This interdependence is accentuated by his request. He asks for what he will provide *for her.*

The importance of reciprocity in relationship is critical for understanding the Fourth Gospel's construct of discipleship. Although the initial invitation to the first disciples was to follow, the discipleship that Jesus has in mind will be companionship, friendship, and taking on the ministry of Jesus at his death. While a hierarchy of social, religious, and political elements will place limitations on the relationship between Jesus and the woman at the well, the conversation that follows will call out these inequities and hegemonies so as to underscore further the closeness of relationship that Jesus offers. True relationship, true intimacy necessitates mutuality, equality, and regard.

The parenthetical (in English translations) remark that "the disciples had gone to the city to buy food" is by no means tangential. That the disciples are absent, presumably in Sychar to gain provisions for their ongoing journey, means that Jesus and the Samaritan woman are alone at the well. The boundaries crossed in this encounter continue to build. We have a man speaking to a woman, a rabbi speaking to a woman, a Jew speaking with a Samaritan, a Jewish rabbi speaking with a Samaritan, and now, we find out, they are *alone.* Verses 7 and 9 repeat her identity as a "Samaritan woman," not just a Samaritan and not just a woman, so as to underline the unfathomability of the exchange that will follow. For all intents and purposes, this conversation not only should not be happening, but it stands way outside the realm of possibility. The impossibility of the encounter and its location and setting further highlight the extent of God's love, the lengths toward which God will go to demonstrate love for the world.

The woman's response to Jesus' request reveals that she is fully aware of the realities and ramifications of Jesus' simple appeal. She names every boundary that has already been crossed just by Jesus' presence and his need. Jesus is a Jew asking a drink from her, a woman, of Samaria. She knows her place very well, she knows the rules, but there is also a sense that she is willing to call Jesus on it. She does not immediately submit to his request. She does not run away when realizing the jeopardous situation in which she has found herself. Instead, she questions Jesus, almost as if she is saying to him, "Do you have any idea what you just did? Any idea at all?" A sermon based on this moment in the text might ask, what does she see in Jesus that compels her to stay?

The comment in parentheses that follows is perhaps the greatest understatement in the entire Bible (4:9). Jews indeed do not share things in common with Samaritans, nor do they come in contact with them for any reason whatsoever. To do so would necessitate a return to Jerusalem for Jesus, a ritual cleansing from the contamination. Jesus' answer is similar to the obscure response given to Nicodemus after his first words in his conversation with Jesus (3:4). The first words of both Nicodemus and the Samaritan woman reflect their sense of place and identity, an awareness of who they are but at the same time intimating who they might become.

Jesus' answer stands in the grammatical construction of a contrary-to-fact condition. What Jesus offers is named as "gift," a term that appears only here and in 15:25, "It was to fulfill the word that is written in their law, 'They hated me without a cause.'" Jesus gives specificity to the water that he offers, living water, thereby making an attempt to help the Samaritan woman see something beyond the immediately observable in Jesus. Her answer parallels that of Nicodemus in 3:4. She states the obvious, that Jesus does not have a bucket, which makes it exceedingly questionable as to how he might have this living water. It is hard to know how she hears the adjective of "living" water. Literally, the verb *zaō* connects to life, having to do with life. She may interpret this as simply basic water needed for sustaining life.

JOHN 4:11-15
THE POSSIBILITY

There is a certain tone of "who do you think you are?" in the woman's next question for Jesus. Her reference to Jacob as "our ancestor" once again emphasizes the same ancestry for both Jews and Samaritans and, in this case, also demonstrates that she understands fully where they are sitting and talking, at Jacob's well. Her description of the well, "and with his sons and his flocks drank from it" (4:12), stresses the theme of provision underlying this entire scene but also helps make sense of her misunderstanding. She knows that this well has provided for God's people for centuries. And now, in Jesus, she is being invited to see that God is still providing for God's people.

In verses 13-14, Jesus demarcates between the water in the well and the water that he provides by introducing the concept of thirst. Jesus attempts to move the woman beyond the literal concept of water and what it satisfies to a different idea of what it means to be thirsty and for what we thirst. At the same time, it is couched in the very bodily, incarnational reality of what water gives. When God becomes human, there is grace upon grace (1:16) which is as simple and as profound as our essential needs. Moreover, the water that Jesus provides, unlike a well, will never dry up, never run empty. The last participle, "gushing up to eternal life," is a present participle, emphasizing the never-ending, ongoing presence and reality of God as the source of life. That this promise is true into eternal life gives further accent to the enduring quality of what God makes available in a relationship with the Father.

Verse 15 indicates that the Samaritan woman is still making sense of Jesus' words from a literal perspective, but there are three significant aspects of her response that disclose how far the conversation has advanced. First, she reiterates Jesus' description of the water he provides, "this" water. She is able to distinguish a difference between the water that Jesus offers her and the water she has had to come and draw each and every day. Second, something has changed for her to state that she will never be thirsty—of course she will. That is a basic state of the makeup of the human body. She has shifted her understanding of thirst to something else, yet not quite certain of what that "something else" might be. She has moved, however, in her understanding of who Jesus might be, from a thirsty Jew who needs to learn some manners to someone who has something that she needs at a very basic level. The final section of her answer divulges the totality of her certain situation. As a woman, she would have been required to visit the well twice a day, in the early morning and the early evening, to fetch water in buckets, probably two each time, to return to the village with the fresh water. That she would not have to engage in that expectation of her lot and place in life—what would she be thinking in this moment? Will our sermons give her a chance to voice what it would mean to be relieved of that ritual? Might there be something in the emphasis on "here" that calls attention to the poignancy of her plight, the plight of the Samaritans alongside the Jews?

JOHN 4:16-19
THE HEART OF THE MATTER

The next section of the dialogue seems abrupt. Why would Jesus ask the woman to call her husband at this point? How does her marital status or the presence of her husband have anything to do with the conversation thus far? A reading forward to the Samaritan woman's response to Jesus' request is a helpful entry into the purpose of this brief section—she will see Jesus as a prophet (4:19). What he knows about her is not purely general information about her life but the most painful reality in which she has lived and now tries to survive.

For the writers of the New Testament, there is no understanding of prophecy other than what is presented in their Scriptures. Unlike our present perceptions of prophecy, which tend to view it as prediction alone, for the Israelites and, therefore, for the Jewish Scriptures, prophecy is history. The prophets are considered historical books because they narrate the events in Israel's history through the role of a particular prophet in that moment in history. The woman sees that Jesus is a prophet, not because he has predicted something yet to happen in her life but because he has named the truth about her life, a truth that is heartbreaking and most likely the reason she finds herself alone at the well at the wrong time of the day. It also situates the reason for the subject of this portion of the dialogue. The conversation between Jesus and the Samaritan woman at the well has the potential to progress beyond that between Jesus and Nicodemus. Jesus instigates this progression by going to the heart of the matter and why he had to go through Samaria in the first place. For the woman to be able to recognize who Jesus is means that Jesus has to reveal not only who he is but also who she is. Her need for him must be named so as to make sense of the mutual dependence between believers and Jesus.

This text continues to demand careful reading and careful interpretation. Jesus' reason for asking about her husbands is not to condemn her for her past. She is not a "five time loser" or a tramp as many sermons still claim. There is no proclamation of forgiveness for her questionable morals. There is no exclamation of judgment for her assumed sin of sexual impropriety. Yet she is continually blamed for her plight and charged with behavior for which there is no textual or historical proof. Lest the preacher think that the twenty-first century church is beyond such misogynistic conclusions, this story, like no other in Scripture, continues to prove otherwise. Sermons on this story will continue to need to free her from a hermeneutic that perpetuates the sexism that is alive and well in the church today.

The dialogue between Jesus and the woman at this point also reiterates her situation. Jesus could have solely stated her situation succinctly without the need for her to respond with "I have no husband." Her brief statement is heartrending . It is not only a statement about her marital status but an assertion about her marginalized status. She is a woman, a Samaritan woman, without a name, who has been married five times. To have been married five times in ancient Palestine would be evidence of circumstances completely beyond the control of any woman at that time. Likely widowed or divorced, the fact alone of having had five husbands would have indicated some sort of curse against her or her family. What on earth did she do, or her ancestors, that she would be subject to such destitution? In order to survive, it was necessary for a woman to be married, thus the numerous injunctions in Scripture to care for widows. To have had five husbands could also mean that the woman had been divorced, often for trivial matters, but more likely because she was barren. If she was barren, that would mean that she would not have family to turn to in the case of being widowed, which would further exacerbate her dependent status. The fact that she is currently living with a man not her husband does not correspond to a modern-day "shacking up" or "living in sin." Rather, her situation was probably a levirate marriage. By law (Deut 25:5-10), the brother of the dead husband was obliged to take in his dead brother's wife, either by formal marriage or by living arrangements of some kind.

An awareness of the woman's situation that is historically informed is a necessary correction to the countless sermons preached that continue to banish and berate Jesus' first witness in the Gospel besides John. At the same time, recognizing the magnitude of the situation of the woman at the well is a theological necessity for the Fourth Gospel. Jesus' revelation to her is not just that he knows *about* her; rather, he knows what it means to *be* her. God is revealing God's self in the Fourth Gospel as the Word made flesh. At stake in this encounter is the incarnation itself. For Jesus to name anything else about her other than that which has completely defined her reality up to this point would be to not take the incarnation seriously. Moreover, as the conversation progresses, her reality and identity will shift dramatically. To sense the impact of this astonishing change, we need to know how unexpected it would be.

JOHN 4:20-24
THE INQUIRY

When the woman sees that Jesus is a prophet (4:19), she then questions Jesus about the most important theological dispute that remained at the heart of the discord between the Jews and the Samaritans—where to worship God. That she asks this particular question of Jesus should not be overlooked. First, she asks a theological question. Regardless of historicity or probability, the fourth evangelist puts on the lips of this Samaritan woman the theological issue at the core not only of the rift between the Jews and Samaritans but of the Gospel itself. Upon the return to Palestine after the exile, the Samaritans built their temple to worship God on Mount Gerizim. The Jews began their rebuilding of the temple on the Temple Mount in Jerusalem. Reference to these building projects is not about worship convenience or religious disagreement. They have everything to do with the belief in and commitment to God's presence. Central to John, and essential for all of the Gospels as post-70 writings, is the location of God. Our interpretation and understanding of all of the Gospels necessitate locating their witness after the destruction of the city of Jerusalem and of the temple. The primary theological question each Gospel answers in the person and portrait of Jesus is, where is God? How each Gospel writer answers this question is key to the interpretation of Jesus presented in each.

In John, moving the temple incident to the second chapter made clear that the presence of God is no longer in the temple but here, now, right in front of you. That is what is at stake to claim that the Word became flesh. The fact that it is a woman from Samaria who first asks of the presence of God is profound. It is another means by which to emphasize 3:16, "For God so loved the world." God will first reveal God's self to her. There are plenty of characters who might have been offered as witnesses to God's revelation in Jesus, Nicodemus, as noted above, or the disciples, yet it is a Samaritan woman who is the example of what might happen when one abides with Jesus. This is another reason why the characters of Nicodemus and the woman at the well must be juxtaposed in interpretation and preaching. The contrasts between these two characters are striking and suggest that reading forward will anticipate similar disparities. This will indeed be true when, only two chapters later, we will be introduced to Judas by the prediction of his betrayal even before his identity as a disciple in chapter 6. The possibility of seeing who Jesus is, of believing in who Jesus is, is immediately manifested in a universal claim. That is, for this Gospel to fulfill its theological purpose (20:30-31), it has to, on the front end, demonstrate its truth. In other words, if these words are written for the sake of creating new believers and for sustaining current believers, then the story must introduce us to a character who has yet to believe. In the Samaritan woman, we encounter such a character. She is someone whom we would least expect to recognize who Jesus is and to whom we would never imagine that Jesus would reveal his identity. That this Gospel situates its beginnings, and the beginnings of Jesus, before creation, in the beginning with God, suggests that the entirety of God's creation is at stake and is involved in God's commitment to becoming human.

In other words, to place Nicodemus alongside the Samaritan woman at the well is a new creation story. The presentation of a male and female as encountering God revealed in Jesus only a few chapters after the opening verses of the Gospel intimates that, throughout this Gospel, Genesis 1 and 2, the creative activity of God—God creator, creation, and new creation—is a central theme.

Jesus' response to the Samaritan woman confirms the essence of her inquiry. "Neither on this mountain nor in Jerusalem" could be a title for John's story of Jesus. Jesus' answer foreshadows the response of the man born blind, who, when Jesus finds him after being expelled by the Pharisees, says, "'Lord, I believe.' And he worshiped him" (9:38). To recognize who Jesus is to worship who he is (4:22-24).

JOHN 4:25-26
THE REVELATION

The woman's response to Jesus' injunctions about worship names another partial truth—he could be the Messiah. She has moved to another level of understanding of who Jesus is. At the same time, Jesus is the Messiah, but there is more to the story. That there is more to Jesus, more to know and understand about him then anticipates Jesus' rejoinder. Jesus' reply to the woman's belief in the Messiah is the first "I AM" statement in the narrative. There are two different categories of "I AM" statements in the Gospel of John. The first type is the absolute "I AM" statement, which occurs nine times in the Gospel of John (4:26; 6:20; 8:24, 28, 58; 13:19; 18:5, 6, 8). Most translations "I AM he" are misleading by including the pronoun "he" after the "I AM." The "he" does not exist in the Greek text and takes away the impact of the "I AM" standing on its own. The absolute "I AM" statements are meant to be direct claims of who Jesus really is, the Word was God, the Word made flesh, God incarnated, God revealing God's self, as God did to Moses (Exod. 3:14), but now in a new and unique way. Preaching on this text, or any text with an absolute "I AM," especially if the preacher chooses to focus specifically on the "I AM" statement, should read the text aloud in worship without the "he" inserted. Let the congregation hear what the hearers of this Gospel would have experienced, what the Samaritan woman at the well experienced. Rather than read the passage as translated and then explain in your sermon why the "he" should not be there, let the effect of hearing these words from Jesus do what they intend to do. Remarkably, Jesus reveals the entirety of who he is, in all of its intimacy, vulnerability, and awe, to her.

The second variety of "I AM" statements in the Gospel of John are those with a predicate nominative (6:35, 51; 8:12; 9:5; 10:7, 9, 11, 14; 11:25-26; 14:6; 15:1, 5). These statements are the familiar images and metaphors by which Jesus describes himself, and they form the major taxonomy for John's portrait of Jesus. Using primarily inanimate objects or concepts, the fourth evangelist creates a diverse collage of ways by which to reveal the meaning and ministry of Jesus. These images seek to give specificity and particularity to what Jesus offers his believers. The only predicate nominative that does not fall into this category is the figure of the Good Shepherd in chapter 10. "I AM the good shepherd" stands out as the single predicate nominative connecting who Jesus is to the activity of an actual kind of person. The predicate nominative "I AM" statements are not only unique to John; they are an essential aspect of the primary theological assumption of this Gospel, "and the Word became flesh." The fourth evangelist undergirds a theology of incarnation by locating a description of Jesus in physical, material, and tangible realities.

JOHN 4:27-30, 4:31-38
THE INVITATIONS

The response of the woman to Jesus' revelation is interrupted by the return of the disciples, who had been off in the city to purchase food. They are surprised when they stumble upon the scene and find Jesus speaking with a woman, a Samaritan woman! The reaction of the disciples is strange at best. Whether because of fear, misunderstanding, or astonishment, none utters a word about Jesus' encounter. At the same time, this brief interlude between the first "I AM" statement and the woman's departure has four functions. First, it gets the disciples back to the well, and we will then anticipate Jesus' explanation to them of what he has been up to since the disciples have been gone. Second, it emphasizes further the shocking nature of this encounter, lest we forget after the lengthy conversation up to this point. The second question of the disciples, why are you speaking with her?, stresses the improbability of this conversation yet again. One might imagine a particular emphasis on "with her" in reading the passage out loud. Third, reminding us once more of the boundaries that have been crossed in this encounter at the well accentuates the woman's response, what she has learned, and our expectations of what she will do after this dialogue. Fourth, the questions the disciples ask reiterate key themes in this passage and in the Gospel. "What do you want?" (4:27) is better translated, "What do you seek?" The answer, of course, is her. He came to the well; he had to go through Samaria to find her. Jesus' first words to his disciples in 1:38 use the same verb, *zēteō* ("to seek"), "what do you seek, what are you looking for?" The tables are turned, so to speak. Jesus asked them, "what are you looking for?" They now ask the same question of him. He is looking for believers, disciples. They were looking for him. This is another instance of the mutuality of relationship between Jesus and believer.

The detail provided in verse 28, "then the woman left her water jar" is a sermon on its own. The Samaritan woman will go back to her town and tell her people of her encounter with Jesus, but first John mentions that she leaves her water jar at the well. Why? What does this seemingly unimportant element have to do with her return to the city and her conversation with Jesus? Is she in a hurry, excited about sharing what happened at the well? Did she simply forget and now she will have to return later in the day to pick it up? If we press a theological question, what did she leave behind at the well? The verb can also be translated "let go." She leaves behind her ostracism, her marginalization, her loneliness, because Jesus has brought her into his fold. She leaves behind her disgrace, her disregard, and the disrespect she has endured to enter into a new reality, a new life that is abundant life. The juxtapositions of what she leaves behind and what she gains are striking. As noted in our discussion above, she is probably barren. Her barrenness is answered by her birth of new believers. Her rejection is replaced by a renewal of hope, in Jesus as the promised Messiah, in her own sense of purpose. Her absence of any individuality is interchanged with a new identity of being a witness. What happens to the woman at the well is a microcosm of the larger appositions that permeate the Gospel as a whole: human and divine, flesh and Spirit, light and darkness. The woman's transformation is no mere new vocation or passing conversation with Jesus. Her encounter with the Word made flesh brings her into the theological reality that undergirds the entire Gospel. She is not only an example of what it means to be a witness. She embodies fully the transition from darkness to light, from outsider to insider. She is reborn.

Verses 28-29 narrate the woman's return to her city. The first words in her invitation to the people are the same words Jesus utters in the calling of the disciples (1:39) and which Peter speaks to Nathanael (1:46). Jesus first says to the disciples, "what are you looking for?" after they have been following him. As discussed in chapter 1, the disciples' question "where are you staying?" is central for this Gospel. They ask Jesus where he is abiding. To know where Jesus is abiding, which is right here and right now as the Word made flesh, as this unique revelation of God, is all that is needed for a relationship with Jesus. Jesus answers the disciples, "come and see." They do and abide with Jesus. The woman at the well invites her townspeople to the very same possibility.

Certainly there are other reiterations of witness that the woman could have expressed. That her words are an exact replication of Jesus' words and also Philip's should invite significant pause for interpretation. What does this mean for the woman at the well? How is it that the words she speaks underscore who she has become? The fact that she uses identical words as Jesus also anticipates the final conversation with Jesus and Peter in chapter 21, where Jesus tells Peter that he will need to feed, tend, and shepherd Jesus' sheep once Jesus ascends to the Father. The woman at the well is not only a witness. She is Jesus, the "I AM" in the world, for her people. The same thing will be true for Peter. Jesus will ask him to be the "I AM" in the world when he cannot be. To be a disciple of, a witness for, Jesus is no second-rate position. It means embodying fully the ministry of Jesus for the sake of those yet to believe.

Remarkably, the woman's invitation to the members of her community comes without certainty. The question in Greek, "he cannot be the Messiah, can he?" (4:29) expects a negative answer. A more accurate translation might be, "Surely, this cannot be the Christ, can it?" There is undeniable promise in this moment of uncertainty. It suggests that to be a disciple or witness of Jesus does not demand full and complete knowledge or conviction. It intimates the primary mystery, the unbelievability of what God has done in becoming human. For the woman at the well to be certain of her encounter with and discovery of Jesus would take for granted what God has done, as if God becoming human was a most ordinary, understandable, and expected choice on God's part.

JOHN 4:31-38
THE INVITATIONS PART 2

In response to the woman's words, the people leave the city and are on their way to meet Jesus. In the meantime, there is an interruption. The encounter with Jesus is postponed, anticipated, for expectation and effect. The interlude offered in verses 31-38 at first glance seems like a bizarre break in the action. The interchange between Jesus and the disciples mimics the conversation between Jesus and Nicodemus and the Samaritan woman at the well, an initial misunderstanding of Jesus' words. The disciples are convinced that Jesus must be hungry, and they urge him to eat. Jesus responds ambiguously which then leads to a literal interpretation. The humor should not be lost in this interchange but in humor is also truth. The questions of the disciples "Did you bring him lunch?" "No, did you?" "When did he eat?" expose their confusion. The use of misunderstanding in the Gospel of John is not just a rhetorical, grammatical, or syntactical tool but is meant to emphasize how really astonishing this all is. It underscores the improbability of what is being presented theologically, that God decided to become human.

The farming image used by Jesus in verses 34–38 has a dual function. It provides the disciples with a vivid picture of what discipleship looks like for this Gospel. Playing with this image, turning it around to discover its various facets is essential for the kind of impact it is meant to have. The picture suggests the profusion of possibility to transform people into being witnesses to or disciples of Jesus. That the field is ripe for harvesting intimates abundance, a major theme of the Gospel and the disciples cannot fail to notice *who* can be a disciple. "Four months more" points to urgency. The disciples need to see that the opportunity to invite people into being witnesses to or disciples of Jesus is here and now because of the temporariness of the incarnation.

The second function of the image is how it works as Jesus' commentary on his conversation and encounter with the woman at the well. In some respects, what happens to the woman at the well is like a sign that Jesus must interpret. It is not only that the woman at the well becomes a witness for Jesus, even though this is miraculous, especially when compared to Jesus' encounter with Nicodemus. The meaning of the encounter, the "sign," also exists beyond itself, beyond the obvious, and points to what is possible. The image also foreshadows the last verses of this section of chapter 4 and the response of the Samaritan townspeople, the harvest will indeed be bountiful.

The language of sower and reaper further unpacks the image for the disciples by suggesting that their witness, their discipleship, is indistinguishable from Jesus' own. The understanding of discipleship that will be presented in the Fourth Gospel has the disciples doing the very works of Jesus, "you will do greater works than these" (14:12). The picture of discipleship in John underscores the reliance on and necessity of the incarnation. Once Jesus returns to the Father, it will be the disciples who will be the presence of the "I AM" in the world when Jesus is not. The incarnation is critical even beyond the incarnated Word. That is, the incarnation is not just a claim about God but a claim about the importance of humanity. This Gospel takes seriously what it means to be human. This emphasis on the incarnation means that at stake for discipleship, for being a believer, for being a witness, is the full and embodied expression of what it means to be human. The woman at the well, who she is and what she represents, is representative of this claim. She reveals that God has in mind the entire spectrum of humanity. What it means to be human will not be limited to certain groups or constituencies. The fullness of the Word made flesh, its abundance, and the theological claims of the incarnation would fall flat if the totality of the expressions of humanity were not represented.

JOHN 4:39-42
THE WITNESS

The last portion of this pericope returns to the Samaritan response to the witness of the woman at the well. Verse 39 reports that many of the woman's townspeople believed in Jesus because of her witness to them. Her testimony is summarized in a brief and somewhat puzzling statement, "he told me everything I have ever done." There certainly could be other statements that might capture better the conversation with Jesus and the woman's testimony. Why this particular distillation of what happened at the well? What exactly did the woman *do*, particularly thinking back to the most revealing part of the conversation, the questioning about her marital status? It may be that by describing Jesus as one who "told me everything I have ever done" points to the expectation of the hearers. They believe that her place in life is the direct result of her own actions. She names that as true but we now know something different.

The Samaritans respond to the woman's testimony and invitation to "come and see" by going to Jesus and inviting him to "stay" with them but the verb is *menō*. As discussed in chapter 1 with the calling of the disciples, *menō* functions as a synonym for relationship with Jesus. To abide with Jesus is to be in an intimate relationship with him. The Samaritans are not asking Jesus to hang out for a few hours. They are speaking the primary language of relationship according to this Gospel. As a result of this abiding, more Samaritans believe. Once again, there is an overlap of terminology that serves to underscore the intimacy of relationship into which this Gospel invites the reader. Abiding and believing are synonymous, and the first persons beyond the first disciples to experience this relationship with Jesus are Samaritans. We are once again reminded of 3:16, "For God so loved the world." This entire story of Jesus in Samaria is an embodied presentation of what this verse means. Jesus, the Samaritan woman at the well, and her villagers have acted out what God loving the world looks like.

The comment of the Samaritans to the woman (4:42) in no way discounts her witness. Rather, it points to a central theological commitment of the Fourth Gospel, that to believe in Jesus must come down to an individual encounter and *krisis* according to 3:17. To believe in Jesus is not assent to avowals made *about* him but to be in relationship *with* him. This Gospel insists that in order to come to believe in Jesus as the Messiah, the Son of God, and to have life (20:31), you must have your own encounter with Jesus. Once again, the essentialness of the incarnation is given emphasis. The incarnation must be experienced and not merely affirmed. That God became human demands that God be fully experienced, encountered, and embodied.

The final confession of the Samaritans about who they perceive Jesus to be is nothing short of incredible. The only time Jesus is called "savior" in the entire Gospel of John is here and by outsiders. Nicodemus was not capable of seeing this possibility of Jesus' identity and not even the disciples will name Jesus as "savior." Though it is a well-known and oft-used descriptor for Jesus, the title *savior* appears infrequently in the Gospels (Luke 1:47; 2:11). What does it mean for the Samaritans to recognize Jesus as savior of the world? This combination, "savior of the world," encapsulates the breadth and depth of God's purpose in becoming incarnate in Jesus. The Samaritans are themselves the world, representing what the world can and should look like when it comes to the ministry of Jesus. The emphasis on the world in the Fourth Gospel intimates God's intention to love the entirety of God's creation in that the outward focus of this Gospel cannot be separated from its creational claims. This Gospel is deeply rooted in the creation story, and therefore God's coming into the world as Jesus must be for all of God's creation.

At the same time, this unique declaration of Jesus' identity, particularly coming from the Samaritans, demands the question, what does it mean to be saved, especially for the Samaritans? The usual definitions of salvation, particularly if they come from vague and dislocated dogmatic, doctrinal, or postbiblical arguments, will not suffice for this Gospel and especially for the Samaritans. For a Gospel that has as its central theological statement that God became flesh, salvation cannot be an abstract assertion or a declaration uprooted from reality. This would be to say that the incarnation is a generic construct, and it would undermine completely the theology of John.

To preach Jesus as savior in the Gospel of John must attend the particularity of salvation in the encounter itself that is then contextualized within the larger claim of abundant and eternal life. Salvation for this Gospel is relationship, here and now, for the Samaritans, for the woman at the well, for anyone who has an encounter with Jesus. While there is certain promise of life beyond death that is imagined as being at the bosom of the Father at the ascension, to know abundant life means that abundance is not capable of being delayed. As a result, salvation is present, an eschatological promise that is in the moment as well as in the future. Preaching the meaning of salvation from the particular witness of this moment in John will invite a different and perhaps more robust soteriology than what preaching tends to proclaim.

CONNECTIONS TO THE LECTIONARY

The Samaritan woman at the well appears on the third Sunday of Lent in Year A and follows the story of Nicodemus. The verse parameters exclude 4:1-4. Essential for the preaching of her story is to include these four verses of the chapter, which set the stage for why Jesus is going through Samaria in the first place. The juxtaposition of these two characters in the lectionary provides numerous possibilities for preaching, as were outlined in the commentary above. Preaching on this conversation between Jesus and the Samaritan woman at the well should ensure that the reading of the text is indeed conversational. To have one person read this story from a lectern works against the very dynamic in the text that leads to her openness to and new identity in Jesus. If the conversation is staged as a reader's theater, the congregation would experience the importance of conversation for discipleship, that dialogue is essential when it comes to belief. The preacher can then drop down into the portion of text determined for the sermon that day, but with the benefit of the entirety of the conversation in mind. Listening in on this conversation would also offer places in which the hearers might enter the dialogue. Where are they in their understanding of Jesus as embodied by the progression of knowledge witnessed in the woman at the well?

John 4:43-54
The Healing of the Official's Son

The last section of chapter 4 narrates the second sign in the Gospel of John, the healing of the official's son. Jesus has finally made it back to Galilee, the trip that he started at the beginning of the chapter (4:4). "When the two days were over" (4:43) refers to the two days that Jesus stayed with the Samaritans. Verse 44 notes his avoidance of Nazareth. The Fourth Gospel does not include traditions of Jesus returning to his homeland as we find in Luke, for example (Luke 4:16-30). Jesus' homecoming in the Gospel of Luke has a prominent role, functioning to set up the theological theme of the rejection of Jesus by his friends and neighbors in Nazareth and then again by his disciples, who reject his resurrection in 24:11 as *lēros,* literally "garbage" or "crap." The entirety of Jesus' ministry in Luke is framed by his rejection. For the Gospel of Luke, this is also a christological issue in that Jesus' finds himself to be as much of an outcast as those he came to save. This brief discussion of Luke helps us see that Nazareth has a different kind of christological function in John's Gospel. The mention here of the dishonor toward Jesus in his home country highlights the hospitable reception he receives on either side of his hometown, the invitation from the Samaritans and the welcome from the Galileans. Moreover, it is another reminder that where he comes from is not Nazareth. He has no need to go to *this* home.

The Galileans welcome him because they had observed "all that he had done" in Jerusalem. The only specific event narrated from his time in Jerusalem for Passover in chapter 2 is the temple incident. The only other mention of what Jesus did while in Jerusalem is in 2:23, "When he was in Jerusalem during the Passover festival, many believed in his name because they saw the signs that he was doing." At the end of chapter 20, the fourth evangelist reminds us that there were many other signs that Jesus did that are not included in his story of Jesus (20:30). There will be other references to generic "signs" that Jesus' performs throughout the Gospel, typically with the caveat that one cannot simply see the signs and believe. The mention of what Jesus has already done also anticipates Jesus' response to the royal official in the healing story to come, "Unless you see signs and wonders you will not believe" (4:48).

The specific location for the second recorded sign is back at Cana, where we are reminded that Jesus had turned water into wine. The setting and the repetition of what happened last time Jesus was in Cana heightens the anticipation of what might again occur in Cana and the potential of abundance. A royal official has learned that Jesus is back in Galilee. The description of the official as an employee of Herod who resides in the northern part of Galilee in Capernaum suggests that he could be a gentile. On the heels of Jesus' presence in Samaria is now his mission to the gentiles. The world that God loves just keeps getting bigger. The official begs him to come and heal his son, who is so ill that he is almost dead—in the Greek, "about to die." Jesus' response is hard to interpret and one's understanding of it has everything to do with how one imagines the inflection of Jesus' words. The phrase is in the subjunctive mood, putting how the official will respond into a condition of uncertainty. "You will not believe" is in the form of a strong future denial, better translated, "you will never believe." This is the only time in the book of John that the term *wonders* appears. As noted above, there is general suspicion of those who only believe in

Jesus because they see the signs that he performs. The signs in and of themselves are miraculous, but their true meaning is found in what they say about the relationship with God that Jesus makes possible as the Word made flesh. In summary, to paraphrase Jesus' words to the royal official, "I wonder what it will take for you to believe. Will it be the signs and wonders, like everybody else?"

The official's answer to Jesus seems to rest on what he knows about Jesus because of the signs, but at the same time, its tone is much like that of Jesus' mother in chapter 2. "Will you please just come and heal him already? I know you can do this, will you just come and get it done?" The proximity of this particular sign to the first sign of turning water into wine invites a number of interesting parallels and entries into preaching. Both episodes take place in Cana. Both signs center in on the relationship between parent and child. In both cases there is belief in Jesus aside from the buildup of miracles Jesus has amassed to prove his identity. At the wedding at Cana, Jesus' mother says to the servants, "do whatever he tells you" (2:5) and that is exactly what the official does in 4:50. When Jesus tells the official, "Go, your son will live," the man believes *the word* Jesus had spoken to him and goes. The royal official does what Jesus' mother has already said, do what he tells you. He believes what Jesus *says* before he believes because of what Jesus *does*. This pattern will also hold true in the healing of the man blind from birth, who first does what Jesus *tells* him to do. He goes down to the Pool of Siloam, washes, and is able to see because that is precisely what Jesus instructed him to do, "Go, wash in the pool of Siloam" (which means Sent) (9:7). The same will be true of the man ill for thirty-eight years (5:8), who also follows Jesus' instructions. The royal official does not believe in Jesus because of the sign Jesus performs for him, even though this sign is incredible, healing his son who is on the verge of death. He first takes Jesus *at his word*. While he will believe after the sign, as will his whole household, what he believes in that moment is not the sign itself but that what Jesus says is true.

That Jesus is the truth himself is a major premise of the Gospel. The Prologue sets out this theme in 1:14, "And the Word became flesh and lived among us, and we have seen his glory, the glory as of a father's only son, full of grace and truth"; and again in 1:17, "The law indeed was given through Moses; grace and truth came through Jesus Christ." What is true and what is truth will have a major role in Jesus' heightened confrontation with the Jewish leaders in chapter 8 (8:32, 40, 44, 45, 46). One of the predicate nominative "I AM" statements is Jesus naming himself as the truth, "I am the way, and the truth, and the life" (14:6). The location of this particular "I AM" statement is important because it is Jesus' words to his disciples in the Farewell Discourse that anticipate his *absence*. The truth of Jesus' words, Jesus as the truth, is dependable even without Jesus present, which is central to the meaning of the healing of the royal official's son. The distance of the healing, that Jesus is not actually present for the healing, functions to put emphasis on the *words* of Jesus and not the healing itself or even Jesus' presence at the healing. The healing is not premised on Jesus' being there but on his word, and it is therefore an embodied event that demonstrates a larger theological issue for the Fourth Gospel, the possibility of believing in Jesus even after his return to the Father (20:30-31). The Farewell Discourse will introduce the Spirit, the Advocate, the Paraclete, the one called alongside the disciples in Jesus' absence, and the Spirit is first described in connection with truth, "And I will ask the Father, and he will give you another Advocate, to be with you forever. This is the Spirit of truth" (14:16-17). One of the primary roles of the Spirit will be to guide Jesus' believers in all truth (16:13).

Of course, to say that Jesus' words are true or that Jesus is truth demands some reflection on what is meant by truth. This story cannot descend into a simplistic moral platitude, what Jesus says is true! Or Jesus is the only Truth! When preaching this story, one must address what truth means in this context and for a life of faith. To say that what Jesus says is true does not mean he speaks verifiable facts. The concept of truth has to be situated in the theological premises of the Fourth Gospel, the primary one being that, in Jesus, God is made known in such a way that there is an intimate, abiding relationship with God. In relationship, truth is about dependability and trust. Jesus is truth because he is the one on whom we can be utterly dependent. Jesus' words are true because there is a correlation between what he says and what he does and who he is. In other words, truth for this Gospel is an incarnated concept, an embodied reality, that connects words and actions and not an abstract claim about fact or historicity or dogma.

Jesus does not say that the official's son will be made well but that his son will live. This association between being made well and life is how Jesus will interpret the third sign, the healing of the man at Beth-zatha, which immediately follows this healing. The healing of the royal official's son anticipates Jesus' discourse on the healing of the man ill for thirty-eight years. To be made well is to be given life. At the same time, therefore, Jesus' interpretation of the sign in the next chapter should inform the meaning of the healing of the royal official's son. Three times the term "alive" or "living," from *zaō*, is used: (a) when Jesus says to the official, "go, your son will live" (4:50); (b) as the man travels down and his servants meet him and tell him that his son is alive (4:51); and (c) when the man realizes that his son was made well at the exact moment Jesus said to him, "your son will live" (4:53). Each time that the son's recovery could have been described as being made well or being healed, it is rather that the son is made alive. Moreover, each occurrence of the verb *zaō* in these verses is not in the future tense, as it is translated in 4:50 and 4:53, but in the present tense, "your son lives." The primary theme in the discourse on the healing of the man at Beth-zatha is eternal life, which is both a present and a future promise. The royal official does not have to look forward to a future life with his son, but is promised life with his son here and now. The belief of the royal official anticipates Peter's confession two chapters later, "Lord, to whom can we go? You have the words of eternal life" (6:68).

One final observation about this story that warrants attention for preaching is that the royal official is given three titles in the story. He is first introduced as a "royal official" in 4:46 and again in 4:49. He is referred to as "the man" in 4:50 and then in 4:53 as "the father." The progression from official, to man, to father is not unlike the progression of recognition of who Jesus is for the Samaritan woman at the well and the man who was blind from birth, from the man Jesus, to a prophet, to Messiah/Lord. It is a progression that signals relationship. While the official first describes his son as his little child, as do the servants, Jesus and the narrative consistently name the child "son." When the official remembers Jesus' words, he quotes Jesus directly, using son, "your son lives." That he is "father" at the end of the story emphasizes that his son "lives." There is a future beyond 4:53 that says that Jesus' words can be believed even beyond the parameters of the Gospel itself. As a result, a preacher might consider renaming this passage, as it has less to do with a healing and more to do with a father who believes Jesus' word. Like the other "signs" in the Fourth Gospel, the sign itself is not necessarily the miraculous moment. In this case, the sign points to the true claim that Jesus' words can be believed, that Jesus' words mean life, and that Jesus' words sustain and promise relationship.

CONNECTIONS TO THE LECTIONARY

The witness of the royal official never appears in the Revised Common Lectionary. After reading his story, the preacher might want to explore where and how his encounter with Jesus might be a part of a congregation's life of faith. Given the themes outlined in the commentary above, there could be numerous settings in the lives of our people in the pews where the royal official's experience would ring true. The preacher might also want to consider adding this story to the list of possible funeral texts provided to those searching for meaningful scripture in a time of loss. To imagine a funeral sermon built around the theme that the words of Jesus can indeed be believed would bring comfort and hope and perhaps a needed unconventional understanding of what belief in the resurrection actually means.

4

The Healing of the Man Ill for Thirty-Eight Years and Jesus as the Bread of Life (John 5–6)

A comparison of the next two signs in the Gospel of John, the healing of the man ill for thirty-eight years and the feeding of the five thousand is valuable for interpretation and preaching these passages because both illustrate the repeated literary pattern in the Gospel of sign, dialogue, discourse. This pattern will occur again in chapters 9 and 10 for the healing of the man blind from birth and in chapter 11 for the raising of Lazarus; it functions as a larger structural pattern for the Gospel as a whole. As discussed previously in this commentary, the structure underscores the main theological point of all of the signs in the Fourth Gospel. Each of the miracles—or signs, as John names them—is miraculous not only on its own terms but also for what it reveals or shows about what it means that Jesus is the Word made flesh. The signs are indeed quite extraordinary: changing water into wine, healing a man ill for thirty-eight years, healing a man blind from birth, raising a man from the dead. They are miracles beyond any comparison and therefore deserving of the attention and reactions they receive. At the same time, the descriptions of the miracles are lean and succinct, occupying little narrative space. Their brevity indicates that the signs themselves are not that on which our focus should be placed. The ensuing dialogue about the sign divulges the many meanings that the miracle might have, and Jesus' discourse on the sign interprets both the act itself and the possible interpretations made known in the conversation.

That our attention should be located more on the conversation and Jesus' interpretation has already been addressed by the Gospel after the first sign, water into wine at Cana. Chapter 2 closes with the statement, "When he was in Jerusalem during the Passover festival, many believed in his name because they saw the signs that he was doing. But Jesus on his part would not entrust himself to them, because he knew all people and needed no one to testify about anyone; for he himself knew what was in everyone" (2:23-25). The signs are a questionable source for assessing Jesus' true self, his true identity. It is worth exploring the reason for the relative downplaying of the signs and the significance placed on Jesus' interpretation of the signs. Theologically, the emphasis on the dialogue and Jesus' discourse suggests that what is critical about the signs is the process of interpretation, what happens in the conversation, as a means of shared relationship. To place weight on the practice of conversation is a relational priority. It is also representative of the foremost theological claim of this Gospel—that the Word became flesh. In that regard, words, Jesus' words, are a significant aspect of the Word becoming flesh.

To know that the full meaning of the sign lies not in the sign itself but in Jesus' interpretation of the sign implies that listening to Jesus, hearing Jesus, is vital. To see the sign, to experience the sign, is not a fully embodied, incarnational experience without listening for its interpretation, its meaning. This serves as another way by which structurally and narratively, the fourth evangelist reinforces theological claims with chosen narrative modes.

JOHN 5:1-47
THE HEALING OF THE MAN ILL FOR THIRTY-EIGHT YEARS

The setting for the healing of the man ill for thirty-eight years places Jesus in Jerusalem for an unspecified festival. Jesus has been in Galilee and is now back in Jerusalem. The commentary on the temple incident recorded in chapter 2 of the Gospel discussed Jesus' regular trips to Jerusalem. Compared to the Synoptic Gospels, we find Jesus in Jerusalem many times, not just for the three Passover festivals noted in 2:13; 6:1; and 13:1. Jesus' recurrent trips to Jerusalem pull the city into the center of the story, not just as a location for events in the narrative but as a theological character. Jerusalem represents the epicenter of Judaism and the political and religious heart of the period of Jesus' ministry. As discussed in the commentary on the temple incident, Jerusalem also denotes the presence of conflict and resistance. Theologically, it is the power and presence of God, and so it makes sense that Jesus would be there frequently. While it symbolizes the forces that stand against Jesus and is the origin of those who will want to kill him, at the same time it characterizes the relationship that Jesus shares with the Father. The closeness of the Father and Jesus the son, so fully developed in this Gospel, is accentuated by the proximity of Jesus to Jerusalem throughout the Gospel. It would make little sense for Jesus to be so far away from God for the entirety of his ministry, as is presented in Matthew, Mark, and Luke. The frequency with which Jesus goes to Jerusalem emphasizes the intimacy between Jesus and the Father. There is only so long a period of time that Jesus can be away.

JOHN 5:1-9
THE HEALING

While there are many sick—the blind, the lame, and the paralyzed—the man ill for thirty-eight years is singled out. The length of time that the man has been ill, given the assumed human life span in the first century, suggests that he has been sick virtually his entire life. The specificity of the number underscores both the length of the illness and the man's difficulties, having to rely on others for support, perhaps at this same spot, these many years. Jesus sees him and knows that he has been ill a long time. Like the encounter with the woman at the well, Jesus is aware of the plight of the man. Jesus' question for the man, "do you want to become well" or "sound," or "healthy" is answered by the man's situation of how to get to the pool.

The healing itself is brief. Jesus commands the man to take up his mat and walk, the man does what Jesus says, and instantly the man is healed, able to act out Jesus' words. As the story progresses, the preacher will want to imagine what the mat symbolizes or represents for the man, like the water jar for the Samaritan woman. We then find out after the fact that the healing occurred on the Sabbath. This pattern will be repeated for the healing of the man born blind (9:14).

JOHN 5:10-18
THE QUESTIONING OF THE MAN

This next section of the healing functions as the dialogue following the sign. In chapter 9, the Jewish leaders question Jesus' actions performed on the Sabbath. Here, the man's actions are questioned, for carrying his mat on a Sabbath day. Verse 10 reiterates that the man has been cured. The Jewish leaders first approach the man, calling out his unlawful behavior regardless of the fact that he has been healed. The man's response calls attention to his healing, "the man who made me well," and brings forward the irony that, while he was cured of the illness he suffered for thirty-eight years, he is accused of breaking Sabbath law by carrying his mat. Jesus' identity becomes the focus of the dialogue, with the man not knowing who healed him. Jesus has disappeared into the crowd.

Jesus will also exit the scene in chapter 9 and will be absent far longer than he is in chapter 5. In both healings, Jesus finds the men: in chapter 5, Jesus finds the man in the temple; and in chapter 9, Jesus finds the man born blind ostensibly out of the temple, having been cast out. To be found by Jesus intimates far more than a reunion after an absence. It is to be brought into a community, restored to wholeness, and to be in relationship with Jesus. According to the calling of the disciples in chapter 1, it is also to become a disciple. That Jesus finds the cured man in the temple is a curious detail. For the past thirty-eight years he would not have been allowed in the temple because of his illness. His destination, once he has been made well, is the temple, presumably to worship God and to be in God's presence. When Jesus finds him, he commands the man to sin no more. The connection between sin and illness is also made in the healing of the man blind from birth, with the disciples wondering who sinned that the result would be this man's blindness (9:2). Though illness is correlated with sin, we have already noted that the function of sin in the Gospel of John is unique. For the fourth evangelist, sin is the state of not being in relationship with God. It is not a category of morality or that which is punishable by illness; sin represents not believing in God, particularly, not believing that, in Jesus, God is present. When Jesus tells the healed man to sin no more while he is in the temple (5:14), Jesus is intimating that the temple is not where the man will know a relationship with God. The altered chronology of the temple incident, moved to the beginning of Jesus' ministry, and Jesus' conversation with the Samaritan woman at the well about the proper place to worship have set the stage for Jesus' words to the man in chapter 5.

The closing verses of the dialogue section of the healing call attention to the growing tension between Jesus, now mentioned by name, and the Jewish authorities. The man ill for thirty-eight years progresses in his recognition of who Jesus is, now identifying Jesus by name. Knowing Jesus by name prefigures the same pattern of perception that the blind man will demonstrate. Furthermore, knowing Jesus' name foreshadows the discourse on the healing of the man born blind, that Jesus' knows his sheep by name. The affinity between Jesus and his disciples is once again highlighted. At first, Jesus is the object of persecution for his Sabbath law-breaking. When Jesus equates his work with that of God, however, he becomes targeted for death. Verse 18 is a summary of the fundamental theological assertion of this Gospel, "For this reason the Jews were seeking all the more to kill him, because he was not only breaking the Sabbath, but was also calling God his own Father, thereby making himself equal to God." That Jesus is God is never more clearly stated than in the Fourth Gospel.

JOHN 5:19-47
THE DISCOURSE ON THE SIGN

Preaching on the discourses in the Gospel of John demands that these words of Jesus never be dislocated from the sign that elicits Jesus' reflections. These are not general thoughts that Jesus chooses to share but are deeply lodged in an event, an encounter that is in need of interpretation. The opening verses of the discourse on the healing of the man ill for thirty-eight years answer directly what this sign points to: that in healing the man on the Sabbath, Jesus is revealed to be God. Verses 19-20 establish the intimate relationship that Jesus has with God, which makes possible the sign he performed. The Father and son relationship is not merely the reason for Jesus' ability to heal the man but emphasizes the dependence of the son on the Father. This relationship is indicative of Jesus' power, to be sure, but, moreover, points to the vulnerability that comes with being human. The reference to greater works than what has just been witnessed in the healing of the man sick for thirty-eight years heralds the signs to come in the narrative, particularly the raising of Lazarus, to which verse 21 alludes: "Indeed, just as the Father raises the dead and gives them life . . . ." At the same time, "and he will show him greater works than these" also anticipates Jesus' own promise to his disciples of what they will be able to do, "greater works than these" (14:12). At that moment in the Farewell Discourse, the disciples are invited to think back on this healing and know that their greater works are possible because of their dependence on Jesus, just as Jesus is dependent on God.

Verse 21 is the pivotal verse that interprets the meaning of the sign. In healing the man ill for thirty-eight years Jesus gave him life. To be cured, to be made well as it turns out, is more than being healed of a sickness, even that from which one has suffered as long as the man at Beth-zatha. He was given life, which is connected to resurrected and ascended life. The central theme of this entire discourse is life and what life means. Put another way, the healing of the sick man is a resurrection, a transformation from being dead to being alive—it is to be born again. The rest of the discourse will unpack what it means to have life, what that life looks like, and what it means. Once again, there is an auguring of the raising of Lazarus, with that last sign in the Gospel having an impact on the meaning of the sign in chapter 5.

Verses 22-24 specify the reaction of the Jewish leaders to Jesus' miracle on the Sabbath as having to do with judgment. The commentary on chapter 3 and Jesus' encounter with Nicodemus reviewed the concept of judgment in the Fourth Gospel. God does not judge or condemn, but judgment or condemnation is brought on one's self depending on one's response to Jesus. The statement in verse 23, that any dishonoring of Jesus is dishonoring of God means that Jesus is not a mere divine representative. To honor God in this particular context would be to recognize that only God can grant life on a Sabbath day. Verse 24 is clear that belief is connected to judgment and that believing in Jesus as the Word made flesh is to move from death to life. What will become more clear, particularly in the raising of Lazarus, is that "from death to life" is not limited to the promise of the resurrection at the end-times. To pass from death to life is the promise of life now. For the man of Beth-zatha, his healing is a passing from a certain deathlike existence of rejection and loneliness to life that is about acceptance and community for the rest of his earthly life.

The expression "very truly I tell you" is a regular formulation for Jesus that first occurs in 1:51 and lastly in 21:18. John 5:25-29 focuses on hearing Jesus' voice, which the man of Beth-zatha heard and obeyed, as did the royal official, as will the man blind from birth. Verse 28 is another foreshadowing of the raising of Lazarus, which reinforces how critical that final sign is for the interpretation of the healing in chapter 5 and what it means to "be made well" for this Gospel. "Resurrection of life" and "resurrection of condemnation" are seemingly odd phrases but not when situated in the Gospel's understanding of life and judgment. Life coupled with resurrection means that what happens for the man of Beth-zatha is nothing short of a resurrection, and like Lazarus, a resurrection to life here and now, to relationship with Jesus.

Verses 30-38 revisit the theme of witness and testimony first introduced in the Prologue, particularly in connection with the character of John the Witness. As this is the first sign that introduces the structural pattern of sign, dialogue, and discourse, the importance of the theme of witness as it is expressed by Jesus in this first discourse needs attention. In other words, to what extent are Jesus' discourses about the signs acts of witness or testimony? It is not enough to observe the sign, but it demands a theological response, a testimony of what it purports. As a result, the discourses of Jesus are not only interpretations of the signs he performs but his own testimony to what they mean—for himself, for God, for discipleship, and for his incarnation in the world, "the works that the Father has given me to complete, the very works that I am doing, testify on my behalf that the Father has sent me" (5:36). Jesus' words about John are not a dismissal of John's testimony or of his identity as witness. A comparison of Jesus' words here and the Samaritan response to the testimony of the woman at the well is helpful, "They said to the woman, 'It is no longer because of what you said that we believe, for we have heard for ourselves, and we know that this is truly the Savior of the world'" (4:42). Jesus' comments about John the Witness are meant to be understood in this light, that while John's role as witness and his testimony were absolutely essential (5:35), one's own experience of Jesus, one's own encounter with Jesus is critical, emphasizing once again the theological importance of the incarnation. Confessing the presence of God in Jesus must be followed by knowing the presence of God in Jesus. Verse 37 includes even the Father in the role of testimony, something that will be revisited in the Farewell Discourse both for the Father and for the Spirit, the Advocate. The mutual testimony of Father, Son, and Holy Spirit for the sake of the other is the kind of testimony to which the believer is called to give. Testimony, giving witness, to the presence of God in Jesus, the activity of God in Jesus, is to take part in the very activity in which the Father, Son, and Holy Spirit engage. To be a witness is an undertaking of discipleship, but it is also evidence of a believer's relationship with Jesus.

Verses 37-47 must be construed from the perspective of the social, religious, and political backdrop of the community to which this Gospel is addressed. Nonetheless, the tone of Jesus' words to the Jewish leaders is shocking and even abhorrent. The polemic and vitriol will only get worse, particularly in chapters 7–8, but to have it present this early in the Gospel is challenging at best. A first step in making sense of Jesus' words here is to be reminded of the setting, a healing, on the Sabbath, during a festival, in Jerusalem, where Jesus' gift of life is rejected. The primary accusation Jesus lodges against the Jewish authorities is their lack of belief. Jesus will make this allegation to any who reject him, who do not recognize who he is. At this juncture, we need to remember that the debate extant in the Fourth Gospel is primarily an intra-Jewish conflict. To make sense of Jesus' words, this setting must be kept in mind. At the same time, acknowledging the difficulty of this conversation, especially with regard to the devastating history of interpretation when it comes to the Fourth Gospel, is crucial. Regardless of historical knowledge, the effect of such words in a public setting without attention or interpretation or focused proclamation results in a perpetuation of misinterpretation of the Fourth Gospel, but more tragically, justification for anti-Semitism. Verses 38-39 point to the way in which Scripture plays a crucial role in how the writers of the New Testament sought to make sense of God's activity in Jesus. These verses also extend beyond their immediate function and suggest to readers of this Gospel that Scripture, the Word, is a "living" witness to God's activity in the world. This claim is elemental to the larger theological claim of the Fourth Gospel. If the Word becomes flesh, God's Word in Scripture must somehow maintain the same inherent characteristic of incarnation. These verses stress the importance of approaching God's Word—even before Jesus—as embodied, changing, and dynamic. Jesus relies on that which he is, the incarnated Word of God that adapts to and manifests itself in the changing realities of God's purposes and the needs of God's people. One of the remarkable features of this passage for preaching is the way in which Jesus relies on Scripture for interpretation of and argumentation for who he is in the world.

The reference to Moses in verses 45-46 intentionally sets up how the role of Moses will play a part in the meaning of the next sign, the feeding of the five thousand in chapter 6. The reference to Moses also recalls the provision of life on which the feeding of the five thousand will be based in the next chapter and recalls the protection of life alluded to in 3:14. This is yet another way in which life for the man ill for thirty-eight years is recast. His new life is situated in this larger history, context, and framework of God's provision of life for God's people from the beginning. To recall Moses at this point is to give tangibility to what life means for the man of Beth-zatha, for eternal life. Life is not a generality, but that which secures provision as Moses himself witnessed as emissary of God.

CONNECTIONS TO THE LECTIONARY

The only time this passage appears in the lectionary is as the alternate reading, Year C, Easter 6, and then only 5:1-9 as a substitute reading. It is no wonder, therefore, that few preachers are aware of the structural pattern primarily established by the story of the healing of the man in chapter 5 of sign, dialogue, and discourse. Were a preacher to select this substitute text for this Sunday, reading beyond the healing itself would be essential. At the same time, this is yet again a massive text to handle. While it is certainly unfortunate that our congregations may never hear this moving story of a man's restoration to life, the preacher can at least give him life as one who shapes and informs preaching on the signs and what life means in the Fourth Gospel. Knowing the story of the man at Beth-zatha cannot help but make preaching the rest of the Gospel more substantive and meaningful.

JOHN 6
JESUS AS THE BREAD OF LIFE

There are perhaps few texts that strike trepidation and exasperation in the hearts of preachers more than the five consecutive Sundays in the season of Pentecost, Year B. How much can you preach on Jesus as the Bread of Life? Perhaps our viewpoint might change when we appreciate fully the pattern exemplified in chapter 5 that is then repeated in chapter 6.

JOHN 6:1-15
THE SIGN

The sign that elicits the Bread of Life discourse is the feeding of the five thousand, which is narrated in each of the four Gospels (Matt. 14:13-21; Mark 6:31-44, Luke 9:10-17) and is the only miracle that appears in all four. Once again, a comparison of John and the Synoptic Gospels yields important differences and underscores particular theological themes in the Gospel of John. The setting has a specific detail unique to John: that of *much* grass (6:10). This description alludes to and foreshadows the presentation of Jesus as the Good Shepherd in chapter 10. The pasture for the sheep signals provision and abundance of life and this abundance is clearly present in the feeding of the five thousand. We are reminded once again that abundant life can be as simple as the basic necessities to sustain life. It is abundance reconfigured through the concept of relationship. Life cannot be abundant if it is not grounded in intimacy and relationship and security. Abundant life cannot be felt or experienced if the knowledge and promise of provision are not assured. Abundant life is predicated on the human necessity of dependence and reliance. Above the minimal needs comes abundance and the ability to thrive.

Another unique detail in John's narration of the feeding of the five thousand is that Jesus himself feeds the crowd. Contrary to the Synoptic Gospels, where the disciples are given the loaves and fish to distribute, it is Jesus alone who metes out the food. This underlines the emphasis on relationship noted above. Not only is Jesus the source of abundant life, but it is being in relationship with him that is also the source. Abundance cannot be separated from its source. For Jesus to feed the crowd is another means by which this Gospel restates 1:18, "No one has ever seen God. It is God the only Son, who is close to the Father's heart, who has made him known." To be at the bosom of the Father is to know that every necessity for life is bestowed. John 1:18 establishes the provision and love on which the entire Gospel is based.

Paying attention to the textual differences in John from Matthew, Mark, and Luke gives a fuller picture of what the concept of abundant life means in the Gospel of John. In addition, it situates the framework for abundant life clearly in the relationship with God that is possible in Jesus Christ. As a result, the discourse that follows can be recast as not simply an explanation of the sign but an invitation to abiding in the relationship that Jesus is offering. To interpret the sign as that which embodies what true sustenance might mean is essential for understanding who Jesus is. Jesus as the Bread of Life cannot be understood as merely metaphor, but rather as a literal revelation of who Jesus is and what abundant life entails. Bread, an essential component of daily life in the ancient world, is what Jesus is. This promise hinges on John's central theological claim of the incarnation. If the incarnation is only euphemistic imagination, then it defies its own logic. To stake an entire theology and Christology on God becoming human requires that at every turn the incarnation is completely present. As a result, Jesus as the Bread of Life, first and foremost, before rendering its interpretation through the lens of the Old Testament or eucharistic liturgical practices, must be grounded in bread as a necessity for sustenance as a human being. Anything less could very well undermine what is at stake in the contention that the Word became flesh.

JOHN 6:16-21
WALKING ON WATER

The feeding of the five thousand is followed by the feat of Jesus walking on water, the fifth sign (cf. Matt. 14:22-33; Mark 6:45-52). This is not a stilling of the storm but a sign of presence. There is no rebuke on Jesus' part for the winds to cease (Luke 8:22-25) or even mention of calm (Matt. 14:32; Mark 6:51). The absence in John of the calming of the storm, the act of controlling nature on the part of Jesus, should make sense set against the larger theological context of this Gospel. For Jesus to demonstrate his power by stilling the storm would be counterintuitive to his identity. This Gospel does not demand proof of his divinity; it assumes it. More miraculous is the revelation of "I AM" and not the capability of manipulating Mother Nature. This is the second absolute "I AM" in the Gospel, the first being for the Samaritan woman at the well in 4:26. The chaos of the sea and the reference to darkness as the setting for this revelation of Jesus make his appearance and his "I AM" statement all the more significant in this moment. As with each absolute "I AM" statement, contextualizing the appearance is essential to imagining its function in this instant in the narrative. Why this "I AM" statement here and now?

An important question for preaching this episode in the Gospel of John is why the fourth evangelist separates the sign of the feeding of the five thousand from its dialogue and discourse. If the pattern holds true—that sign, dialogue, and discourse—is a primary structural pattern for this Gospel, then why the interruption of 6:16-21? What interpretive purpose does it serve beyond including an event recorded in other Gospels? Taking this narrative interruption sincerely might yield several perspectives on the dialogue and discourse meant to give meaning to the feeding of the five thousand. One such perspective would suggest that the "I AM" is necessary before the dialogue and discourse that follow the feeding of the five thousand. The discourse on the feeding of the five thousand is absolutely premised on 6:20. It would not make sense if it were not because the discourse assumes God's presence in the wilderness. We are reminded that the words Jesus shares in his interpretation of the feeding of the five thousand will come from his identity as the "I AM" in the world.

CONNECTIONS TO THE LECTIONARY

Few preachers need a reminder of when the Bread of Life passages occur in the Revised Common Lectionary. John 6:1-21 (Proper 12 [17]) begins the five Sundays dedicated to this chapter in the Gospel of John in Year B, the year of Mark. The preacher will note that both the feeding of the five thousand and Jesus walking on the sea are included in the lection. This incorporation alone will demand that the preacher make some decisions as to the thematic directions preaching might take over the course of the next four weeks. Selecting those issues that the preacher would want to carry forward will create focus for interpretation and preaching a series of texts that for many seems insurmountable at best and plodding at worst. Preaching the feeding of the five thousand in John or the walking on the sea would also lift up their unique presentations in John and what that might mean for a life of faith, for an understanding of who Jesus is, and for a sense of what God is revealing about God's self in becoming this one and only God.

JOHN 6:22-71
THE BREAD OF LIFE DIALOGUE AND DISCOURSE

The Bread of Life Discourse is broken up into four sections in the Revised Common Lectionary. Immediately, the preacher should notice the overlapping versification for the designated pericopes, thus pointing to one of the difficulties of preaching John, its exceedingly long narratives and the interconnection of the entirety of the Gospel. The lectionary dictates false sections of texts doing the best that it can with what it has. For the preacher, this means approaching the designated lections with a loose commitment to the set verses. The determined lectionary boundaries may be better suited when imagining the specific theme or progression on which the preacher chooses to focus for the week.

With that generosity in mind, we can move through the discourse with a sense that progression is not defined by set parameters of passages, but rather by a movement of themes. At the same time, no section of the discourse can be understood or interpreted without recognizing its complete reliance on the feeding of the five thousand. The Bread of Life discourse is first and foremost Jesus' interpretation of this sign. That point alone might ease the homiletical angst that seems to surround this particular series from John. If the preacher approaches the entirety of the passage with the same interpretive sense as that of the discourse on the healing of the man in chapter 5 and the healing of the blind man in chapter 9, there may be an openness to the ways in which Jesus seeks to explain this miracle so as to reveal something about himself that we need to know.

In other words, what is new that Jesus actually says in each carefully delineated pericope according to the lectionary is perhaps is the wrong question to ask of the evolution of Jesus' discourses. While it is a seemingly small distinction, the development of the discourse is less about what is new than about the deeper meaning and possibility of what the sign means. For a preacher to approach each pericope, each section of the Bread of Life discourse as expecting a fresh perspective works against the theological nature of the Fourth Gospel, that the intent of the discourse is a desire to pull the believer deeper into abiding with Jesus, not to gain some further knowledge or insight.

JOHN 6:24-35
THE BREAD FROM HEAVEN

6:22-23 appear somewhat meaningless, unimportant transitional sentences, which is probably why they are omitted from the lectionary. Yet these verses are all about searching and finding and set up the situation in verse 24 that opens the lectionary pericope. It would be important to include these verses in this lection. The crowd finds Jesus on the other side of the sea, indicating the mutuality of relationship between Jesus and those who believe. There is much about the Bread of Life discourse that mimics the conversation between Jesus and the Samaritan woman at the well. There is an intermingling of dialogue and discourse, so that noticing the pattern of conversation can lead to certain interpretive possibilities. In other words, the preacher needs to attend carefully to the questions, comments, and responses by all parties to track the progression of the discourse.

Looking for Jesus recalls Jesus' first words to the first disciples, "What are you looking for?" (1:38). This has been a central question of the Gospel, one that will be repeated, albeit in a different form, at the arrest of Jesus (18:4, 7) and at the resurrection appearance to Mary Magdalene (20:15), "Who are you looking for?" Jesus' first words in the discourse call attention to a clear misinterpretation of what the sign might mean, that the need for food is fulfilled in Jesus' feeding of the five thousand. Verse 28 should recall that to do the works of God is really quite straight forward, to believe in Jesus as God incarnate. In 6:30 the crowd wants a sign, some manifestation of the power of God that will enable their own ability to react. In response, Jesus will unpack the sign he has just performed, the feeding of the five thousand. That the crowd wants or needs a sign exposes their inability to recognize the meaning of the sign and therefore the necessity of Jesus' discourse. Even witnessing the sign itself will not necessarily result in belief.

Verse 31 represents a certain level of listening, of understanding, on the part of the crowd, not unlike the Samaritan woman at the well, whose questions of Jesus centered on the provision of water (4:12). The response of the crowd, like that of the woman at the well, is an instinctive reaction to that which Jesus is providing. While one interpretation might assume a choreographed conversation on the part of the fourth evangelist, another response might be to acknowledge that in each circumstance there is a visceral, primitive recognition of need and that what Jesus provides, is that which is basic, indispensable for life. In this way, the crowd connects Jesus' feeding of the five thousand with the God's provision of manna in the wilderness. How do they make this connection? One could argue for the redactional activity of the fourth evangelist, who manipulates the encounters with Jesus to suit the theological claims at stake.

Another approach might be to take seriously the theological premise of the Gospel, that if the incarnation is true, then perhaps those who come in contact with Jesus recognize this embodied reality. That is, if Jesus can feed five thousand people himself, to what might one connect that theologically? How does one make sense of that scripturally? When, where, and how have masses of people been fed like this? The primary resource is God's provision in the wilderness, the gift of manna. As a result, the connection is made. There is no answer to what has happened other than what has already been revealed, what is already known, what has already been experienced. That God is the source and possibility of the feeding of the five thousand is the only logical theological answer. John 6:31 acknowledges that truth on which then Jesus builds his discourse.

Verse 32 signals a progression in the conversation, in the discourse, like that presented in chapter 5. "Very truly I tell you" is a marker of response and change of focus, which is why versification of chapter 6 and the discourse as a whole presents such difficulties. Jesus' response is an attempt to move the conversation forward and move understanding forward as to what the sign means. The source of the bread from heaven, even in the wilderness, was not Moses but "my father." The first person singular possessive pronoun, not "our" or "your" father connects Jesus with God, which is the theological move that Jesus will soon make. The second alteration Jesus makes to the confession in verse 31 is to add the adjective "true" to bread, thereby distinguishing himself from the manna in the wilderness. Verse 33 provides even more detail about the bread from heaven, now making the distinction that it is the "bread of God," not Moses. God was and is the source of the bread from heaven, and this bread gives life to the world. Jesus now offers two more unique features of this bread, that it gives life and that it is for the world. It is significant here that Jesus' conversation partner is not the Jewish leaders or the disciples but the crowd, the five thousand people whom Jesus fed. They are the world, the world that God loves (3:16). The feeding of the five thousand is a sign of God's abundant love for the world. What does abundant grace, abundant love, look like, even *taste* like? It tastes like enough fresh bread and fish to satisfy your hunger and more so. This bread also gives life, quite literally in that it is food to sustain life.

The crowd's response to Jesus' words in 6:34 is much like that of the Samaritan woman at the well, "Sir, give me this water, so that I may never be thirsty or have to keep coming here to draw water" (4:15). For the Samaritan woman at the well and now for the crowd, this is an instance of realization, albeit incomplete, that Jesus is the source of something that they need. While it is still a moment of misunderstanding, nevertheless there is some advancement in the recognition of who Jesus is. The Samaritan woman at the well goes from viewing Jesus as a thirsty Jew who needs to learn to say please to someone who is able to satisfy her basic human need of water. The same pattern holds true in the dialogue portion of response to the feeding of the five thousand. There is first a recognition of shared ancestry and history, "Our ancestors ate the manna in the wilderness; as it is written, 'He gave them bread from heaven to eat'" (6:31), to a nascent sense that Jesus might be a source of the basic human need for food.

As a result of this slight progress, Jesus seeks to move the conversation forward with his next statement. Jesus says to them, "I am the bread of life. Whoever comes to me will never be hungry, and whoever believes in me will never be thirsty" (6:35). "I AM the bread of life" is significant here on several levels. First, this is the first "I AM" statement with a predicate nominative in the Gospel (6:35, 51; 8:12; 9:5; 10:7, 9, 11, 14; 11:25-26; 14:6; 15:1, 5). That the first predicate nominative "I AM" statement is connected to that which is needed to maintain life underscores the incarnational theology of the Gospel as well as that of 1:18—that a relationship with Jesus, believing in Jesus will mean that everything necessary for your life to be sustained will be provided by God. This first predicate nominative "I AM" statement can be interpreted metaphorically, and what follows in the dialogue and discourse is certainly an invitation to imagine emblematic meanings at work in this symbol of bread. At the same time, there has to be a literal component in any interpretation of Jesus as the Bread of Life for the promise of the incarnation to have its full impact in this Gospel.

Second, this is the first direct revelation that Jesus himself is the bread with the first person singular claim. Bread has been connected to heaven (6:31-32) and to God (6:33), but now it is directly linked with Jesus. Third, the bread is given a modifier, "of life." What "of life" will then mean, beyond its literal promise will be one of the primary directions for the rest of the chapter. One who believes in Jesus with never be hungry or thirsty. The inclusion of thirst here offers three allusions for meaning. First, it recalls the conversation with the woman at the well. Jesus has already revealed himself to be the source of living water. If that is the case, then Jesus as the living bread is also an expectation that may very well be met. As a result, the link between bread and water affirms that, in Jesus, God provides essential needs for life. Second, it anticipates Jesus' claim in 7:37-39. Third, the reference to water makes sense in the larger context of God's provision for God's people in the wilderness. The discourse thus far has already recalled the point in the Israelite history when God sent manna from heaven to God's hungry people. Water was also provided for the Israelites by Moses striking the rock at Horeb as God commanded (Exod. 17:1-7). That which God afforded God's people, bread and water, Jesus now offers to the crowd. Jesus is able to give what God is able to give. Bread and water are quite literally bread and water, but they also represent life, especially life in the midst of dire circumstances. This is also a place for the preacher to remember the situation of the community for which this Gospel was written. In this regard, bread and water symbolize abundant life. Abundant life with God is not a postponed promise for the end-times but a present materiality here and now.

JOHN 6:35, 41-51
THE BREAD OF LIFE

In the Revised Common Lectionary, 6:35 both closes out the first of the four passages dedicated to the Bread of Life discourse and begins this second passage. The overlap of verses intimates the difficulty of breaking up this chapter into manageable sections for preaching. We have already commented on 6:35 above, but a few additional notes are helpful here, as this verse now functions to introduce a section rather than close one out, at least according to the lectionary. In 6:35 Jesus associates his identity as the Bread of Life with believing. Verse 36 reproaches the crowd for seeing Jesus (ostensibly seeing the sign he performed) yet not believing. Verses 36-40 is not included in the lectionary reading, yet the issue that elicits complaints from the Jews in 6:41, that Jesus said, "I am the bread that came down from heaven," does not make sense without Jesus' statement in 6:38, "for I have come down from heaven." Incorporating these verses removed from the lectionary provides the necessary background for what is to be the subject matter of belief in this moment. To believe in Jesus here is to make the connection that he is both the bread God provides that gives life and also *the source* of the bread. This particular construal of belief underscores once more that believing is not an assent to some specific doctrine or cognitive decision about Jesus but has everything to do with relationship. To believe in Jesus as the Bread of Life is primarily to acknowledge the relationship between God and God's people. The bread from heaven is provided for the Israelites whom God loves and will not abandon. In the wilderness, God is present, providing for God's people, and God's people rely on God for that provision. To believe in Jesus as the bread from heaven is to recognize that relationship. It is to believe in the relationship and what that relationship means, both then and now.

That relationship also means being in community. In verse 37 the term *ekballō* ("throw out") foreshadows the plight of the man born blind, who will be thrown out of his community for what he confesses about Jesus (9:35). This is a glimpse into the situation of this community but also represents a central theological image of this Gospel, that relationship also means being in community. The promise of Jesus in verses 39-40 imagines rising up on the last day not only as the resurrection but also as the ascension. One of the reasons these verses may not be included in the lectionary reading is a lack of certainty as to how this imagery fits into the dominant image of the bread of life. At the same time, the bread that comes down from heaven means that the promise of heaven exists for all believers. What heaven means for this Gospel, of course, is being in the presence of God. Heaven and earth are no longer locations but a truth about God's character, that God's presence is wherever the believer is. "All who see him may have eternal life and I will raise them up on the last day" (6:40). What eternal life means in this context looks forward and not just backwards. Eternal life is the certainty of provision, the source of what sustains life that you know and trust witnessed in the feeding of the five thousand. At the same time, it is this same promise carried into the future that Jesus prepares for all believers.

The "complaining" in response to Jesus' revelation, "I am the bread that came down from heaven" (6:41), is the same word that occurs in the Septuagint in Exodus 16. The provision of bread and water in the wilderness is the underlying scriptural story that gives the fourth evangelist the imagination for how to interpret the feeding of the five thousand. At the same time, the feeding story is located in this Gospel and reinterpreted. Like the shepherd imagery in chapter 9, Old Testament allusions cannot be the only interpretative move to understanding the meaning of the feeding of the five thousand. The allusions are recast to underscore the evangelist's interpretation of Jesus. Verse 42 summarizes one of the three primary assertions of 1:1, Jesus' origin. Where does Jesus come from? He is, of course, not the son of Joseph but the son of God. Interesting about this verse is that knowledge of Jesus' father and mother are in the present tense. This subtle detail emphasizes Jesus' humanity at the same time that the evangelist is making a weighty argument about Jesus' divinity. The reference to Jesus' mother here is a reminder of her presence at the beginning of Jesus' ministry, the wedding at Cana, and at the end of his ministry and life, at the foot of the cross.

In addition to its function as the interpretation of the feeding of the five thousand, the Bread of Life passage also interprets 1:51, "And he said to him, 'Very truly, I tell you, you will see heaven opened and the angels of God ascending and descending upon the Son of Man.'" The story of God's provision in the wilderness makes the connection that the *origin* of the food and water for the Israelites was from heaven, from God. Jesus is now also the source of such food and water, but, in addition, this is where he comes from and where he will return. As a result, this story has the function of reiterating the theological sequence on which the plot of the Fourth Gospel is premised: the incarnation, crucifixion, resurrection, and ascension. Jesus comes from the Father and will return to the Father. The manna in the wilderness as the story that helps make sense of the feeding of the five thousand then emphasizes several key points at once: Jesus' origin, Jesus' identity, and what a relationship with God looks like and means, all three themes having been laid out in the very first verse of the Gospel, "In the beginning was the Word, and the Word was with God, and the Word was God."

The question of Jesus' origin, the knowing of his mother and his father, Joseph, is what prompts Jesus' next words, which seek to clarify his origins and who his father really is. In verses 44-45 Jesus further develops what his relationship with the Father means, for him and for those who believe in him. If there appears to be a certain circularity in these verses, there should be. Jesus is trying to make the case that what the Jews know about their history, what is recorded in scripture and in the prophets, how they have heard and learned from God, all of this is now located in his revelation as the Word made flesh. Without these working assumptions, for Jesus to say "I AM the bread of life" would make little sense.

Verse 46 recalls 1:18, "No one has ever seen God. It is God the only Son, who is close to the Father's heart, who has made him known." Jesus has seen the Father because he comes from the Father and he is God made flesh. The reason for the incarnation is for us now to see God, to experience God in the fullness of relationship that was assumed in God's relationship with God's people but could be known only at a certain level. In part, Jesus is saying, "in me you do see God in a way you have never seen God before."

Verse 47 names the promise of eternal life again (cf. 6:40), setting up the next verses, that add more detail to what Jesus means by eternal life yet at the same time state it clearly enough to anticipate the conflict and difficulty ahead. In verse 48 Jesus repeats the primary "I AM" statement of this discourse, "I AM the bread of life," but what follows is a significantly stronger claim. Thus far, Jesus as the Bread of Life has been described in moderately acceptable theological arguments. The straightforward statement, "Your ancestors ate the manna in the wilderness, and they died," should cause suspicion of any easy acceptance of what Jesus has said thus far. This is Jesus at his transparent best. The blatancy of the allegation "and they died" stands in direct contrast to the imagery of eternal life developed up to this point. As a result, "eternal life" is reevaluated through this disturbing truth. Two additional details should elicit significant pause. First, Jesus uses the second person possessive pronoun, "your ancestors," not "our ancestors." Whether a play on the question of Jesus' ancestry recently discussed or a subtle reminder of the very real situation of the audience of this Gospel, this has the effect of augmenting potential conflict already simmering in this dialogue. Second, the term "ancestors" illumines the already established theme of relationship, parenthood, family, and community. It raises a larger theological issue at stake here and for the rest of the Gospel, who is family? Can ancestry look forward and not just backward? Is God imagining a larger familial structure in drawing persons in (6:44) who are not of this fold (10:16)?

Verse 50 is a moderate, third person demonstrative contention, "*this* is the bread that comes down from heaven" before the more upfront self-revelation in 6:51, "*I* am the living bread that came down from heaven." While verse 51 both closes this lectionary passage and opens the next pericope, it is perhaps best located as the latter because it clearly introduces a new level of interpretation of the sign, the connection of the bread from heaven with Jesus' own flesh. In this sense, for the sake of preaching through the Bread of Life discourse, the preacher might want to consider having 6:50 be the conclusion to the previous lectionary passage of the Bread of Life discourse and reserve verse 51 for the next week. When verse 50 closes out this section of the discourse, "This is the bread that comes down from heaven, so that one may eat of it and not die," the meaning of the opening verse, Jesus as the Bread of Life (6:35), and the emphasis on eternal life are given a particular focus, the promise of the absence of death. As a result, one strategy for preaching the second section of the discourse according to the lectionary is to start from the end and work backwards.

JOHN 6:51-58
TRUE FOOD AND TRUE DRINK

The lectionary articulates 6:51-58 as the fourth reading in this five-Sunday series. Looking ahead, the final section will include a three-verse overlap with this fourth section to round out the discourse. While there is a natural break at 6:59 to establish the setting for the discourse, the synagogue in Capernaum, the response of the disciples in 6:60 is premised on Jesus words prior to 6:59, and not just verses 56-58. The fluidity of parameters aside, the commentary on the penultimate reading from the Bread of Life discourse that follows will focus on the unique ideas introduced in this particular section.

While there is much that seems repetitive in the opening claim of verse 51, "I am the living bread that came down from heaven," this is a different assertion in many ways. New is the phrase "living bread" a present tense masculine nominative singular participle of *zaō*, "to live." This same participle will be used to describe the Father later in this passage, "Just as the living Father sent me" (6:57). The present tense is noteworthy, calling attention to the ongoing, unending "life" or "living" of Jesus as the bread, a central characteristic also of the Father. The unendingness of life is another way to articulate what eternal life mean. At the same time, the present tense is premised on 1:16, "grace upon grace," the abundance that Jesus has come to give. This particular participle also appears in the encounter with the Samaritan woman at the well, where Jesus describes the water he offers as "living water"—"If you knew the gift of God, and who it is that is saying to you, 'Give me a drink,' you would have asked him, and he would have given you living water"—the description used again in her response to Jesus, "Sir, you have no bucket, and the well is deep. Where do you get that living water?" (4:10-11). The use of the participle to describe both the water and the bread that Jesus provides reiterates the connection made earlier in the discourse and discussed above, "Whoever comes to me will never be hungry, and whoever believes in me will never be thirsty" (6:35). The promise made to the woman at the well, living water, is now for those listening here, living water *and* living bread, and serves to underscore the truthfulness of Jesus' words.

Verse 51 is also the first connection made between the nature of the bread, "living bread" and its source, "came down from heaven." To eat this bread means life forever, abundant life, eternal life, living life, all seeking to describe what life with God means. Moreover, this bread is given for the life of the world, not just for those who make confident and convinced claims about ancestry and God's activity. Jesus then makes the boldest statement yet, "and the bread that I will give for the life of the world *is my flesh*." The commentary on chapter 6 thus far has deliberately postponed a discussion of communion, the Lord's Supper, the Eucharist, and its role or lack thereof in the Fourth Gospel, because it is here that we can most readily see how the fourth evangelist might be working with this known tradition. Whether John is aware of the Last Supper traditions found in the Synoptic Gospels is an issue that does little to engage a homiletical imagination about this portion of the Bread of Life passage. That which is absent in John should not be the primary homiletical impulse when it comes to this portion of the discourse and, moreover, perpetuates John's place as the supplemental version to the Synoptics. In John's Gospel, there are no Words of Institution, no Lord's Supper per se that informs current liturgical practices of the Eucharist. With that knowledge in mind, it is not fair to this Gospel, nor to the community for whom it was originally written, to import our theologies about or preferences for communion practices. Rather, we can ask how this passage might shape our contemporary imagination for theological understanding and practice of the Lord's Supper in our various ecclesial communities.

A careful reading of 6:51 will also take note that Jesus bypasses language about the bread as his body altogether and equates this eating of the bread of life with his flesh. This is, of course, the same word used in the Prologue, "And the Word became flesh" (*sarx*, 1:14). As a result, 1:14 must be brought forward when interpreting the meaning and function of Jesus' words in 6:51. That the bread of life is Jesus' *flesh*, not his body, not only emphasizes the importance of the incarnation as the principal salvific premise for John but also reiterates all that Jesus as the Word made flesh contributes to our interpretation of the promise of abundant life and eternal life, so very prominent in this discourse.

The dispute among the Jewish leaders is thus very much expected. How can Jesus say that he is giving us *his flesh* to eat? It is important to note as well that the Jewish leaders call Jesus "this man" and do not use his name. The offense is that this mere man is making these radical claims about God. This particular moment is worth contemplating when it comes to our sacramental theology around Holy Communion—To what extent do our practices and our imagination around our celebrations of the table have a marked domesticity about them, as if we have forgotten the radicalness of what Jesus actually did and said? When Jesus offers himself as the Bread of Life, his flesh to eat, at least according to John, it is not limited to the offering of his life on the cross. That allusions to the Lord's Supper are relocated from the events surrounding the death of Jesus to the middle of his earthly ministry suggests that the offer of his flesh is first and foremost connected with abundant life here and now and not just the resurrection, and certainly, not just the crucifixion. If there is any eucharistic theology to be gleaned from the Gospel of John, it needs to be one that is a celebration of abundant life with God now and not a remembrance of Jesus' life soon to pass away.

In 6:53-55, Jesus responds to the debate with an even more outrageous inclusion, drinking his blood. Now presumably the water that he is able to provide, as the bread becomes flesh, becomes his blood. With the commentary above in mind, we can imagine what this might mean for ways to think about flesh and blood, bread and wine, true food and true drink (6:55), when it comes to the Lord's Supper. There is something quite visceral in this staggering claim, that the life Jesus offers us is not just his life on the cross but his flesh and blood life here and now. Eating Jesus' flesh and drinking Jesus' blood means eternal life and being raised up on the last day. What does that really mean? The clue to interpreting this statement comes in 6:56, "Those who eat my flesh and drink my blood abide in me, and I in them." The larger theological presupposition behind the entirety of this discourse is the Gospel's central means by which to articulate a relationship with God and Jesus, that of abiding. To be raised up on the last day does not have the resurrection in mind, but the ascension, "And if I go and prepare a place for you, I will come again and will take you to myself, so that where I am, there you may be also" (14:3). The mention of abiding here is another prompt to situate the whole of this discourse as the interpretation of the feeding of the five thousand. That essential provision is a marker of what it means to believe in Jesus, to be in relationship with Jesus. This is why, then, Jesus makes note in 6:55 that his flesh and blood are true food and true drink. While we are tempted to allow our present ecclesial practices to sentimentalize the Lord's Table or label the sum of the Bread of Life chapter as one big metaphorical exercise, the fourth evangelist stations Jesus' discourse in the very real event of the feeding of the five thousand, where Jesus himself fed them, not the disciples.

Verses 57-58 round out this lectionary portion with another way to convey how the feeding is connected to life. The commentary above noted that the participle "living" is used here to describe the Father. It is a central characteristic of who God is, the giver of life, creator, and, in Jesus, God is a living human being. In verse 57, all impediments, bread, flesh, blood, are removed, "whoever eats *me*." Verse 58 repeats verse 49, "your ancestors ate the bread from heaven in the wilderness and died." There is an interesting move to a third person reference here, from the first person petitions Jesus has been making up to this point, "the one who eats this bread." "This bread" recalls the reason for this discourse in the first place, the feeding of the five thousand. The bread that Jesus gave to the five thousand, that bread, was his very self and the life that only he can provide. "To live forever" links life here and now, as the promise of the resurrection, with life in the future, as the assurance of the ascension.

JOHN 6:56-71
RESISTANCE AND BETRAYAL

According to the lectionary, the last section of the Bread of Life chapter backs up three verses into the previous pericope but stops short of extending to the end of the chapter. Not included in the lectionary are the last two verses of the discourse, 6:70-71. The discussion on these verses will address the possible reasons for this omission and make the argument that these verses be included in the reading for this Sunday. The commentary has already addressed 6:56-58, so we begin with 6:59. Verse 59 affords a critical detail about the setting of this conversation and discourse, the synagogue at Capernaum. We know that Jesus was in Capernaum according to the earlier reference in the chapter (6:24), and to discover that this conversation and discourse have taken place not in the city of Capernaum in general but in the synagogue might explain the sudden appearance of the "Jews," the Jewish leaders. More explicit now, less clear in 6:24-25, is that the disciples have also overheard Jesus' words thus far and it is now their turn to weigh in on Jesus' interpretation of the sign they witnessed. In fact, the rest of the discourse is directed chiefly to the disciples.

The first reaction of the disciples is that this teaching is "difficult." The term *sklēros* can also be translated as "hard," "harsh," or "unpleasant." This is either one of the more understated rejoinders to Jesus' ministry or it is just the opposite, naming the truth about how demanding it can be to hear and make sense of what Jesus has to say. The NRSV translates the latter portion of this verse, "who can accept it?" but a more accurate translation would be "who is able to hear it?" To be a disciple of Jesus, to be in relationship with Jesus, is to hear him, listen to him. One possible entry into preaching this section of the discourse is to give voice to these words that perhaps we wish we could be allowed to say. Acknowledge the difficulties in what has been heard in this conversation and discourse. Why is it hard? What makes it harsh? Are we willing to admit that it is difficult? That we now know that the disciples have also been present throughout the entire discourse reiterates that these words of Jesus were also reflections on the nature of discipleship. That the disciples have also heard Jesus' discourse underscores the fact that this was indeed an interpretation of the feeding of the five thousand, the sign, for them.

The disciples are found to be grumbling like the Jewish leaders, like God's people in the wilderness. When Jesus learns of their complaining, his question, "does this offend you?," is literally, "does this scandalize you?" The verb is *skandalizō*, "to anger, offend, shock, to cause one to stumble, or cause one to sin." This last possible translation is perhaps the most fitting in the context of the Fourth Gospel, where sin is equivalent to the absence of a relationship with God. In other words, the disciples hear Jesus' words and are led to a possible position of unbelief rather than belief. This reading anticipates the crisis Jesus' names in 6:64, "'But among you there are some who do not believe.' For Jesus knew from the first who were the ones that did not believe, and who was the one that would betray him." Verse 62, therefore, has a critical place in the overall Bread of Life discourse as an unexpected cause for scandal. We anticipate that predictions of the crucifixion would cause resistance, but that the ascension would trigger dissention? Why the ascension here and now? What is scandalous in Jesus' return to heaven, to the Father? Perhaps it would then make all of what this Gospel has presented so far actually be true. That Jesus really does come from God. That he really was in the beginning with God. That he really is God. In the end, this is by far more outrageous than the death of Jesus.

The restatement of the ascension here and now also calls attention to how critical this theological presupposition is for this Gospel's construal of what life with Jesus and because of Jesus means. The ascension of Jesus will bring the fullness of life of which this Gospel speaks and witnesses. Abundant life, eternal life, life forever, is fully realized and known in the act of Jesus' return to the Father to prepare an abiding place for his own.

The Spirit as the source of life is also somewhat of a surprise at this point, given the emphasis on Jesus and God as the source of life thus far, but is grounded in an inseparability of relationship. The reference to the Spirit foreshadows the gift of the Spirit in 20:22, where Jesus will literally "breathe into" the disciples the Spirit, the breath of God. The reference to the Spirit here also looks toward the expanded presentation of the role of the Spirit in the Farewell Discourse. The conversation between Nicodemus and Jesus in chapter 3, "What is born of the flesh is flesh, and what is born of the Spirit is spirit" (3:6) also comes to mind.

Verse 64 is the first reference to Judas in the Gospel of John and marks a shift in the discourse to focus primarily on the disciples. Imagine being introduced for the first time not by your name, or what you have done, but in reference to what you *will* do. Such is the case for Judas in this closing section of chapter 6 in John's Gospel, "For Jesus knew from the first who were the ones that did not believe, and who was the one that would betray him." Typically, we are recognized by our past, whether achievements or hardships, with some evidence of behavior, some documentation of performance that reveals one's character. But not for Judas. There is no mention of Judas before this moment in the narrative. As a character in the unfolding story of Jesus, he is first known by and immediately indicted for an act he has yet to commit, betraying Jesus. Perhaps not fair, but every bit true. That the concept of betrayal is introduced at this point in the story necessitates extended commentary here on how betrayal is uniquely presented in the Gospel of John.

Important to note is that to which betrayal is immediately connected—believing. Betrayal in the Gospel of John is far more complex than going back on a promise. The story of Judas narrates one such complication. The word translated "betray" means "to hand or give over." Judas will betray Jesus, but not in the way we think, or in the way we come to know from the other Gospels. Judas's last appearance in John's Gospel before accompanying the soldiers to arrest Jesus is during the final meal shared between Jesus and his disciples. Satan enters into Judas and he exits, going out into the night (13:30). He has crossed over to the dark side. When we get to the arrest scene in John 18:1-13a, Judas himself does not actually hand Jesus over to the authorities. In the other Gospels, Judas identifies Jesus with a kiss but in John's Gospel, there is no kiss, no identification at all of Jesus. We know only that Judas "was standing with *them*" (18:5) presumably with the Jewish police representing the chief priests and Pharisees and the Roman soldiers. Jesus comes forward, out of the garden, of his own accord and willingly gives *himself* up to the authorities.

The arrest scene is the last we ever hear of Judas in John's story. There is no recounting of remorse or repentance to explain Judas's actions. Greed is never given as a justification of his betrayal, and there is no act of suicide to assuage guilt. Instead, John leaves us hanging, without answers, without reasons for Judas's behavior, and with the lingering question of why? The answer to that seemingly simple question might be equally simple. Only a few verses before the introduction of Judas, many of Jesus' disciples say, "This teaching is difficult; who can accept it?" Jesus responds with his own question to them, "Does this offend you?" (6:60-61) What if affronted by the challenges of Jesus' words, and even offended by them, Judas has no choice but to betray his teacher? It's Jesus' fault.

When all is said and done, the true nature of Judas's betrayal is not in response to Jesus' unfaithfulness or inability to fulfill promises. In fact, Jesus will be faithful to the end and will come through on every single promise he ever uttered, abundantly so. At the heart of the betrayal of Judas is his own disbelief. He does not believe that Jesus is who he says he is, the Word made flesh, the very presence of God right in front of him. It cannot be. That is not the God he has known. That is not the God that he really wants or can accept. This is difficult, even offensive. He did not sign up for this God. And as soon as we construe God in ways that demand that God conform to our standards, there is no choice but to fault God for betraying *us*.

For preaching, the story of Judas in the Gospel of John calls attention to those times when being offended by or disappointed in someone is really more about us than about the other. Rather than take responsibility for our own sense of betrayal, we cast blame. Instead of questioning the appropriateness of our reaction or asking why our response is allegations of dashed hopes, we accuse, as if others are obligated to fulfill *our* expectations. That may be a bit hard for us to hear, that sometimes feeling betrayed has less to do with the conduct of another than with our own conduct; that the impression of betrayal comes not from a deliberate act perpetrated against us, but from the fact that we have made the other something or someone they are not. And then it is *we* that have done the betraying by being unfaithful to another person's true self. Of course, this is certainly not always the case. Examples of intentional duplicity and deceitfulness in our world more than abound. But the story of Judas exposes the intricacies of betrayal that we would rather ignore or to which we rarely admit. Judas reminds us that sometimes the origin of our hurt lies deep within ourselves.

This theological presentation of betrayal invites us to listen carefully to those who feel let down by others. Were they really betrayed by the person in whom their hope was placed? Or did the person end up not being the person they wanted him or her to be, as determined by their standards, their set beliefs, their ideals? We might also ask, when someone slights our confidences, why is it that betrayal is so close at hand as an accusation? What makes the power and potency of betrayal take hold so quickly? The story of Judas asks us to look long and hard at our own, possibly unreasonable, expectations of the other, and to speak the truth about what stands behind our own disappointments. John 6:65 is a summary of this truth.

The referent of "this" in verse 66 is not necessarily the most immediate words Jesus has spoken, but could very well represent the entirety of the discourse, much as 18:1, "After Jesus had spoken these words," where "these words" signifies the whole of the Farewell Discourse. There is a marked poignancy in this verse, that there were other disciples besides the Twelve, who at this point will no longer follow Jesus. While we know in theory that there were other followers of Jesus in addition to the named dozen, to be told this early in the Gospel that they could not believe in Jesus should elicit a certain amount of grief. Preaching this text might put the listener in the place of these disciples who turn back and pose Jesus' question, "Do you also wish to go away?" (6:67).

In view of Peter's response in the next verse, there are some parallels in this section of the Bread of Life discourse with the passion predictions and Peter's confession at Caesarea Philippi in the Synoptic Gospels (Matt. 16:13-20; Mark 8:27-30; Luke 9:18-21). This is a moment of decision, of response, of commitment, of crisis. Considering that the next chapters will describe the level of opposition against Jesus by the Jewish authorities, now may very well be a good time to get out. While much of what the disciples will face is made more explicit in the Farewell Discourse, the attention to the betrayal of Judas and Jesus' very candid question to the disciples at this point in the narrative is another means by which, like moving the temple incident, the very real conflict that is the difficult context of this community is made known. The crisis of judgment outlined in the Nicodemus narrative is always present in this Gospel. It is important to note that what Jesus has revealed in this discourse, which is found to be difficult and ultimately rejected, is not predictions of suffering and death but visions of eternal life. Perhaps there is only so much of a good thing we can take. There is something painfully true about the human condition that is named in this last section of Jesus' discourse that interprets the feeding of the five thousand—our tendency toward suspicion when things seem too good to be true; our disbelief in a God whose sole purpose is the giving of life, especially forever, eternal, and abundant life for the world; but even more so, our general difficulty with a God who wants to be as close as the God of the Fourth Gospel. That life, eternal, abundant, and forever, is the primary point of impediment is affirmed by Peter's response to Jesus' question in 6:68, "Lord, to whom can we go? You have the words of eternal life." Peter's answer serves to summarize the entire discourse and thereby the meaning of the sign itself. Who else but Jesus is the source of eternal life? The sign, dialogue, and discourse have sought to make that abundantly clear, that Jesus, as from God and as God, is the giver of life, life that is now sustained by that which is essential for living, food and water, and life to come because the bread that came down from heaven will return to heaven to prepare an everlasting abiding place for all believers.

Preachers in liturgical traditions will connect Peter's words with the Gospel acclamation used in worship, "Lord, to whom can we go? You have the words of eternal life." Making that connection when preaching on this passage would help congregations realize that listening to the Gospel text is more than hearing a story about Jesus' ministry. It is to anticipate encountering Jesus so that abundant life, perhaps only briefly, might actually be experienced. Peter's second acclamation is yet another summary of the sign, dialogue, and discourse, and also encapsulates the meaning of discipleship for this Gospel (6:69). Both verbs, to believe and to know, are synonymous in that they indicate being in a relationship with Jesus. To believe Jesus and to know Jesus are the same as to say one is in an abiding relationship with Jesus. In addition, both verbs are in the perfect tense. In other words, this relationship is already set and the effects of this relationship—in the case of the Bread of Life chapter, provision of life—are an ongoing reality. That Peter articulates the existence of this relationship with Jesus as the "Holy One of God" is the meaning of this particular sign and its dialogue and discourse. Peter could well have formulated realizing a relationship *with Jesus.* Instead, he expresses the truth of this relationship as *with God.* The central imagery by which Jesus interprets the feeding of the five thousand assumes that God's provision for God's people is now that which Jesus also provides because he is from God and is God, the Holy One from God. The

"Holy One" can be another way to understand the meaning of, or to translate, the phrase in 1:18, "God the One and Only" (NIV).

The lectionary brings the passage to a close at 6:69, Peter's confession. A cursory read of 6:70-71 indicates why these verses are omitted from the lectionary. To cast Judas as a "devil" even "the devil" or "the slanderer" creates all kinds of challenges for preaching, but if the text raises these difficulties, perhaps we should address them in our preaching. The reference looks forward to the moment of Judas's betrayal, when Satan enters into him and he retreats into the night (13:27-30). The language of "choice" resonates with the larger theme of this Gospel that those who encounter Jesus are put in a position of choice, a position of crisis, decision, and therefore judgment. Even though Jesus chooses Judas, Judas must still choose Jesus. The issue of choice, of coming to belief in Jesus, is essentially about relationship. True relationship is mutual and reciprocal. While Jesus may have invited Judas to follow him, there is still accountability on Judas's part to enter into this relationship fully. Given the setting of the feeding of the five thousand and the provision of food and water by God for the Israelites in the wilderness, critical is how God's people respond to God's desire for relationship. For the Fourth Gospel, encountering God in the Word made flesh, Jesus, is a crisis moment.

For some denominations, the idea of decision or choice when it comes to a relationship with God will be resisted and even rejected; for others, central and celebrated. Ownership of one's own denominational biases is essential when it comes to preaching, especially preaching biblical texts with integrity and truthfulness. There will be some preachers who will ignore these verses altogether, thankful that the lectionary has eliminated for them a "choice" they did not want to make. Yet, to exclude these verses from the lectionary passage and from one's own theological wrestling is to risk casting a blind eye to the very real presence of evil that this text acknowledges and that exists in all of us, even preachers.

These last verses of chapter 6 attempt to articulate what is, in the end, unexplainable: why some people believe in Jesus—particularly who Jesus is in this Gospel as God incarnated—and some do not. Most certainly, this was an ecclesial, communal, and theological crisis for the community to which this Gospel is addressed. How do they make sense of those who have not chosen to follow Jesus, who do not recognize who Jesus is, especially those *closest* to them, friends, family members? Why are they not able to see what they see and hear what they hear? How can we explain it or understand it? Part of what this Gospel acknowledges is that we cannot. Those who attend our churches experience the same crisis. Do we talk about this in our sermons or only when asked within the protected walls of our church studies or individual conversations? Yet there is honesty in how this Gospel gives witness to the reasons why some believe and some do not: we do not know and it may very well be the presence of the other power at work in the world, Satan. As this Gospel begins with a cosmological birth story, it realizes the cosmological dimensions behind what is operative in the world, both on a national, worldly level and on the communal, intimate, and individual level.

These verses, then, are essential when it comes to interpreting the character of Judas in the Fourth Gospel. As noted above, Judas is first introduced in the story at 6:64, not by name but by his action of betraying Jesus. Verse 71 describes Judas again as the one who will hand Jesus over (future active participle masculine nominative singular of *paradidōmi*), but it is also the first place in the Gospel that the *name* of Judas is mentioned. To name Judas at this moment is significant because the reference is located in the midst of language of intimacy and relationship. Twice these verses call attention to the Twelve, the Twelve Jesus chose, and that Judas was one of the Twelve. The one who betrays Jesus is not a nondescript someone who happens upon Jesus sometime in his ministry. It is not even one of the disciples who turned away after Jesus' challenging words. It is one of the Twelve, one from the inner circle, one closest to Jesus, whom Jesus knows by name, because he knows his disciples by name (10:3).

CONNECTIONS TO THE LECTIONARY

The lectionary connections for the Bread of Life passage in John's Gospel have been postponed until this point in the commentary because most of the comments about lectionary issues related to this chapter were included in the discussion above. 6:24–35 is Proper 13[18], Year B, but is also the designated lection for Thanksgiving (6:25–35) in Year C. Each liturgical setting could yield interpretive value when it comes to preaching this portion of John 6. Intended in the commentary above was to point out specific textual issues and themes present at this initial stage in the dialogue and discourse on the feeding of the five thousand. All of these might be considered when it comes to preaching some of the particularity of this section of the chapter. For the first section of the Bread of Life dialogue and discourse, it would be essential to explain how in this passage Jesus begins to articulate what the sign actually means. Each section of this discourse reveals something new about what happened on that knoll of much grass for five thousand people. That this passage is chosen for Thanksgiving on its own, separated from the sign on which it comments, necessitates relocating it as commentary on the feeding of the five thousand for the sake of an embodied understanding of what it means to give thanks for what is provided.

All in Year B, 6:35, 41-51 is Proper 14[19], 6:51-58 is assigned to Proper 15 [20], and Proper 16 [21] is 6:56-69. The commentary on the verses themselves argues that 6:70-71 should definitely be included in the last reading. To reiterate, one of the significant challenges of preaching this chapter is exposed by the lectionary itself. It is almost impossible to separate manageable lections for preaching when the whole of the chapter builds and is based on what has come before and points to what lies ahead. A preacher's best strategy is to plan ahead; in doing so the preacher will certainly discover new moments of revelation in each subsequent pericope which the commentary above intended to establish. At the same time, one direction for preaching might tell the story up front, that is, start at the end and work backward. This might lend a new perspective to how both preacher and parishioner experience a rather anticipated miracle.

5

Conflict with the World (John 7–8)

Unless you happen to select the alternate Gospel reading for the Sunday of Pentecost in Year A or you are Lutheran and the Gospel reading assigned for Reformation Sunday in every lectionary year is John 8:31-36, you will never have to preach any portion of chapters 7–8 in the Gospel of John. If these two chapters are eliminated by the lectionary why should a preacher keep reading this chapter in this commentary, especially a non-Lutheran preacher? Preaching the Gospel of John with integrity, particularity, and especially with nuance and dexterity necessitates a diligent reading through and careful analysis of these chapters. The primary goal of this chapter of the commentary is to demonstrate the multiple ways in which thoughtful attention to chapters 7–8 will make one a better preacher of the rest of the Gospel. The imagery and symbols, the social, political, and religious contexts, as well as the theological and christological themes presented in these two chapters flesh out and help interpret the whole of the narrative.

Any preacher knows that sections of texts, large or small, overlooked by the lectionary should prompt suspicion. These are usually texts that are deemed "difficult" either theologically or as topics of faith best avoided by the common believer. In this regard, chapters 7–8 meet those criteria. There is little that is easy about these chapters. The setting is new, one of the three pilgrimage festivals, and will necessitate explanation both historically and in terms of how it functions in the chapters. There is no real "event" on which the dialogue hinges, no sign or miracle, which makes the discussion appear to lack a kind of grounding. The exception, of course, is the woman caught in adultery in 8:1-11, which most Johannine scholars argue was not original to the Fourth Gospel. Finally, the polemic between Jesus and the Jewish authorities reaches its most vitriolic tone, with words on Jesus' lips that should cause deep concern when it comes to the ever-present reality and persistence of anti-Semitism today. The difficulties that abound in these chapters are all the more reason to pay them sustained attention.

Before any verse-by-verse commentary on these chapters, we need to be reminded of the brief discussion on the audience of the Fourth Gospel presented in the Introduction. If, indeed, the Johannine community represents a Jewish group that has been excommunicated from a more dominant representative Judaism, the language of chapters 7–8—and even the language of Jesus in these chapters—is consistent with a sectarian perspective that sets itself in opposition to the principal party. The differentiation of the ostracized group over and against those with the prevailing power is essential because it is identity building. The people of the Johannine community find themselves expelled from their community and, therefore, from virtually every communal aspect they have ever known. Separation from friends, family, synagogue, social structures, and, in the case of a gathering together (what *synagogue* means) for worship of God, separation from God is their crisis. This very real situation of the Johannine community must be ever-present in our discussion of chapters 7–8. As noted in the Introduction, the Gospel of John represents an intra-Jewish debate in the first century with not one dominant Judaism at the time of Jesus but multiple "Judaisms," so to speak. In part, this is the reason that the Jesus movement had the "success" that it did. For the Gospel writers especially, in a post-70 milieu, ideas concerning correct interpretation of Scripture, where to worship, and the presence of God were all up for debate when it came to making sense of what God was now doing in the person and ministry of Jesus Christ.

Critical for the interpretion and preaching of chapters 7–8 in the Gospel of John is the role of these chapters as justifying anti-Semitism. Omitting these verses from the lectionary, however, is not going to erase this situation, nor will it solve the difficult truth that many believers continue to ask the same question as that of the Johannine community—why don't the "Jews" believe in Jesus? We will perpetuate ill-advised and ill-informed interpreters of the bible by preaching and by ecclesial decisions that eliminate unpleasantries in the history of biblical interpretation. Chapters 7–8 in the Fourth Gospel may also very well be one of the reasons preachers have difficulty preaching John. In the little time allotted for a sermon, it seems unfeasible to take on the historical issues of first-century Judaism, Jewish–Christian debate, and anti-Semitism—not to mention the host of theological issues raised in all three topics. The irony should not be lost that the one passage that finds itself in the Revised Common Lectionary from chapters 7–8 is for Reformation Sunday, when Martin Luther's writings about and against the Jews are well known.

It is no accident, then, that the primary setting for such identifiers and distinctive claims about God is the Festival of Booths, that is, the Feast of Tabernacles, or Sukkot (7:2). The Festival of Booths was one of three pilgrimage festivals that brought Jews from all regions of Palestine to Jerusalem and the temple (Exod. 23:14-19; 34:22-24; Lev. 23:33-43; Num. 29:12-38; Deut. 16:16-17; 31:9-13). It was the culminating festival of the year, a fall festival that celebrated the end of harvest, particularly the grape and olive harvest. As its name intimates, part of the week-long celebration included building temporary shelters, "tabernacles" or "booths," in which to live during the festival that thereby recalled God's protection in the wilderness wanderings. Its essential celebratory focus is the presence of and provision from God in the wilderness. The two primary celebrations during the festival marked God's provision of both water and light during the wilderness wanderings of the Israelites. It will be against this backdrop that Jesus will identify himself as the source of water (7:37) and the light of the world (8:12). John is the only Gospel to mention the Feast of Tabernacles directly.

One final introductory note before moving to the commentary on the chapters is to inquiry about the function of these chapters, particularly as they stand alone as dialogue with and discourse from Jesus apart from a narrated event or sign. That this question is rarely asked or minimally addressed may be another reason why these chapters are overlooked in our homiletical lectionary. When sections of text do not seem to have an identifiable purpose, it becomes difficult to justify their usefulness for faith reflection. The function of chapters 7–8 may be answered in three possible ways. First, they bring another central festival of the Jews to the forefront of interpretational imagination when it comes to christological reflection for the fourth evangelist. John weaves the entirety of who Jesus is through the essential stories and festivals that marked God's relationship with God's people. This is yet another point of contact to discount any and all use of this Gospel as a means to justify anti-Semitism. While any categorization of the Gospels as more or less "Jewish" or more or less "gentile" is a false dichotomy, there is everything to suggest how thoroughly Jewish the Gospel of John is. Moreover, the festivals are by definition acts to maintain relationship with God and remembrances of God's relational commitment and covenant. As a result, they underscore the Gospel's important theme of relationship with Jesus and God.

Second, within the overall narrative itself, chapters 7–8 bridge chapters 6 and 9 in such a way as to link the two primary symbols of water from chapter 6, "I am the bread of life. Whoever comes to me will never be hungry, and whoever believes in me will never be thirsty" (6:35) and light in chapter 9, "As long as I am in the world, I am the light of the world" (9:5). Beyond a simple bridge section between chapters 6 and 9, chapters 7 and 8 build on, inform, anticipate, and help interpret what precedes them and what follows them. As a result, preaching the Bread of Life discourse should draw on the development of Jesus as the source of living water (7:37), and preaching on the healing of the man blind from birth and its discourse should refer to Jesus' revelation as "the light of the world" in 8:12.

Third, these chapters pull together into one section the conflict that was intimated in chapter 2 with the temple incident and that has been increasing ever since. Chapters 7 and 8 assist in making sense of the conflict that will continue to intensify in the chapters that follow, especially in the response to the raising of Lazarus. As a result, these chapters can function to inform the passages where dialogue between Jesus and the Jewish leaders seems at its most controversial.

John 7:1-13
Conflict Everywhere

Chapter 7 opens with a change of setting from Jerusalem and Judea in chapter 6. "After this" refers to the entirety of chapter 6, the feeding of the five thousand and the dialogue and discourse that followed. As a reminder, the setting for the feeding of the five thousand and the Bread of Life discourse was Jerusalem for the Festival of Passover. The first verse of chapter 7 indicates and anticipates the severity of the situation between Jesus and the religious authorities. Jesus stays in the Galilee region because of the threat to his life from the Jewish leaders. Verses 3-9 are a unique glimpse into Jesus' family life. Jesus has brothers! While known about Jesus, the role of Jesus' brothers here is not just to give evidence for Jesus' siblings. That Jesus has brothers underscores his humanity. Jesus had a mother and brothers. Chapter 7 will call attention to Jesus' divinity now through the lens of God's activity particularly in the celebration of the Festival of Booths. The mention of Jesus' brothers mandates once again that Jesus' humanity and divinity be held together. Jesus' brothers are introduced with narrative proximity to the first encounter with Judas, reiterating that even those closest to Jesus are not able to recognize who he is. The interjection of siblings here in these particular chapters points to the reality of the Johannine community; community members are separated from their families, forced out of their synagogue for believing in Jesus. Jesus experienced the denunciation even of those closest to him, just as those who believed in him would face the rejection of those they love.

The Festival of Booths was near, which would mean travel to Jerusalem. Jesus' brothers urge him to go to Judea for the festival so that the works he has been doing, evidently in the Galilean region, may be seen by the disciples, perhaps sent ahead by Jesus with his plan to stay behind. The works to which his brothers might be referring are not necessarily signs or miracles not recorded in the Gospel, but rather the act of believing in Jesus. The parenthetical remark in 7:5 intimates this connection between works and belief. The irony in 7:4 is more than apparent. For Jesus to be widely known means that he offers the relationship he has with the Father to all those who believe. In fact, Jesus has not acted in secret, and all that he has done up to this point in the Gospel has been for the sake of the world. Jesus' mention of his "time" recollects Jesus' hour, which refers to the events of his crucifixion, resurrection, and ascension. This is a unique description found only here in 7:6 and 8 in the Gospel.

The use of the term "hate" in 7:7, particularly connected to evil, draws on Jesus' words to Nicodemus. "For all who do evil hate the light and do not come to the light, so that their deeds may not be exposed" (3:20). That 3:20 also raises the idea of being exposed makes another connection to chapter 7 and the concern for Jesus showing himself. The opening verses of chapter 7 draw significantly on Jesus' words to Nicodemus, particularly 3:16–21. The NRSV's translation "deeds" in 3:20, "so that their deeds may not be exposed," is the same word that occurs in 7:7 but here it is translated as "works."

Verse 8 anticipates the conflict that would result were Jesus to go to Jerusalem for the Festival of Booths. Of course, this is not just any everyday conflict, but a confrontation that will precipitate the actual events of the hour. Verses 10–13 bring the setting to Jerusalem for the festival, with Jesus having decided to go regardless of the inevitable opposition with the Jewish authorities. During the first three days of the festival, we find the Jewish leaders looking for Jesus and the crowds complaining about him, the same grumbling as that of the Jewish leaders in 6:41 and of the disciples in 6:61. The very real fear of what the Jewish leaders might do to one found speaking of Jesus—being thrown out of the synagogue—anticipates the concern of the parents of the man born blind and the fate of their son in chapter 9. This is the first time in the Gospel that the phrase "fear of the Jews" appears. The reason for the secret-disciple status of Joseph of Arimathea is his "fear of the Jews" (19:38), and in the resurrection narratives, we find the disciples hiding behind closed doors for "fear of the Jews" (20:19). In 12:42, fear is connected directly with the idea of being put out of the synagogue—in this instance by other Jewish authorities who will not confess their belief in Jesus because of the Pharisees. Family members, disciples, even some Jewish authorities all know the certainty of what befalls those who testify openly to believing in Jesus. Such fear and all too certain consequences raise the stakes considerably when we think about the act of witnessing. By definition, testimony is public. It is observable verification of beliefs and as such is vulnerable and exposing. A sermon on the potential costs of open expression of faith would capture some of the simmering issues in these opening verses of chapter 7.

John 7:14-29
Arrival at the Festival:
Where Does Jesus come From?

In the middle of the week-long festival, Jesus goes up into the temple to teach. This is a much different scenario from how the chapter began, with Jesus' reluctance to attend the festival at all. Moreover, he is not teaching somewhere outside the city walls or someplace in the city streets, but in the temple itself. Why the temple? Why would Jesus be here when it is not his time and when he knows the response that his presence and his teaching will prompt? Why would he purposefully make himself a possible subject of attention? These are not mere rhetorical questions in this case because, given the introduction to these chapters outlined above, this move on Jesus' part activates the most intense disagreement between Jesus and the religious leaders in the entire Gospel. To answer these questions requires christological wrestling with who Jesus is, theological grappling with the nature of a God who would choose altercation, and ecclesiological struggling with how we go about public testimony to our faith. Knowing the identity of Jesus in the Fourth Gospel, it should not be surprising that he is the instigator of encounter rather than waiting for it to come to him. Jesus' as initiator of the events of the hour is foreshadowed here. That Jesus attends the festival may also be that he cannot help himself given who he is in this Gospel. He cannot *not* be present in the temple during the Festival of Booths because the purpose of the festival is to commemorate God's presence.

The Jewish authorities are amazed at his teaching, especially for one who has not been taught, or at least has not been taught in the ways they deem acceptable. Their reaction leads Jesus to reference the origins of his authority, but it also points to the larger political and religious situation of Judaism in the time of Jesus, with a focus on interpretation of Scripture, particularly claims about God. In some ways this is no different than what we are about today as Christians, vying for correct views of the Bible, arguments for who God is and who or what God is for, and questioning the authority of all such testimony.

What we will see in these two chapters in the Gospel of John is a glimpse into the struggles of the witness of faith, then and now.

The topic of the dialogue moves immediately into the question of the sources of Jesus' teaching, or, put another way, Jesus' origin (1:1). Jesus is sent by God and is God. Where did Jesus come from? is a major theme for this Gospel, as we have already noted. Jesus' origin is always an issue especially in how he will identify himself in the context of the Festival of Booths. In many respects, chapters 7–8 are Jesus' discourse on the one work he mentions in 7:21, his one work of making God known. This section is moving toward Jesus' statement, "I know him, because I am from him, and he sent me" (7:29). One helpful strategy for preaching this portion of chapter 7 is to begin with 7:29 and work backwards.

The introduction of Moses in verse 19 reveals that much of what is at stake in these chapters is interpretation of the law, the reading of Scripture, and an understanding who God is now in the revelation of Jesus. Verse 23 refers back to the healing of the man in chapter 5, who was made well on the Sabbath. The man born blind will also be healed on the Sabbath, which this chapter then foreshadows. At first glance, verse 21 seems to be referencing the healing of the man at Beth-zatha as the one work. A broad perspective on the Gospel, however, suggests that the one work is what was noted above, making God known. In fact, Jesus has already performed other "works"—water into wine, the healing of the official's son (4:43-54), the healing of the man at Beth-zatha, and the feeding of the five thousand. The argument on the basis of Moses and circumcision for Jesus' healing on the Sabbath is a direct reference to relationship. What is it that circumcision symbolized? It was the mark of covenant, a symbol of relationship with God. Before the people now stands that which makes relationship with God possible, Jesus. In verses 25-27, Jesus is the man they are trying to kill, the Messiah, and a man whose origin they know, presumably Nazareth. In Jesus' reaction is a palpable tone of frustration, "You know where I am from"—but they do not.

John 7:30-36
Where I Am, You Cannot Come

These verses continue the theme of where Jesus comes from but now include where he is going. Where Jesus is going is returning to the Father who sent him, and the ascension is the full circle of the revelation of God, "the work" that Jesus came to "perform." Jesus' exclamations about his origins, however, are now cause for an interest in his arrest. The desire to arrest Jesus appears initially in this chapter of the Gospel, first as a response to Jesus' claims about his origins and, second, because there are some listening to Jesus who now believe in him (7:32, 44, 45; 10:39; 11:57). In the Synoptic Gospels there is little hesitancy or delay in arresting Jesus. In John, there are numerous references to wanting to arrest him as well reports of difficulty in making the arrest happen (8:20, 59; 12:36). When Jesus begins to talk about going back to where he came from, there is misunderstanding (7:35). The language of searching or seeking in these verses recalls Jesus' very first words to his disciples, "what are you looking for" (1:37). The multiple responses to Jesus in the previous verses suggest that none of the characters is certain for what or whom they are looking or what or whom they see in Jesus. As a result, what follows in the next section of chapter 7 is a means by which Jesus' counters this confusion.

John 7:37-52
Living Water Revisited

The setting for this last large section of chapter 7 is now the last day of the festival, the great day, which was the water festival celebrating God's provision of water in the wilderness wanderings. In the midst of this commemoration Jesus suggests that he is the source of water by which no one will ever be thirsty. Jesus has already made similar claims in the discourse on the feeding of the five thousand and, more personally, in his revelation to the Samaritan woman at the well. Jesus is the source of living water, which is then connected to the believer's heart and the Spirit. There is a prolepsis in verse 39, anticipating the giving of the Spirit in 20:22. Verses 40-44 articulate again the confusion around who Jesus is and where he comes from. The pattern of seeing Jesus as a prophet and then as the Messiah has already been acted out with the Samaritan woman at the well. Verse 42 points to the awareness of the tradition that the Messiah will come from the house of David, a theme that Matthew develops most thoroughly in his Gospel. For John, however, Jesus is the Word made flesh who comes from God. Verses 45-52 reintroduce the character of Nicodemus to the plot of the narrative—a leader of the Jews who first came to Jesus by night (3:2). The temple police wonder about Jesus, "Never has anyone spoken like this!" (7:46). The Pharisees inquire as to why the temple police did not arrest Jesus, accuse them of being deceived by Jesus, inquire if any other authorities have come to believe in him, and dismiss the crowd's reaction to Jesus because it knows nothing about the law. In this fourfold reaction of the Pharisees to the various responses to Jesus' words, Nicodemus seems to come to Jesus' rescue, his question for the Pharisees anticipating a negative answer:

"Does our law condemn anyone without first hearing him to find out what he is doing?" (7:51 NIV). Of course not! What should we make of Nicodemus and his triumphal return to stand up for Jesus? While his question appears sincere, nonetheless it is a third-person remark that says little about either his own belief or his willingness to testify publicly to that belief. As much as we may want to rehabilitate Nicodemus—and perhaps even more so at his reappearance to assist Joseph of Arimathea in burying Jesus—he nonetheless offers no more than his own interpretation of the law and nothing about who he thinks Jesus might be. The Pharisees, on the other hand, conclude that, while some may think Jesus is a prophet, no prophet ever came from Galilee (7:52). The irony, of course, is that the prophets were sent from God. Were Nicodemus to defend Jesus as a prophet, there may be more hope for his character at this point in the story.

One avenue for preaching this chapter is to zero in on Nicodemus and his role here against the backdrop of the entire story. Why here and why now does Nicodemus enjoy a reappearance in the narrative? How does he function as a character in the story, particularly at this juncture? We noted above that the opening verses of chapter 7 rely on the latter section of Jesus' words to Nicodemus in chapter 3. We might ask in what ways the Nicodemus story stands behind the themes presented in chapter 7: water, Spirit, judgment, to name three. Chapter 7 is also a moment of judgment for a number of characters, as to whether or not they recognize who Jesus is. The language of "lifting up" stands behind any discussion on or assumption of the ascension. Allowing some of the themes with which Nicodemus must struggle as they are now rearticulated in chapter 7 might bring to the surface aspects of this passage that are easily reduced to Jesus saying more of the same.

John 7:53—8:11
The Woman Caught in Adultery

For a passage that never appears in the lectionary, the story of the woman caught in adultery has managed to take on an extraordinary life of its own in the theological imaginations of many who listen to our sermons. The story of the woman caught in adultery is not found in the oldest and most reliable Greek manuscripts we have of the Gospel of John, and most critical study Bibles will demarcate the text in double brackets with an accompanying footnote explaining this text-critical issue. Nevertheless, like the disputed endings of the Gospel of Mark (16:9-18), the story of the woman caught in adultery is still included in modern versions of the Bible that people read and interpret. As a result, the responsible preacher will decide to preach on this text every so often in her ministry so as to offer additional lines of interpretation besides those in general lore. To bypass this story because it is not included in the lectionary and is not original to the Fourth Gospel only marginalizes this woman even more.

To be sure, there are many aspects of this story that are outside the thematic bounds of the Gospel of John, of which the commentary that follows will take note. At the same time, we find her story here, in the text of John as it stands, and dismissing it does not help our understanding of the Gospel. There are many avenues for preaching this text on its own terms as well as in its location in the Fourth Gospel. To be honest, the story seems out of place in these chapters, much like the woman is. We could easily jump from 8:2 to 8:12 and never know she existed. The preceding scene ended with everyone going home, perhaps tired of arguing for one day, with Jesus retreating to the Mount of Olives which is across the Kidron Valley from the west gate of the temple mount. This is an interesting geographical detail. Why does Jesus leave the temple? Why go to the Mount of Olives which is the only time this location is mentioned in the Gospel of John? Early the next morning Jesus returns to the temple and starts up his teaching again. Enter a snare of sorts, which is very much how this story sounds, especially compared to the controversy stories in the Synoptic Gospels. It has every element of entrapment that we are accustomed to seeing in the other Gospels. Indeed, that the whole episode is meant to test Jesus is made clear in 8:6. This test, however, is not a general trap but one that might lead to a reason for Jesus' arrest.

The Pharisees bring before Jesus a woman caught in adultery and make her stand before *all* of them, and we have already been told that "*all* the people came to him" (8:2) when he returned to the temple in the morning. This act alone, the objectification of this woman at the hands of the religious leaders makes a point worth exploring in a sermon. Like the woman at the well, her "sin" is too easily judged until we remember that both the woman and the man caught in adultery were guilty and sentenced to death. Where is the other party in this parade? A similar question might be asked of the men who found some necessary little fault in the woman at the well so as to divorce her. The woman in chapter 8 is further trivialized by how she is introduced to Jesus, "this woman," as if being caught in the *very act* of adultery did not include a man. The narrative pace between their question for Jesus and Jesus' response slows down enough to create a feeling of anticipation of how this will turn out, for the Pharisees, for Jesus, and for the woman. Jesus' act of playing in the dirt with his fingers appears to be a downright dismissal of both the trap and the charge. When Jesus finally stands, his words are ones that have entered into contemporary vocabulary much like the Prodigal Son and the Good Samaritan,

"Let anyone among you who is without sin be the first to throw a stone at her" (Joh 8:7) Even to preach this passage, relocating this pithy saying of Jesus back into its literary setting is worth a sermon or two. The absurdity of Jesus' response, however, is lost in how this phrase has been reduced to a moral quotable quote. This is not a saying for us to go around repeating as if to self-justify our own sin. In fact, this too-often quoted dictum of Jesus has little to do with morality and everything to do with a conflict of interest. In other words, we all have sinned, and the Pharisees sin, by bringing only the woman and not the man involved for a verdict. The sin here is not adultery or any other identifiable sin, but that they have objectified her, condemning her without fair judgment of both parties. Verses 8–9 offer a glimpse into a moment of the condemnation of the self. In the larger context of this Gospel, where judgment is not something that Jesus, or God for that matter, has come to do, but is a moment of self-judgment as to whether or not one believes in Jesus, Jesus here provides the moment for that realization. It is something we might imagine doing in our preaching. Rather than naming the sin, naming the wrong, the realization is naming the human condition, giving space for ample contemplation for how to respond to Jesus' question, "Where are they? Or "Where are you?" (8:10). That "one by one" they depart, leaving just Jesus and the woman alone provides significant space for reflection, given the "all" that came in the first place. This part of the scene is drawn out for a reason, to give narrative emphasis on the moment of judgment that this Gospel has already suggested will indeed happen.

Against the backdrop of what condemnation means for this Gospel, there is no way that Jesus can judge her. One of the likely reasons for why this passage is out of place in this Gospel is verse 11 and its perceived presentation of sin. Jesus tells the woman to sin no more, presumably referring to her sin of adultery. Since sin in the Gospel of John is a category of relationship and not a moral construct, Jesus' words do not ring true, at least for John. At the same time, one could imagine that in the case of the woman caught in adultery, to sin no more is to solicit thought about the complexities and demands of relationship. That the "sin" of the woman here has to do with relationship and that sin is equivalent to a lack of relationship in the Gospel of John invite parallels and possibilities for preaching on how we talk about the levels and meanings of relationship in our lives. In other words, the very concept of adultery alludes to what true relationships need and on which they rely.

John 8:12–20
Jesus as the Light of the World

"I am the light of the world" (8:12) is the third predicate nominative "I AM" statement in the Gospel of John after "I am the bread of life" (6:35) and "I am the living bread that came down from heaven." This same "I AM" statement will recur in the healing of the man born blind (9:5) so that how Jesus expresses that identity here should inform interpretation of its repetition in the context of chapter 9. The celebration of light in the Festival of Booths, like the water celebration, was central to what the festival commemorated. The light celebration observed God's provision of light in the wilderness wanderings by lighting massive bowls of oil filled with thousands of wicks at the four corners of the temple. The temple, lit up and on the mountain, could be seen for miles, a kind of experience of light that would not be known in the ancient world outside of this sort of event. In the midst of this remembrance, Jesus proclaims himself to be the light of the world when literally the temple appeared to be lighting up the world. Verse 12 also draws on the claims made about the Word in the Prologue, particularly 1:2–5, and "the light shines in the darkness and the darkness does not overcome it." Verses 13–20 focus on the concepts of testimony and judgment, both themes critical to this Gospel. While the Pharisees charge Jesus with testifying on his own behalf without any other witnesses involved, Jesus will assert that even the Father testifies on his behalf so that the Pharisees' charge, narratively, is not true (8:13). There have already been witnesses to Jesus who have demonstrated what testimony looks like, John the Witness and the Samaritan woman at the well. A primary mark of discipleship will be testifying on behalf of Jesus, giving witness to his presence in the world. Jesus names the law of the time, that two witnesses are necessary to give account of one being judged, but the fact is that Jesus has multiple witnesses, including the Spirit and even the Father. Verse 19 in some respects is a response to verse 16: Jesus does not judge, but he does state the truth about a situation. In this case, the Pharisees are not able to see that in Jesus is the Father.

John 8:21–30
Predictions of What is to Come

After confirmation that we are still in the temple, adding to the conflict and tension, Jesus continues the dialogue, a rather frustrating conversation about the crucifixion, resurrection, and ascension and the meaning of sin. Jesus will be going to the cross, to the tomb, to the resurrection garden, with the final destination being a return to the Father. This language here is critical because the relationship with the Father about which Jesus speaks is premised on his origins and his ascension. "You will die in your sin" means that the kind of life Jesus makes possible because of a relationship with him will not be possible for his current audience. They will die in their unbelief because the opposite of life, which Jesus has offered, is death. Verse 22 narrates a typical moment of misunderstanding for this Gospel, where the Pharisees think that Jesus is going to kill himself because of his language of where he is going. Verse 23, while not precisely the same terminology, recalls Jesus' statement to Nicodemus, unless you are born from above. Jesus is from above. To be born from above is to be made a child of God (1:13), to enter into the utterly and completely dependent relationship God has in mind. Verse 24 is one of three absolute "I AM" statements in chapter 8 alone. There have been two absolute "I AM" statements prior to chapter 8, for the Samaritan woman at the well (4:26) and Jesus walking on the water (6:20). The next "I AM" statement will be for the disciples, but not until the foot washing (13:19). That three "I AM" statements are concentrated in chapter 8 alone of the Gospel should invite curiosity at best and ultimately should help make sense of the polemic between Jesus and the Jewish authorities, which will reach the peak of its intensity in this chapter.

Verse 24 is one of only two places where "sin" is plural in the Gospel of John, the other use being 9:34 for the man born blind, "'You were born entirely in sins, and are you trying to teach us?' And they drove him out." As has already been discussed, sin in the Gospel of John is representative of not believing in Jesus, and here Jesus makes that direct connection. That sin is plural here reiterates the repeated refusal, rejection, inability, and self-condemnation of the Jewish leaders when it comes to believing who Jesus is. The question in 8:25 is an extraordinary question when it comes to preaching. "Who are you, Jesus?" How we answer that question individually, communally, denominationally, ecclesiologically, has everything to do with our christological and theological perceptions and commitments. We may not want to answer this question the way the Gospel of John answers the question.

There is marked exasperation in Jesus' comment, "why do I speak to you at all?" Jesus is talking about the Father, which his opponents are not capable of realizing. Are we? Are we able to hear in Jesus' words that everything he says about himself is a statement about God and vice versa? Are we willing to have our theology and Christology intertwined to that extent? Or are we more comfortable with separate claims about Jesus and God that categorize our beliefs in such a way that make both more understandable (8:27). Verse 28 is usually determined to be a clear reference to the crucifixion, particularly with the second-person address on the part of Jesus. At the same time, for Jesus to be lifted up in this Gospel means the crucifixion, resurrection, and ascension. With the multiple references already in these chapters to where Jesus is going, the ascension must also be assumed in the "lifting up" here. Moreover, the second absolute "I AM" statement appears here, so that a full realization of Jesus as the I AM requires the full expression of his revelation of God, incarnation, crucifixion, resurrection, and ascension. In verse 29 Jesus gives witness to the presence of the Father who is with him and who has not left him alone.

JOHN 8:31-59
CLAIMS OF ANCESTRY AND DISCIPLESHIP

Because of what Jesus has said, many believe in him, and it is to them that these next words are addressed. As discussed above, 8:31-36 is the only passage from chapters 7 and 8 in the Gospel of John that appears in the lectionary—and only if you preach in a denomination that celebrates Reformation Sunday. The commentary on these verses will insist that interpretation of this passage for preaching maintain the integrity of this portion of John 8 as it is found in these particular chapters in the Gospel of John and as it is located in the Gospel as a whole. To conflate its commitments and claims with other texts dedicated to Reformation Sunday will overlook its unique contribution to what it means for a denomination to identify itself as a reforming church. In verse 31 Jesus directs his comments to the Jewish leaders who show belief in what he has said thus far. The preacher would imagine locating the listeners in the same position: What have the designated believers heard that now Jesus articulates these particular words here for them? Bring the listeners up to speed. Put them in the place of those who have heard Jesus' words up to this point. What is it that they need to hear that is revealed in what Jesus has to say now?

Verses 31-36 function as the introduction to the closing section of chapter 8, which is primarily a focused argument on claims of ancestry with Abraham. The clause "If you continue in my word" (NRSV) is better translated, "if you abide in my word." The verb *menō* here is the same verb that is used throughout the Gospel, variously translated as "remain," "stay," or "abide." The mood is subjunctive, conditional. That is, this is a moment of crisis for these nascent believers. The sense of the subjunctive condition is, "If you abide, and it will certainly be questionable as to whether or not you will . . .". "You will be set free" appears only here in the entire Gospel of John, which makes it all the more likely that preachers will yoke it with Romans 3. To be set free in the context of the Gospel of John is not the same as Martin Luther's angst vying for a way to escape the weight of his own decrepitude. To be set free here and now, according to Jesus and according to the fourth evangelist, is to be free to see that, in Jesus, God is here, present, offering a relationship that is one of abiding, love, provision, sustenance, nurture, and protection—a relationship that is not bound by the constraints of past worship and sacrifice because it cannot be, a relationship that is not limited to what is prescribed by limited perceptions of God, because God loves the world. The only way one can preach this text as freedom from sin is to say that in Jesus, there is the possibility of intimate relationship with God, not the liberation from your sinful nature. That this has everything to do with relationship is found in Jesus' claim, "you will know the truth." To know the truth is synonymous with being in a relationship with Jesus.

The rebuttal to Jesus' invitation refers to Abraham and ancestry when Jesus is making possible being children of God for the world. The truth is Abraham's ancestors were slaves to Pharaoh. Verse 34 reiterates the concept of sin, the sin of unbelief when it comes to this Gospel and verse 35 contrasts the position of a slave with that of a child, and to be a child of God is a fundamental promise of this Gospel. The glorious end of the lectionary pericope, "So if the Son makes you free, you will be free indeed" (8:36) is not end of this chapter. A Reformation preacher might imagine extending this pericope for a change, to explore the ways in which this Gospel actually might give witness to the struggles of the Reformation itself rather than simply its outcomes. Jesus does not stop talking in 8:36, and perhaps the preacher should not either when it comes to wrestling with concepts of God which are actually at the heart of the Reformation.

In 8:37 Jesus acknowledges the Abrahamic ancestry of his audience and, in doing so, conveys again the conflict that permeates the entirety of this Gospel. One of the theological questions at stake is which Jews represented in this Gospel, those who believe in Jesus or those who think they are loyal to God, can claim the promises of God made to Abraham? Jesus is trying to get them to see God the Father as present and active but yet beyond Abraham, just as God promised to Abraham. The answer is "Abraham is our Father." This misstatement is not unlike that which will be uttered during the trial narrative, "we have no king but the emperor" (19:15). While not as tragic, it nevertheless indicates that those in the audience are not able to imagine God beyond what is or has been already known. Verse 39, "what Abraham did," in the context of the Fourth Gospel would suggest Abraham's willingness to follow. The focus on Abraham here is critical and is worth sustained attention when it comes to preaching. Why Abraham? What about the Abraham story finds new meaning for the Johannine community? It may be the promise to Abraham of multiple descendants in which the audience of this Gospel might very well see themselves as those "not of this fold" (10:16).

John 8:41 takes an ominous turn in the dialogue, a reference to who their father might be, which is clearly neither Abraham nor God. Jesus' audience now makes the contention that they have one Father, God. Yet that it is first Abraham and then God exposes a sense of misunderstanding, a lack of openness, a disturbing mood of uncertainty, even fear, that falls back on the known so as not to entertain the unknown. The contrary-to-fact condition in verse 42 exacerbates the polemical possibilities even more, "If God were your Father (and he is not), you would love me (but you do not)." Jesus continues by saying that is he from God, God sent him, and they simply cannot accept what he is saying. Before taking Jesus' side too quickly, we might do well to imagine both the content and the context of Jesus' words. It is important to recall at this point that the audience is the Jewish authorities. Just who does Jesus think he is?

John 8:44 may stand as one of the most troubling verses in the entire Bible. That the accusation that the father of the Jewish leaders is the devil is put on the lips of Jesus should send chills up and down the spine of any person coming in contact with this text. Jesus said *what? when?* And to *whom?* This verse is all many need as proof of even modest interest when it comes to the fate of the Jews. All too often, of course, Jesus' words are thought to be directed to the Jews in general, thereby justifying anti-Semitism in the minds of many. While not a means of rescuing Jesus from his position in this Gospel, it may be helpful to recall the way in which Judas's betrayal is intimated at the end of chapter 6. Judas's inability to believe in Jesus is blamed on evil, plain and simple, the work of the devil, alive and present and active. At the same time, these words come from the mouth of Jesus, the only justification necessary for many of the atrocities lodged against the Jewish people. Once again, were preachers actually to preach on this text, perhaps our listeners would be better equipped to speak about a God who did not and cannot give up on the people God chose.

In 8:45-47 Jesus talks about truth, which will surface again in his trial before Pilate, the connection again between sin and belief, and hearing the word of God. Hearing God and hearing God's word, the voice of God, will be front and center in the next chapters in the healing of the man blind from birth and the discourse in response to the healing. Hearing Jesus, listening to his voice, is a mark of discipleship. The next brief section, verses 48-51, draws on and reiterates more themes in the Gospel. To call Jesus a Samaritan recalls the Samaritan woman at the well, who represents God's love for the world. That Jesus has a demon will be a charge that will resurface at the end of the Shepherd

Discourse (10:19-21). In other words, there is an anxiety here on the part of the religious authorities to explain, understand, make sense of, what they are hearing in, about, and from Jesus. He must be a Samaritan! Or, he has a demon! A mood of desperation to gain any knowledge of who Jesus is and what Jesus means, or, to dismiss him altogether, has infiltrated the conversation.

Perhaps this is exactly what happens when we latch on to what is known and comfortable and secure instead of risking that which is unknown and unstable and insecure when it comes to God. This makes sense and an expected reaction on the part of those who seem to have God all figured out. At the same time, how and where and why we challenge such assumptions about God may very well be how and where and why this text should be the subject of a Sunday sermon. Verse 52 is the primary example of such resistance. Clearly, Jesus must have a demon or be a demon if he can make any claims that look death in the face and declare its own death. Verse 53 echoes the question of the Samaritan woman at the well, "Are you greater than our ancestor Jacob, who gave us the well, and with his sons and his flocks drank from it?" (4:12). She and the religious authorities here in chapter 8 have every reason to say to Jesus, "just who do you think you are?" Of course, the identity of Jesus is the key question for the Gospel, with which everyone who encounters Jesus in this narrative must come to terms. In 8:54, Jesus raises the concept of "glorify," which is its first occurrence in the Gospel and which will have a more dominant role after this introduction (12:28; 13:32; 16:14; 17:1, 5; 21:19). The expansion of this concept later in the Gospel should inform interpretation of 8:54. Verse 55 accuses the Jewish leaders of not knowing God, and, for the fourth evangelist, this means that they do not know a full relationship with God because of what they are unable to recognize in Jesus. Verses 56-57 narrate another Johannine misunderstanding: the Jewish leaders think that Abraham has literally witnessed Jesus' ministry, but Jesus is calling to mind the promise made to Abraham that his descendants would number the stars above and be to the ends of the earth. This particular verse foreshadows 10:16, "I have other sheep not of this fold," but the abundance of which it speaks has already been witnessed in the encounter with the woman at the well and the signs Jesus has already performed and will be witnessed again in the signs to come. John 8:58 is the third absolute "I AM" statement in chapter 8, "Very truly, I tell you, before Abraham was, I AM." The entirety of verses 31-59 has been leading up to this statement. The reliance on Abraham, on any ancestry, cannot be the defining factor for this community of what it means to be a child of God. If that ancestry is stripped away when one is expelled from the synagogue, then conceptions of community and belonging must shift. Much of this comes from the very claim of the Prologue, "But to all who received him, who believed in his name, he gave power to become children of God, who were born, not of blood or of the will of the flesh or of the will of man, but of God" (1:12-13).

CONNECTIONS TO THE LECTIONARY

The commentary above noted that the only lections from chapters 7 and 8 in the Gospel of John are 8:31-36 for Reformation Sunday and 7:37-39 for Pentecost Sunday in Year A. For the latter, however, a preacher would have to explain the reasoning for choosing a passage from chapter 7 over John's Pentecost narrated in 20:19-23. The primary challenge for the Lutheran preacher will be to preach the John text without imposing on John's witness the other quintessential Reformation texts. Perhaps there might be a way that John's Gospel could provide a lens through which to understand and experience the Reformation that does not necessitate a conglomeration of passages. Rather than preaching Reformation themes, the preacher might consider the ways in which the John passage helps us see new aspects of Reformation themes. John 7:37-39, albeit a brief text, introduces some fascinating ways by which to preach the meaning of the Spirit. The Spirit is connected to the quenching of thirst and to the gift of living water. These characteristics of the Spirit would be well worth the preacher's time in a sermon for Pentecost Sunday.

6

The Healing of the Man Born Blind and Jesus as Door and Shepherd (John 9–10)

The healing of the man born blind and what is typically designated the "Shepherd Discourse" narrates one event in the Gospel of John and follows the same structural pattern as outlined in chapters 5 and 6 of sign, dialogue, discourse. Unfortunately, contemporary versions of the Bible with their convenient chapter and verse settings have separated these two chapters that belong together. While chapter 9 ends at 9:41, Jesus does not stop talking. The Revised Common Lectionary has taken its cue from the set chapter designations, dividing the unit into three distinct parts, separating the sign from its discourse by multiple Sundays and over the course of two years. This decision is both liturgical and ecclesiastical, because Easter 4 has been assigned "Good Shepherd" Sunday—no matter that there is another primary image by which Jesus describes himself in the Shepherd Discourse, as the door or the gate for the sheep. The lectionary locates the sign itself of the healing of the man born blind on the Fourth Sunday of Lent, Year A. On Good Shepherd Sunday in Years A and B, the Fourth Sunday of Easter, 10:1-18 is separated into two parts, 10:1-10 in Year A and 10:11-18 in Year B. John 10:19-21 never appears in the lectionary, yet this is the conclusion to the passage and provides a critical summary of the events of chapters 9 and 10. For Good Shepherd Sunday in Year C, the pericope is 10:22-30. Although these concluding verses of chapter 10 use the same imagery of shepherd and sheep, this passage has nothing to do with the healing of the blind man and is set at a completely different time of the year, the Feast of Dedication, "At that time the festival of the Dedication took place in Jerusalem. It was winter" (10:22). This commentary will work out of the premise that 9:1—10:21 is all one unit of text, with careful attention given to the multiple levels of interconnectivity throughout the entirety of the passage. To interpret any part of chapter 9 without chapter 10 ignores Jesus' own understanding of the miracle he has performed. To preach chapter 10 without chapter 9 is an attempt to make sense of Jesus' words without the act that precipitated this discourse.

Before moving through sections of verses individually, it is helpful to have an overall sense of the trajectory of this particular sign and its interpretation. Like the other signs in the Gospel of John, the sign itself is narrated succinctly. The man is healed, and Jesus disappears from the story until 9:35. In the meantime, the dialogue ensues in the form of inquiry of the man's neighbors, and then questioning of the man's parents, and the man himself. When the formerly blind man is thrown out, Jesus then reappears, finding him, and there is a brief conversation between the two. The Pharisees overhear this exchange and ask Jesus about their own blindness. The verses that follow constitute Jesus' discourse, or interpretation, of the sign for the Pharisees, the blind man, and the disciples who are also witnesses of the sign (9:2-7). In the discourse, Jesus' depicts himself as both the door and the shepherd, and these images are meant to unpack key themes presented in chapter 9. In other words, the blind man and Jesus have already acted out Jesus' words in 10:1-18. As a result, to separate the sign from the discourse is to dislodge the full meanings of Jesus as both door and shepherd and to reduce the healing and witness of the blind man to just one more fantastical miracle of Jesus.

As noted above, these two chapters as one large unit of text have the same organizational configuration as the signs of Jesus in chapters 5 and 6. In the case of the healing of the man blind from birth, the structural pattern is as follows: Sign (9:1-7), Dialogue (9:8-40), Discourse (9:41—10:18), and Conclusion (10:19-21). The outline below divides the passage further, particularly the dialogue, in which various characters engage in conversation about the healing. This outline will serve as the structural basis for the commentary that follows. The rest of chapter 10 (22-42) is addressed separately later in the commentary.

9:1-7	The Sign
9:8-12	Dialogue between the Blind Man and His Neighbors
9:13-17	First Dialogue between the Blind Man and the Pharisees
9:18-22	Dialogue between the Parents of the Blind Man and the Pharisees
9:24-34	Second Dialogue between the Blind Man and the Pharisees
9:35-38	Dialogue between the Blind Man and Jesus
9:39-40	Dialogue between Jesus and the Pharisees

John 9:1-7
The Sign

In many respects, to call this large unit of text "the Healing of the Man Blind from Birth" is a misnomer, yet it is the key to its interpretation. It is incongruous in that, like the other signs in the Gospel of John, the actual miracle is exceedingly short. The first scene sets the stage for the healing, narrates the miracle, and, raises themes and issues that will need to be present in the minds of the hearers as they listen to the story unfold. Only two of the seven verses in this first scene describe the sign. The dialogue and Jesus' discourse attempt to make sense of the healing and what it points to beyond the sign itself.

The first verse immediately invites a sense of intrigue. Jesus comes across a man who has been blind since his birth, a detail on which we should pause. What difference does this make? The details of his blindness recall the length of time that the man at Beth-zatha was ill. These particulars not only emphasize the miraculousness of the healings but also provide specificity to each individual healed. That he has been blind from birth exacerbates his blindness. This is obvious, of course, yet when we come to the end of the dialogue we realize how much more he is able to "see" than the Pharisees. The detail also gives greater magnitude to the healing, which will be acknowledged in 9:32 by the Pharisees, "Never since the world began has it been heard that anyone opened the eyes of a person born blind." This will be a miracle of unprecedented proportions, yet the miracle itself is almost incidental compared to what it means for the blind man, for those who believe in Jesus, and for understanding who Jesus is. This is not to say that the healing is not without significant consequence for the man's physical state, nor is it to discount what a difference this would have made for the man's life. This is especially true when it comes to preaching this passage, a necessary sensitivity to those who pray for a healing such as this in their own lives. There will be people who cannot get past the absolute need and desire for the miracle alone, much like other characters in the Gospel. At the same time, Jesus has been clear to disclose that the signs he will perform are, by themselves, not creditable for trust and belief in him. As miraculous as they are, the signs are but the invitation to the possibilities of abundant life. In other words, the structure itself of sign–dialogue–discourse underscores the primary theme of grace upon grace. The sign itself is grace, but what it signifies is grace upon grace.

The disciples assume that anyone born with or stricken by a physical ailment is suffering from sins committed by previous generations. Their question, however, exposes their misunderstanding of what sin represents now that Jesus is in the world. Throughout the passage, the concept of sin will be subject to discussion and the dialogue portion will close with Jesus and the Pharisees debating the topic of sin. As has already been argued, sin in the Gospel of John is not a moral category but a category of relationship. To be in sin or to sin is to not be in relationship with God, not to believe that God is present in the Word made flesh. Jesus' response to the inquiry of the disciples indicates that they are misled, both in their understanding of sin and in their interpretation of the situation of the blind man. It is important to note that as the disciples are introduced in the first scene of this passage, there is never any indication that they are not present to overhear the dialogue and the discourse that follow. This means that they, as part of the audience of Jesus' discourse along with the Pharisees, will hear Jesus' interpretation of the sign. The healing, the dialogue, and Jesus' discourse, therefore, will have a central theme of discipleship. The initial interaction between Jesus and his disciples suggests that what follows will be a revelation of what discipleship looks like. In fact, the response of the blind man to his healing will embody what discipleship is.

At first, the man born blind appears to be only a pawn or a prop in a plan about which he has no knowledge. Furthermore, Jesus seems to justify the man's blindness for a good cause, the revelation of God's works. Yet this is not Jesus' first reaction to the blind man. As Jesus is walking along, he *sees* the blind man. We discover only later where or how Jesus saw him—the man was begging, likely daily, outside of the city walls. In this man blind from birth, Jesus *sees* a disciple, a witness, just as he did with the Samaritan woman at the well. Since "works" is synonymous with believing, what will be clear at the end of the story is the blind man's "work" of believing in Jesus when he worships Jesus. Jesus then invites the disciples into this work of believing, of recognizing disciples and witnesses. The theological theme of light and darkness returns and is itself incarnated in the man born blind. The person for whom this miracle is performed has always, literally, been in the dark. He will then move from this literal darkness and figurative darkness of unbelief into the light. He symbolizes wholly and completely that which this sign primarily communicates. He is not only the object of the miracle but embodies it.

Light and darkness have symbolized belief and unbelief, respectively. Nicodemus came to Jesus by night; the Samaritan woman meets Jesus at noon.

That night is coming when no one can work foreshadows the approaching end of the Book of Signs. There will only be one more public sign, the raising of Lazarus, before the hour arrives.

Verses 6-7 narrate the sign itself. Jesus makes mud with his saliva and commands the man to go to the pool of Siloam and wash. The making of mud recalls how this Gospel begins, in the recollection of creation. While not the same word, "dust" in Genesis, "mud" in John 9, the allusion to the creative act of God is unquestionably at work. The man goes to the pool, washes, and comes back able to see. A critical note: the blind man listens to Jesus' voice and follows Jesus' directions—what Jesus' mother first suggested, echoing the response of the royal official in chapter 4 and the man ill for thirty-eight years. Hearing the voice of Jesus, as well as seeing, will be important when it comes to discipleship. The blind man first hears Jesus, just as Jesus' sheep hear his voice in chapter 10.

John 9:8-12
Dialogue between the Blind Man and His Neighbors

Verse 8 begins the dialogue about the sign with characters entering and exiting with each scene change. The first portion of dialogue occurs between the blind man, his neighbors, and general people who have observed him sitting on the ground, begging, outside the city, all of these years. All of the verbs in this verse are present participles, which emphasize the blind man's daily reality. He was a beggar, every day and all day relying on the regard of others for his survival. The question of the neighbors is primarily focused on his identity because his identity will change over the course of the narrative, from a beggar, blind from birth, to a witness for and disciple of Jesus.

Questioning of the blind man's identity continues into verse 9 with the imperfect verb tenses indicating ongoing cross-examination. How the blind man answers his so-called neighbors should sound familiar. While English translations include "the man" as the predicate nominative, the Greek has no such construction. The blind man simply says, "I am," ego eimi, the same words that Jesus has uttered so far in the narrative in 4:26; 6:20; 8:24, 28, 58. The relationship between Jesus and the formerly blind man that began when he heard Jesus' voice is emphasized by their shared words. Investigation continues in verse 10, again with the use of the imperfect verb highlighting the persistence of the questioning but perhaps also exposing the on-going incredulity of the sign itself. The man's answer in verse 11 is a straightforward summary of what happened, with one exception—that he now knows the name of Jesus. That Jesus is here called "the man named Jesus" recalls the progression in recognition by the man ill for thirty-eight years. Furthermore, that Jesus is "the man" Jesus will juxtapose his humanity with the inquiry about his divinity by the Pharisees later on in the dialogue. In the last verse of this scene we discover that at some point in time during this initial dialogue Jesus has disappeared. When the man answers "I don't know" to the question of Jesus' whereabouts, knowing Jesus, a fundamental category of relationship developed in the Gospel as a whole, is introduced. What it means to know Jesus will take center stage when Jesus begins to interpret the sign in chapter 10.

John 9:13-17
First Dialogue between the Blind Man and the Pharisees

The neighbors and cohort bring the blind man to the Pharisees, indicating a shift in scenes. The miraculous nature of the man's healing is underscored by the description of him as "formerly blind," which, of course, we knew already. Verse 14 adds suspense and intrigue. Like the healing of the man at Beth-zatha (5:9), the healing of the man born blind takes place on the Sabbath, raising the stakes when it comes to the healing and the healer. The Pharisees begin their questioning of the man, who repeats the event as he did for the neighbors. "Where is he?" was the response of the neighbors. "Where does he come from?" is the question of the Pharisees, evoking the theme once again of Jesus' origin. Because Jesus has healed the man on the Sabbath, then clearly he cannot be from God. The issue of sin surfaces again, this time in reference to Jesus. Jesus must be a sinner if he has healed on the Sabbath; moreover, only God is able to heal on the Sabbath. Divided, the Pharisees ask the blind man who he thinks Jesus is. The blind man's answer indicates his growing understanding of who Jesus, "he is a prophet." Like the Samaritan woman at the well (4:19), the blind man progresses in his recognition of Jesus. For the blind man, this advance in perception of Jesus' identity takes on additional meaning because of his sight having been restored. His physical sight was returned to him, but what he will see about Jesus and in Jesus is also at stake. It is not evident whether the blind man has actually seen Jesus yet. He heard Jesus' voice and obeyed his request, but it is unclear when Jesus actually departs from the drama. The man's "sight" is progressing without Jesus being extant, a significant theme throughout this Gospel, "blessed are those who do not see and yet come to believe" (20:29). The blind man will develop in his belief in Jesus not with Jesus being present but by witnessing to Jesus' presence in his life. The actual act of testimony has everything to do with the capacity to believe.

John 9:18-22
Dialogue between the Parents of the Blind Man and the Pharisees

Twice in verse 18 the blind man is referred to as the one "who received his sight." The repetition of the healing as well as his chronic condition, "the once blind man" emphasizes his former state and the miracle itself. The Jews here are the Jewish leaders, the Pharisees. They summon the parents of the blind man to interview them about the healing of their son. The man's blindness is again underscored, "he was born blind." They know their son but have no knowledge of how he received his sight or who performed the miracle and place the onus back on him. They are afraid that they will be *aposynagōgos*, "put out of the synagogue." This is the first reference to the specific consequences of the Johannine community for believing in Jesus—separation from their entire social, religious, communal life (12:42; 16:2). That the situation of the Johannine community and for the parents of the blind man is first explicitly described here is significant for this particular story. The blind man will indeed be cast out for his confession of who Jesus is. That Jesus provides a community for those who have been expelled from their own is a major subtext of Jesus' interpretation of the healing of the blind man in chapter 10.

To say to the Jewish leaders "he is of age, ask him" is a rare glimpse into what would have been a certain actuality for families divided over Jesus' ministry. Members of families who chose to follow Jesus would be leaving their families for good. This would have been a complete break from every communal structure that constituted society in the ancient world. We find similar sorts of phrases from Jesus in the Synoptic Gospels about hating your mother and brother (cf. Luke 14:26). In our present-day familial structures, there is certainly no lack of discord, with multiple issues causing strife and animosity—religion, faith, and belief constructs being no exception. To enter into commentary, dialogue, and proclamation about the pain and loss that result from disagreements about faith, particularly differences about theological claims in the Fourth Gospel, would be a sermon worth hearing.

JOHN 9:24–34
SECOND DIALOGUE BETWEEN THE BLIND MAN
AND THE PHARISEES

The second dialogue between the Blind Man and the Pharisees is lengthier and will be the last. Summoning the man who had been blind again calls attention to the amazement surrounding this miracle. Jesus is a sinner because he has performed an act of healing on the Sabbath, an act reserved for God alone. The blind man repeats what happened to him, "I was blind and now I see. That is what I know." Perhaps repeating the same questions will yield the desired answer, but the man born blind is quick to respond, "and just how many times do you want me to retell my story?" The Jewish leaders are unable to hear the witness of the formerly blind man, let alone the voice of the Shepherd. The man's question, "Why do you want to hear it again?," is direct and devastating. Why do they want to hear it again? What will be gained by a restatement of what has already been said? The blind man's second question, "Do you also want to become one of his disciples?," is the theme at the heart of this entire passage: what it means to be a disciple, what discipleship is, and what the characteristics of a disciple are. The blind man names what is at stake in these two chapters—hearing and discipleship.

The Pharisees state the truth, that the blind man is indeed one of Jesus' disciples. He does not know it yet, but this will be exactly what Jesus will call him in the Shepherd discourse. That the Pharisees are disciples of Moses once again underscores the division in the Jewish community between those who lodge their faith in the God of Moses and those who are seeing a new revealing of God in Jesus. The reference to Moses and not Abraham or any other of the forefathers in the faith echoes the previous allusions to Moses in the narrative, particularly in chapter 6. Moreover, it calls to mind God's revelation to Moses as "I AM", thereby giving emphasis to Jesus' revelation as the "I AM" in this Gospel.

The Pharisees admit that they have no idea from where Jesus comes, which the reader knows is an essential question for this Gospel set out in 1:1. The formerly blind man calls out the lack of knowledge of the Pharisees. Verse 31 is a self-fulfilling prophecy for the blind man and names the sought for response when one recognizes Jesus for who he really is—worship. "Never since the world began" is another reference to Jesus' origins, taking us back to the very first words of this Gospel, "in the beginning," yet also highlights this miracle of abundance. The blind man intimates what he is beginning to believe, hidden in the contrary-to-fact condition that begins verse 33. "If this man were not from God (but he is), he could do nothing (but he can do everything and anything)."

It is this subversive confession and this unbelievable and blasphemous truth, that Jesus is from God, that finally causes the Pharisees to say, "that's enough," and the certain fate that frightened the man's parents now befalls the man born blind. He is thrown out (*ekballō*). One of the compelling features of this particular section of the dialogue is the way in which the blind man models our own need to sort out and sort through who we think Jesus is. Recognition of Jesus, both here and in the case of the woman at the well, is a gradual process that happens in dialogue and even confrontation. A sermon might take up this issue as something we all have had to negotiate in our lives of faith, personally, communally, ecclesially, and denominationally. When the church addresses its primary faith tenets, it is usually within interchange and various levels of conflict.

John 9:35-38
Dialogue between the Blind Man and Jesus

Jesus, having been absent since the healing, *hears* that the Pharisees have thrown out the man born blind, once again underlining the mutuality between Jesus and his disciples who hear him, and it is the hearing of the shepherd's voice that will be immediately addressed in the discourse. The verb "to find" is the same verb used when Jesus calls the first disciples, "The next day Jesus decided to go to Galilee. He found Philip and said to him, 'Follow me'" (1:43) and is a key category for new discipleship. Andrew *finds* his brother, Simon, and announces that he has *found* the Messiah (1:41). In the narrative of the calling of the disciples, the verb "to find" is used five times in only five verses. It is against this backdrop and thematic focus that we are to read and interpret the implications of Jesus finding the man born blind. As a result, the blind man is now a disciple, found by Jesus, a sheep in the fold. While this promise of Jesus' penchant to find the lost and the possibility of new community would have certainly resonated with the Johannine community, we have ourselves experienced communal rejection and have had to seek new sources of community. We are also reminded of those cast out of our own communities, perhaps by our own doing. The story of the blind man rebukes our all too often tendency to expel, over disagreement or judgment, even those closest to us.

Having been found, the blind man will now be asked the principal question of the Gospel of John, does he believe in Jesus. The title "Son of Man" at this point is significant because it is the title given to Jesus at the end of the call narrative of the disciples, "And he said to him, 'Very truly, I tell you, you will see heaven opened and the angels of God ascending and descending upon the Son of Man'" (1:51; cf. 3:13, 14; 6:27, 53, 62; 8:28; 12:23, 34; 13:31). This connection indicates the potential of the blind man for discipleship.

The blind man's response voices another central question of this Gospel, "Who is Jesus?" We know that Jesus' identity is a leading theme in the Gospel, established in the very first verse, "the Word was God." Jesus reveals himself to the blind man, holding together both senses of hearing and sight. The man born blind first heard and now sees who Jesus is, underscoring the fact that the healing of the man born blind is not just about seeing. Hearing will be the focus of the discourse that follows because the blind man first heard Jesus' voice and listened to it and obeyed it. Had he not, the healing, the dialogue, and the discourse would not have happened. Jesus will acknowledge the blind man as a sheep, a disciple, as one who does hear the voice of Jesus and follows.

The formerly blind man's reply, "Lord, I believe," is simultaneously a confession of who he knows Jesus to be and who man has now become. We have discussed before that believing in the Gospel of John is synonymous with relationship with Jesus. To state that he believes in Jesus means that the formerly blind man is in relationship with Jesus, and Jesus' subsequent discourse will describe the features of this relationship. In worshiping Jesus, there is acknowledgment of Jesus' identity as God. The formerly blind man's seemingly simple statement provides an example for how we might answer to the voice of Jesus. When we say, "Lord, I believe," we are not only making a confession of faith but making a claim of the true presence of relationship with Jesus. It is not often that we are invited to imagine belief outside of cognitive and dogmatic criteria. To acknowledge belief as a relational category may very well transform much of how we think church and faith need to be.

JOHN 9:39-40
DIALOGUE BETWEEN JESUS AND THE PHARISEES

Most commentaries will set the last thee verses of chapter 9 as a unit. Categorizing these final three verses has been a challenge for interpreters and preachers, primarily because of the constraint of the chapter demarcations. While the verses function to bring to a close the dialogue about the healing, they also transition into the discourse, as Jesus begins to comment on and interpret the healing of the blind man. It would be easy to overlook the fact that Jesus has a wide audience at this point. There has been no indication that either the man born blind or the disciples have left the scene with only the Pharisees present. Rather, all three, the disciples, the Pharisees, and the blind man will hear Jesus' words that follow in chapter 10. Preaching this passage invites listening to the discourse of Jesus from all three perspectives. What would each individual audience hear? What might they overhear in words perhaps not directly intended for them? By setting up three audiences for this discourse, the fourth evangelist summons the readers and hearers past and present to envisage in which audience they might locate themselves.

That three different audiences—four including the original audience of the Fourth Gospel and even five including present and potential believers—are intended to hear what Jesus has to say is an essential detail for interpreting Jesus' words in 9:39, "I came into this world for judgment." In chapter 3, Jesus announced that the purpose of his ministry was not for judgment, "Indeed, God did not send the Son into the world to condemn the world, but in order that the world might be saved through him," so that Jesus appears to be contradicting himself at this point in the narrative. Judgment in the Fourth Gospel, as discussed before, is not outward condemnation but self-condemnation. Those who do not believe in Jesus bring judgment upon themselves, but it is not from Jesus or God. Judgment does not come from the outside; it has everything to do with one's response to Jesus as the Word made flesh. It is a moment of crisis for everyone who has an encounter with Jesus and demands a response. As a result, all five parties are being judged, or will judge themselves, at this moment in time. While the man born blind has rejoined with his personal profession, the Pharisees and the disciples are have yet to respond to Jesus' query, "Do you believe in the Son of Man?". Not even the disciples have offered a confession like that of the man born blind.

The enigmatic phrase of Jesus in verse 39, "so that those who do not see may see, and those who do see may become blind," will remain so without consideration of these multiple audiences. Sight has now moved beyond the physical sense to the deeper level of recognition of who Jesus is. We are forced to wonder, Who are those who see or do not see? What does it mean to see or not see? What do you see or not see? What does it mean to be blind? The same pattern of misunderstanding and literal interpretation that has occurred up to this point in the Gospel now appears again, this time from the Pharisees. They react to Jesus' statement with a literal understanding of blindness, "Surely we are not blind, are we?" The Greek construction of their question anticipates a negative answer, "of course we aren't!" The dialogue properly ends with their question because beginning in 9:41 Jesus responds to their question and moves directly into the discourse. The final question of the Pharisees mirrors that of

Nicodemus, "how can these things be?" and Jesus will answer their question with his discourse that follows.

CONNECTIONS TO THE LECTIONARY

Connections to the Lectionary may seem premature, given that we have yet to arrive at the end of the chapter determined by our modern Bibles. At the same time, our Bibles today with their chapters, versification, punctuation, and titles have indeed determined lectionary decisions. There is no better example of this than the story of the man blind from birth and his healing. While indeed chapter 9 concludes with 9:41, the full meaning of the healing has yet to be revealed. John 9:1-41 occurs in Year A, Lent 4 and is the third of four readings from John. Lent in Year A begins with Jesus' temptation according to Matthew, but the next four Sundays are dedicated to John and include Nicodemus (3:1-17), the Samaritan woman at the well (4:5-42), the healing of the blind man (9:1-41), and the raising of Lazarus (11:1-45). As discussed in the commentary above, the story of the healing of the man blind from birth does not conclude until 10:21, yet the rest of his story is spread out to Easter 4, Year A (10:1-10) and Easter 4, Year B (10:11-18). It is imperative that the preacher have 9:1—10:21 in full view when preaching any part of this passage. Is this a monumental request? Perhaps, but the formerly blind man deserves in our preaching the recognition that he then receives from Jesus, that he is a disciple who has heard the voice of Jesus, listened, obeyed, witnessed to his experience of Jesus; was thrown out of his synagogue for it; was found by Jesus; and was brought into Jesus' fold. To deny any of this is to return him to his plight as a blind beggar.

JOHN 9:40—10:21
THE DISCOURSE ON THE HEALING
OF THE MAN BLIND FROM BIRTH

JOHN 10:1-5
THE IMAGE OF THE SHEPHERD, THE SHEEP,
AND THE SHEEP PEN

The discourse begins with Jesus' answer to correct the misguided assumptions of the Pharisees. "If you were blind, you would not have sin" is a contrary-to-fact condition in Greek. The meaning of this semantic construction would be the following: "if you were blind (but you are not, literally), you would not have sin (but you do)." Jesus states the truth that the Pharisees are not literally blind, but they are when it comes to recognizing who Jesus is. Jesus confirms this reality with the next statement, "But now that you say, 'We see,' your sin remains." The Pharisees are not able to see, to recognize Jesus' origin and identity, which is absolutely key to a relationship with Jesus, revealed in the Prologue.

It is this relationship that defines what sin is in the Fourth Gospel. To "remain in sin" is not to be in a relationship with Jesus. Said another way, sin is the absence of relationship with God. This is the only time in the Gospel of John that the term *menō*, typically translated as "remain," is connected with a negative reality. Every other instance of *menō* describes an encounter with or proximity to Jesus. As *menō* is the principal term used to depict what it means to be in a relationship with Jesus, its function here exacerbates the state of the Pharisees.

One of the challenges of preaching chapter 9 in the Gospel of John is the tendency to digress into general claims about spiritual sight or blindness. The "literal verses spiritual" discussion that dominates much of contemporary understanding and categories for biblical interpretation is neither helpful nor theologically sound when it comes to the Gospel of John. Jesus is not inviting a dichotomous entry into experiencing the incarnation. To do so would be to counteract the incarnation itself. That is, Jesus as the Word made flesh is quite literally human but also quite literally not. To designate recognition of Jesus as "spiritual" sight disregards John's presentation of the Holy Spirit. The function of the Holy Spirit in the Gospel of John is not simply to provide help when it comes to recognizing the revelation of God in Jesus. Believers will be given the Holy Spirit, breathed into them (20:22). The full extent of the meaning and promise of the in-breathing of the Holy Spirit is dismissed by the term "spiritual."

The primary purpose of the two levels of understanding, or misunderstanding, is to bring the listener/reader closer to the abiding presence of Jesus. This has everything to do with John's principal theological claim, that in Jesus both the human and the divine are held together, constantly. To see only the literal when it comes to Jesus sees only his humanity. To see beyond the literal is to see Jesus' divinity. Such a powerful theological statement cannot be delimited by the word "spiritual." There is too much at stake theologically to reduce an encounter with Jesus to these two simplistic lines of reasoning.

10:1 is the typically the marker for determining the beginning of the "Shepherd Discourse" as this section of the Gospel is usually known. As discussed above, 10:1-18 is spread out over two liturgical years in the Revised Common Lectionary which is determined by the liturgical decision of making the Fourth Sunday of Easter Good Shepherd Sunday. The assigned pericopes, therefore, are 10:1-10 in Year A and 10:11-18 in Year B. In most commentaries the Shepherd discourse is configured with 10:1-6 as a parable about shepherd and sheep and 10:7-18 the explanation to the parable, much like the parable of the sower in Mark 4:1-20.

The bifurcation of the Shepherd discourse into parable and explanation is problematic for preaching on three levels. First, it invites simplistic equivalents to the characters in the parable. The commentary that follows will note the assignments typically given to the various personalities and provide a critique of their limitations when it comes to possible interpretations of this discourse. Second, it tends to ignore that these verses are a commentary on what has happened in chapter 9, the discourse on the healing of the blind man, giving undue attention to a so-called parable. Third, it is not at all certain that 10:1-5 is a parable. If it were, it would be the only time Jesus tells a parable in the Gospel of John. Unlike the Synoptic Gospels, the Fourth Gospel is devoid of parables. Jesus' main mode of speech is imagery and metaphor and discourse but not parable. To assume that 10:1-5 is a parable goes against the rest of the Gospel's presentation of Jesus' words.

One final issue needs to be considered before moving into the chapter itself. Most commentaries on this passage will interpret the meaning of the shepherd imagery primarily through the lens of pastoral practices of ancient Palestine. This is certainly not incorrect, but the strong draw toward determining the background of the imagery, thereby going outside of the Gospel itself to determine the meaning of the imagery, has succeeded in overlooking how the Gospel as a whole might help in the interpretation of the imagery. With that being said, the discussion that follows will assume that the imagery relies heavily on chapter 18 for its interpretation and that the converse is true. These chapters are meant to be in a mutually interpretive relationship.

John 10:1 most certainly marks a shift, as Jesus moves into his interpretation of the healing of the man blind from birth and begins to introduce the imagery that will be further developed in the discourse. This seemingly abrupt change in imagery was certainly the reason for interrupting Jesus to start a new chapter. Verses 1–5 offer a cast of characters that will receive attention as the discourse unfolds: shepherd, sheep, thieves, bandits, gatekeeper, strangers, and, yes, even the gate. Intriguing pictures such as stealthy entrance into the sheepfold, knowing the voice of the shepherd, being someone's own, and having your name called are presented. Verse 6 is a brief interruption in the flow to note the lack of understanding of the audience, which includes, by the way, the Pharisees, the disciples, and even the blind man. Misunderstanding is a frequent reaction to Jesus, to which Jesus typically responds with an invitation to a deeper level of engagement. Any element on which the preacher chooses to focus must be filtered through the experience of the blind man and the consideration of what Jesus has yet to say in the rest of the discourse.

We can look at 10:1–5 as introducing some of the primary imagery and themes that will be carried forward into the rest of the discourse. As noted above, the sudden switch in imagery at 10:1 is perhaps the single most compelling reason why chapters 9 and 10 have been separated from each other when it comes to their relative interpretation. The question that fuels the disconnect is, how do shepherd and sheep possibly have anything to do with the healing of the blind man? Perhaps we should ask, however, what does it mean that Jesus chooses *this* portrait of himself when it comes to interpreting the healing of the man born blind for us? The opening words of 10:1 follow the same pattern as Jesus' other discourses in the Gospel (cf. 5:19; 6:52). "Very truly I tell you" indicates a transference to a new form of speech. While this passage is best known as the Shepherd discourse, the first image introduced and on which Jesus will build in 10:7, is that of a gate. The term "gate" can also be translated "door." It is frequently translated as "gate" here because that makes more sense in the context of building a picture of shepherding and sheep. It is the same word, however, that is used in chapter 20 when the disciples are behind closed doors into which Jesus, as the door, enters. No one can enter the sheepfold unless it is through the door, and specifically named here are the thief and the bandit. This exclusionary clause is frequently connected to a seemingly equally prohibitive claim in 14:6, "I am the way, and the truth, and the life. No one comes to the Father except through me," when the circumstances for each are entirely different. To view "anyone who does not enter the sheepfold by the gate but climbs in by another way is a thief and a bandit" primarily through the lens of 14:6 perpetuates an unfortunate understanding and use of this Gospel as that which insists that the only way for salvation is through Jesus Christ. Neither verse is making that kind of statement, and to argue for such an interpretation sets aside the situation of the original audience for which this Gospel was written.

Looking forward, Jesus will reveal himself to be the door as a life-giving image and not one of condemnation or exclusion. In chapter 18, Jesus will be the gate of the sheepfold, standing between the disciples who are safely in the garden and the soldiers outside of the garden who have come to arrest Jesus. The introduction of the thief and the bandit raises the question of their identity. The hasty answer, when this passage is not integrated into its immediate literary surroundings, is to label the Pharisees as the thieves and bandits. But have the Jewish leaders tried to get into the sheepfold?

The only other time that either the word *thief* or the word *bandit* is used in the Gospel of John is in 12:4 and 18:40, respectively. In 18:40, Barabbas is called a "bandit," where the Jewish leaders are given a choice of whom to release, Jesus or Barabbas, the Good Shepherd or the bandit. In 12:4, Judas is called a "thief," and it will be Judas who returns in chapter 18, standing outside the garden with the Roman soldiers and police from the chief priests and the Pharisees. As a result, an easy assignment of identity will not suffice for interpreting the thief and the bandit. Even a disciple can be a thief, and we should ask how the disciples listening to Jesus at this point might have responded. The disciples already know that one of them will betray Jesus, "'But among you there are some who do not believe.' For Jesus knew from the first who were the ones that did not believe, and who was the one that would betray him" (6:64). They may very well be asking themselves, "Could I be the thief?" This interpretation is not just for the Jewish leaders. It is for the disciples to hear because it is their moment of crisis as well. The contrast between Nicodemus and the Samaritan woman established that discipleship is open to all but that even those we assume will be believers will reject God's revelation in Jesus.

A careful reading of 10:2 yields the simultaneity of Jesus as both gate and shepherd. Both images will be central to Jesus' discourse, yet the image of Jesus as the door is co-opted by the more appealing and approachable presentation of Jesus as shepherd. The gatekeeper opens the gate for the shepherd. While much interpretive energy has been spent attempting to determine the identity of the gatekeeper, knowing the gatekeeper's identity is less important than the relationship between the gatekeeper and the shepherd that is implied. The gatekeeper knows the shepherd, recognizes the shepherd, and therefore lets him into the sheep pen. One of the central themes throughout the entire discourse is intimacy in relationship. The sheep hear the shepherd's voice and listen to his voice, because they know the voice of their shepherd. As noted in the discussion above, the blind man first heard Jesus and listened to his command before he saw Jesus. In these first verses of Jesus' discourse, we are to imagine that the sign of the healing of the blind man was an acting out of the pastoral picture that Jesus is now depicting. The sheep of Jesus' fold will be those who hear his voice.

More often than not, commentators interpret Jesus' knowing the names of his sheep as something typical of shepherding in the ancient world without any assumed significance outside of the pastoral background. Yet, that the shepherd knows his sheep by name foreshadows two episodes to come in the Gospel, the raising of Lazarus and Jesus' resurrection appearance to Mary. It is when Jesus calls Lazarus's name that the dead man comes out of the tomb (11:43). Mary is not able to recognize Jesus until he calls her by name (20:16). That both episodes in which Jesus calls his followers by name are connected to abundant life is no accident. Lazarus is raised from the dead and Mary sees the resurrected Jesus. In moments of life beyond death Jesus' promise of abundant life has its true meaning (10:10). In their particularity, these life-beyond-death stories reveal exactly what abundant life is according to the Gospel of John—life here and now with Jesus and life eternal in the resurrection. Lazarus is raised from the dead and we find him reclining on Jesus at a meal (12:2). This is an image of abundant life. The resurrection appearance to Mary and Jesus' specific words about his ascension promise the same for her. The shepherd leads sheep out into pasture, where there is sustenance, what they need to survive. "I came that they may have life and have it abundantly" (10:10). Once again, this is not just a shepherd feeding his sheep. It points to the reliance and dependence on Jesus to provide everything that we need for our lives to be sustained and experienced abundantly. Furthermore, to listen to Jesus' voice and obey, like the royal official, like the man ill for thirty-eight years, like the man born blind, will indeed result in abundant life.

In 10:4, the sheep are described as the shepherd's "own," further emphasizing the intimate relationship between the shepherd and the sheep. He leads them out and the sheep follow him because they know his voice, they recognize his voice. That this is a story about discipleship is made even more evident by the use of the term to follow. Jesus' next words to his first disciples after "What are you looking for?" are "Follow me" (1:43) and to follow is an essential category of discipleship in the calling of the disciples. Jesus' last request of Peter will be "Follow me" (21:19). The sheep will not follow the voice of someone they do not know, a stranger, but only the one they know, the shepherd. Once again, resolving the identity of the stranger is not a beneficial interpretive goal. The stranger is, by definition, one who is not known, the opposite of the shepherd who is known. Going forward, there will be a host of characters who pose threats to the sheep because they are not the shepherd. The narrative is less interested in who they as it is in what they stand for—those who are not the shepherd, who do not have an intimate relationship with the sheep. Before moving into the next section of the discourse, the preacher could explore how the particularities of this section alone present a number of sermon possibilities. How is it that we recognize a known voice? What does it mean to be called by your name? When have we as disciples experienced these aspects of discipleship?

John 10:6 reports that the hearers to whom Jesus is speaking do not understand the "figure of speech" that he used. The term translated "figure of speech" is *paroimia*, not *parable* (cf. 16:29). Throughout the Gospel, Jesus' words are misunderstood. His puzzling responses are meant to invite further conversation and dialogue, thereby engaging a deeper level of understanding, a deeper level of intimacy and abiding. The interpretation of *paroimia* must be located in the Gospel's larger framework of enigmatic speech and the purpose of conversation and dialogue. It will not be until the Farewell Discourse that the disciples will finally hear Jesus speak "plainly." Verse 6 functions to advance Jesus' interpretation of the sign to a deeper level of meaning. What follows is not an explanation of the "parable" Jesus has offered but a continuing development of the imagery with which Jesus began the discourse.

Jesus first addresses the image of the door with one of two "I AM" statements in chapter 10, the second overall in the entire textual unit with 9:5, "I AM the light of the world." The uniqueness and importance of the "I AM" statements in the Gospel of John have already been discussed earlier in this commentary. This "I AM" statement with the predicate nominative of "the door" or "the gate" becomes the focus of 10:7-10 as an image critical to the understanding of who Jesus is and what Jesus has to offer. The image of the door highlights the notion of inside and outside first articulated in chapter 9 with the blind man being thrown out, being found and brought into community, and now reiterated in the idea of a sheep pen.

The thieves and bandits return as persons, like the stranger, whom the sheep do not know and to whom they will not listen. Each of these sets of characters—the thieves, the bandits, and the strangers—is the counterpoint to Jesus, who is known. Jesus repeats "I AM the gate" in verse 9, giving more specificity to what it means that he is the gate for the sheep. Whoever enters, presumably the sheepfold, through him will be saved, will be able to go in and out and find pasture. Although typically unheeded, it is Jesus as the gate that first offers salvation in this discourse. Preaching salvation here demands a radical contextualizing of its implications. Any amorphous claim about salvation that erases the specificity of its literary location will miss the point of who the subject of this discourse is in the first place. As commentary on the healing of the blind man, what is salvation for him? From what did he need to be saved? To ask these kinds of questions of this biblical text will prevent nondescript definitions of salvation that, if we are honest, will not save anybody. The man blind from birth is saved from isolation and marginalization. His healing saves him from everlasting darkness. Never again will he wonder where his next meal will be or who will answer his pleas as he sits begging outside the city. He will know the safety and sanctuary of community. That salvation in 10:9 is linked to the promise of pasture and protection (in and out of the sheep pen) suggests that the man born blind will know sustenance and security. For the disciples overhearing Jesus' words, what is for the blind man is for every disciple, every believer. The basic needs of life, food, water, shelter, belonging, community, and intimacy Jesus affords, the tangible grace depicted in 1:18, at the bosom of the Father.

The development of the image of Jesus as door or gate concludes in 10:10. The character of the thief returns alone, this time as the one who comes to steal and kill and destroy. In contrast, Jesus comes to provide abundant life. Singling out the thief foreshadows the role of Judas, the thief (12:4) at the arrest of Jesus. Stealing and killing and destroying are all possible outcomes of Judas's arrival at the garden and may explain Jesus' words in 18:9, which have no antecedent, "This was to fulfill the word that he had spoken, 'I did not lose a single one of those whom you gave me.'" When the thief arrives at the garden, Jesus will first be the gate, blocking entry into the garden by the thief so as to protect the sheep.

Preaching this portion of the Shepherd discourse on Good Shepherd Sunday in Year A will take this text on its own terms, as offering a sustained picture of Jesus as door or gate that is every bit as life-giving as that of Jesus as shepherd. Not until 10:11 will Jesus declare, "I AM the good shepherd" because 10:1–10 is all about Jesus as the gate. Twice, 10:7 and 10:9, Jesus reveals himself to be the gate for the sheep before saying he is the shepherd of the sheep. Perhaps for this year, we might find a way to explore the significance of this image of Jesus in relation to Good Shepherd Sunday. This may be challenging on a Sunday labeled Good Shepherd Sunday, but to ignore this portrait of Jesus dismisses the ways in which this image is further established throughout the Gospel. Too many readers and hearers of this particular passage will extract its seemingly exclusionary claims of Jesus as the sole source and way of salvation. To embed the pericope in its immediate and narrative contexts works against such absolute assumptions that are, in fact, counterintuitive to the theological premise of the Fourth Gospel, that God loves the world.

CONNECTIONS TO THE LECTIONARY

The lectionary dislodges 10:1-10 from its natural progression as Jesus' discourse on what he and the blind man have just acted out in chapter 9. As the Gospel reading for Easter 4, Year A, its primary role is to offer imagery for the liturgical decision that the Fourth Sunday of Easter is Good Shepherd Sunday. That the primary image is more the door than the shepherd in these first ten verses of chapter 10 is disregarded in favor of the so-called parable in 10:1-5. Preaching this portion of chapter 10 will relocate it as commentary on the healing of the blind man, as well as explore the idea of Jesus as the door. The preacher could choose to fly in the face of liturgical determinations and preach Jesus as the door for all its worth. Jesus is the door for the blind man. Jesus is his entrance into a new fold, an abundant pasture, and eternal life, which he has never, ever known. That these promises are addressed to a man blind from birth, who, for his entire life, has experienced the exact opposite of that which Jesus describes suggests that this is a moment of rebirth, of new creation. The blind man is born again, to experience a life that could not be more contrary to the one he has already lived.

JOHN 10:11-18
THE IMAGE OF THE GOOD SHEPHERD

The primary image shifts in these verses to Jesus as the Good Shepherd with the second "I AM" statement of this discourse: "I AM the good shepherd." A first pass might rest on what Jesus means by "good" and the implications of this particular adjective. Typically, the source material for understanding Jesus as the Good Shepherd is the shepherding texts in the Old Testament, particularly Ezekiel 34, Zechariah 11. Certainly the Fourth Gospel knew of these texts, yet the full significance of Jesus the "good" Shepherd must also be determined by those activities or behaviors connected to Jesus being good in the entirety of the Gospel of John. Glancing forward in the chapter, the question of what makes Jesus the "good" shepherd is a principal lens through which to view the text. The first claim about the Good Shepherd is that he lays down his life for the sheep. Our cross-centered theologies immediately move to the crucifixion, where Jesus laid down his life for the sin of the world. While there is nothing inherently *wrong* with this interpretative move, situating these words in the context of the whole of the Gospel of John poses two issues. Narratively speaking, Jesus will lay down his life for the sheep before his crucifixion. As noted in the discussion above, the imagery in the discourse on the healing of the man blind from birth is reimagined and embodied in the arrest scene in the Gospel of John. In the arrest of Jesus, which is in a garden (unique to John), Jesus goes out of the garden to face the soldiers and police who have come to arrest him. That is, the shepherd leaves the sheep safely in the fold while he exits to fend off thieves, bandits, strangers, wolves, anything that might try to get into the fold and harm the sheep. In the Gospel of John, Jesus initiates his own arrest. There is no kiss from Judas. The good shepherd willingly lays down his life for the sheep. That laying down his life means more than the crucifixion is addressed also in the Farewell Discourse, where Jesus tells his disciples, "no one has greater love than this, to lay down one's life for one's friends" (15:12–13). The disciples themselves will be asked to lay down their lives for each other, and that cannot be immediately assumed to be dying on a cross. Both of these narrative connections expand the meaning of 10:11 beyond the confines of pastoral life and certainly beyond the constraints of a soteriology that is absent in the Gospel of John. This is not to argue that "laying down his life" does not refer to the crucifixion. It is, rather, to suggest that it means more than that event, especially in the wider context of the Fourth Gospel. When Jesus hands over his life at his arrest, how then is he laying down his life for the sheep? How then are we to imagine laying down our lives for our friends? How do the connections between this section of the discourse and the arrest scene help expand our sensibility of both salvation and discipleship?

Verses 12–13 introduce additional characters that pose a threat to the sheep, the hired hand and wolves. While again much interpretive energy has been spent on the identification of such characters, correctly ascertaining who these characters represent is little help when it comes to preaching this passage. The hired hand is someone who does not care for the sheep, as opposed to the shepherd, who does. The hired hand is clearly not the shepherd. This is not necessarily suggesting that there were false shepherds in the midst of the disciples, or even that the Pharisees were considered false shepherds. Rather, in the situation of this community, the hired hand serves to offer a direct contrast to the relationship between the shepherd and the sheep: the shepherd owns the sheep, the sheep are his very own, and the shepherd remains with the sheep in the face of danger. The hired hand abandons the sheep, leaving them alone to ward off wolves that come to snatch and scatter them. There are numerous resonances in these particular verses with other parts of the Gospel. In the immediate narrative context, Jesus does not abandon the blind man but finds him when he has been cast out of the fold. This will be true for the disciples, "I will not leave you orphaned" (14:18). Verses 12-13 are a promise to the disciples, "I will never leave you," which is now true for the blind man who listened to Jesus' voice. In 16:32, Jesus will predict the scattering of the disciples, "The hour is coming, indeed it has come, when you will be scattered, each one to his home, and you will leave me alone. Yet I am not alone because the Father is with me." To be scattered is the opposite of being one fold, in the sheep pen, safe and protected.

Verse 14 repeats the "I AM" statement not simply for the sake of repetition but so that it brackets the activity of the one who is not the shepherd. What makes the good shepherd *good* is that he does not do what the hired hand does. This is another reason why the image of Jesus as the Good Shepherd cannot be connected to Jesus' death on the cross alone. Verse 14 also provides further description of the relationship between the shepherd and the sheep, between Jesus and his disciples: "I know my own and my own know me." In this statement are both intimacy and reciprocity, which will receive additional attention in the Farewell Discourse, but particularly in Jesus' final prayer for his disciples, that they may all be one. "As you, Father, are in me and I am in you, may they also be in us, so that the world may believe that you have sent me. The glory that you have given me I have given them, so that they may be one, as we are one, I in them and you in me, that they may become completely one, so that the world may know that you have sent me and have loved them even as you have loved me" (17:21-23). The relationship between Jesus and the disciples is modeled after that between Jesus and the Father, "just as the Father knows me and I know the Father" (10:15). Knowing in this Gospel is a category of relationship. To know the Father is to be in relationship with the Father. Once again, the Good Shepherd lays down his life for the sheep. We have already seen that laying down his life is a counter-behavior to that of the hired hand. Verse 16 gains its meaning directly as being interpretive of what the blind man and Jesus have already acted out. The man blind from birth was one of those sheep, not of this fold, who is now a member of Jesus' community of disciples because he listened to Jesus' voice. At the same time, verse 16 both recalls John 3:16 and anticipates one of the essential purposes of this Gospel, that people will come to believe in Jesus and have life in his name (20:30-31). That there will be other sheep not of this fold will also depend on the disciples, who will be sent into the world (20:21). That there will be one flock, one shepherd foreshadows the unity of which Jesus will speak, primarily in the Farewell Discourse, but it is also another way to express the intimacy of relationship being articulated here and throughout the Gospel of John between Jesus and his believers.

The Father loves Jesus because Jesus lays down his life, but now also because he will take it up again (10:17). Just as Jesus has the power to lay down his life, he also has the power to take up his life again. "To take up his life again" is an assurance simultaneously of both the resurrection and of the ascension. That both of these promises are present as accompanying the laying down of Jesus' life also points to the fact that the crucifixion is not the final act of what it means for Jesus to lay down his life, nor the ultimate expression of love in this Gospel. The Father loves the Son because he lays down his life *and* takes it up again. The crucifixion, resurrection, and ascension are all at work when it comes to understanding what salvation means. Moreover, that Jesus laid down his life may also refer to the act of the incarnation. His life in incarnate form was fully present, dwelling on earth for three years, according to John, and to that extent God laid down God's very life by becoming flesh and dwelling among us (1:14), descending to earth (1:51). That Jesus is able to lay down his life and take it up again comes from his power, a power, as we know, whose source is from God because Jesus is from God. God has the power to come out of the garden, say "I AM," and have the six hundred or so soldiers and police fall to the ground (18:3, 6). God has the power to raise from the dead. It is God's power that makes ascension possible.

CONNECTIONS TO THE LECTIONARY

It should be clear by now that this section of chapter 10 belongs with verses 1-10 and that none of it makes sense without Jesus' healing of the man blind from birth. As the Gospel reading for Easter 4, Year B, the blind man is asked to hear the rest of his story a year later. Preaching these verses of chapter 10 must reposition them in their literary context not only for the sake of sound biblical preaching but also for sake of a man who has already suffered a lifetime of disregard. This portion of the discourse is the year to preach Jesus as the Good Shepherd, but to be committed to giving breadth and depth to this depiction of Jesus beyond the confines of the so-called "Shepherd Discourse."

JOHN 10:19-21
CONCLUSION TO THE SIGN, DIALOGUE, AND DISCOURSE
OF THE HEALING OF THE BLIND MAN

As noted above, 10:19-21 are not included in the lectionary, but they are critical verses for the overall unit of 9:1—10:21, closing out the passage and making important connections back to that which was the impetus for Jesus' words about the door, the shepherd, and the sheep in the first place. They are a reminder of how important it is to interpret this section, known as the Shepherd Discourse, consistently with the blind man in mind. The Jewish leaders are divided in their response to Jesus. Jesus is once again accused of having a demon (cf. 7:20; 8:48, 49, 52). This is not a convenient accusation but intimates the larger question of the source of Jesus' power and the origin of Jesus himself. The question posed in 10:20, "Why listen to him?," takes us back to the very beginning of this textual unit and the healing of the man blind from birth. Why listen to Jesus is that doing so leads to life and life abundantly. The blind man listened to Jesus and ended up being a disciple. The blind man followed the words of Jesus and ended up a sheep of Jesus' fold, with access to God's pasture of abundant life.

JOHN 10:22-42
DEBATE WITH THE JEWISH LEADERS

As noted above, the third Good Shepherd Sunday, Year C, is 10:22-30 with 10:31-42 never appearing in the lectionary. The passage in the lectionary ends at verse 30 because it is a convenient place to break the text, but the conversation that Jesus is having with the Jewish leaders continues beyond 10:30. The discussion that follows will offer commentary on 10:22-30, but as this unit functions in its larger literary context.

John 10:22-30 is chosen for this liturgical Sunday because of the topic, shepherd and sheep. The setting and audience, however, are completely altered from that of 10:1-21, and this should have some influence on how this imagery might be interpreted differently. The setting is the Feast of Dedication, better known to contemporary audiences as Hanukkah. Jesus would still be in Jerusalem, but the time frame is two months later, with the Feast of Tabernacles celebrated in the middle of the fall and the Feast of Dedication in mid-December. This is the only New Testament reference to the Feast of Dedication. The festival commemorated the rededication of the temple by the

Maccabees after the revolt in 166 B.C.E. against Antiochus Epiphanes who had desecrated the temple. The Feast of Dedication was also known as the Festival of Lights because at the rededication and the lighting of the eternal flame in the temple symbolizing the presence of God, there was only enough oil for the flame to burn for a day. Yet the flame burned for eight days, when new, purified oil was finally available. This particular feast was not a pilgrimage festival, but Jesus would have certainly celebrated the festival. The central symbol for the festival was light, marking the provision of light and the presence of God.

The central focus of this passage is a debate between Jesus and the Jewish leaders around Jesus' identity. Verse 24 is the only place where Jesus is asked directly if he is the Christ. The Jewish leaders desire plain speech, "tell us plainly" (7:4, 13, 26; 11:14, 54; 16:25, 29; 18:20), in the context of a festival that celebrates light, and intimates exposure and clarity. "Plainly" will be contrasted with "figure of speech" by the disciples in the Farewell Discourse, "Yes, now you are speaking plainly, not in any figure of speech!" (16:29; cf., 10:6). While this might not seem important for interpreting this passage, particularly for preaching, it raises the larger issue of the human need for clarity. One of the difficulties in preaching the Gospel of John is Jesus' seemingly veiled speech, hard to understand, difficult to interpret, as if Jesus is simply repeating himself or talking endlessly around the issue. A theological view might imagine that, while lucidity might be desired, it is not necessarily the ways of God. Moreover, were Jesus to be transparent up front, that would leave little room for dialogue, for conversation, which draws one into relationship when it comes to this Gospel. Part of what this Gospel requires is to figure Jesus out on one's own terms, from one's own encounter, and to abide in the Word. What follows is an example of such conversations. Perhaps rather than construing Jesus' speech in the Gospel of John as mind games or perpetual circularity, it is Jesus' way of inviting one into shared words with him so as to experience what it means to abide in the word (8:31). Perhaps Jesus does not want to let you go.

Jesus responds to the Jewish authorities with similar exasperation, as we saw with the formerly blind man, "I have told you" (9:27). They are not able to believe because they are not Jesus' sheep. They are not sheep because they do not listen to Jesus. They do not listen to Jesus, so therefore they are not Jesus' sheep. While this may appear to be yet another example of Jesus orbiting around the issue, it is meant to reiterate that to be a disciple means to be in a relationship with Jesus. That they ask whether Jesus is the Messiah reveals that they are still far away from recognizing who Jesus is and thereby knowing what it means to be in a relationship with Jesus. The healing of the man blind from birth and the following discourse can certainly assist in interpreting Jesus' words now to the Jewish authorities in this setting. The focus here, that no one will snatch them out of Jesus' hand, that they will never perish, can also be viewed through the lens of the last sign that follows, the raising of Lazarus. Not even death will be able to separate the shepherd from his sheep. That they will never perish is made abundantly clear in chapter 11. This also looks forward to the end of chapter 10, that Jesus does not allow himself to be captured (10:39).

To what is Jesus referring in 10:29, "what the Father has given me"? In this context, and in the larger context of the narrative, "it" is life. The Father has given Jesus life; Jesus gives life to those who believe in him and it is this power that fundamentally defines what it means to "make yourself God" (10:33). When Jesus declares that he and the Father are one (10:30) the response is the desire to stone Jesus. One of the troubling issues with the lectionary boundaries determined for Good Shepherd Sunday is that, when the reaction of the Jewish leaders to Jesus' claim in 10:30 is omitted, the assurances about Jesus as the Good Shepherd are equally truncated. That is, Jesus' identity as the Good Shepherd is about provision and protection, about laying down his life and giving life. The threat to the sheep, the threat to believing in Jesus, the threat to witnessing to the power of Jesus are overlooked when the pericope ends at 10:30.

Verse 32 is a poignant and pointed question on the part of Jesus. The works, of course, to which Jesus refers are believing in Jesus and believing that he is the Word made flesh. Ironically, the Jewish leaders name this, albeit without full awareness of that to which they are testifying. They desire to stone him not for the good works, in their eyes, the signs that Jesus has performed, but for making himself God, which is exactly what the signs indicate. Their reason for wanting to stone Jesus is also the theological promise of this Gospel that is simultaneously its peril, that "the Word was God." Verses 34-36 call attention further to what is at stake—that Jesus is claiming to be God's son.

In verse 37, what the Jewish leaders are not able to see is that to do the Father's works means to believe. Jesus' presence in the world elicits the work of believing. "Even if you do not believe me, believe the works" is an interesting move on the part of Jesus. In the end, the attention is turned to God, the Father. Jesus' presence, his ministry, is not about Jesus but about making God known (1:18). Jesus is asking the Jewish leaders to see in what Jesus has done that God loves the world (3:16), that in the Word made flesh the promise of 12:32 will be fulfilled, "And I, when I am lifted up from the earth, will draw all people to myself." That "the Father is in me and I in the Father" is another expression of the purpose of Jesus' presence on earth, to make God's love known.

The chapter closes with Jesus leaving the temple, crossing the Jordan River, and returning to the place where John had been baptizing. We are reminded in this brief turn of phrase that it was not John who baptized Jesus. John is not the baptizer but the witness and in this recollection, we might cast Jesus' words in 10:31-39 as his own witness to the Father. Jesus abided there ("remained" NRSV), and many came to him, acknowledging that John's witness about Jesus was true. What was John's witness? "Behold the Lamb of God who takes away the sin of the world." In remembering John's witness—that Jesus removes separation from God, that Jesus makes possible a relationship with God—abiding there with Jesus, many believed in him. The reference to John here clarifies verses 37-38. Jesus' works are to witness to God's presence in the world, just as John did of Jesus.

CONNECTIONS TO THE LECTIONARY

The commentary above already pointed out the lectionary issues when it comes to 10:22-30 in the Gospel of John. They are primarily selected for the subject matter of shepherd and sheep so as to round out a three-year reading cycle of Jesus as shepherd for Good Shepherd Sunday, Easter 4, Year C. The challenge to the preacher is to imagine in what ways these particular verses might offer an approach to explore this image of Jesus in a new way. As a result, the preacher could move outside the bounds of the liturgical calendar and the lectionary and preach 10:22-42 as the Fourth Sunday of Easter, about how it speaks to the promise of resurrection, what resurrection looks like. This passage might offer reflection on what it means to live and know a resurrected life, to imagine a relationship with the resurrected Jesus, and to gain a sense that resurrection is not a disembodied anticipation but can be a lived here and now in the present.

7

The Raising of Lazarus, the Anointing, and the Last Public Discourse (John 11–12)

Placing the last sign and the last public discourse of Jesus in the same chapter for interpretive and homiletical consideration is in part to recognize the continuity of Lazarus as a character in the Gospel of John. While the raising of Lazarus concludes with the end of chapter 11, Lazarus appears in the very next scene, and his presence at the anointing of Jesus is critical for interpreting his own resurrection. Furthermore, Jesus' final public discourse will represent a number of themes posed in Jesus' final sign.

John 11
The Raising of Lazarus

The raising of Lazarus is a bit of a misnomer when it comes to the title of chapter 11 in the Gospel of John. Like the previous signs in the narrative, particularly the man ill for thirty-eight years and the man blind from birth, the raising of Lazarus from the dead is exceedingly brief. Jesus calls Lazarus's name, Lazarus comes out of the tomb, and in a matter of only two verses (11:43-44), we have a resurrection. Not a resuscitation but a full-blown resurrection. Moreover, the sign itself does not occur until the very end, with the preamble to the actual moment of raising Lazarus from the dead given the narrative emphasis. The space devoted to the events leading up to the miracle itself is indicative of where the interpretive focus needs to be. This is Jesus' last sign and it is in danger of being misinterpreted. Understanding the implications of this final sign in Jesus' public ministry is critical, for interpretation of the Gospel as a whole, for a full grasp of the purpose of the Word made flesh, but especially for comprehending the meaning of Jesus' own resurrection. As a result, the structural pattern employed for the other signs in the Gospel of Jesus—sign, dialogue, discourse—is reversed for this concluding sign.

For the last miracle in John's Gospel, the dialogue and the discourse occur before the performance of the sign. The reason for the alteration in this structural pattern becomes clear in the interaction between Jesus and Martha about belief in the resurrection. Martha anticipates the promise of the resurrection as a future expectation. Yet this is exactly why Jesus' correction is critical. Martha positions resurrection as eternal life in a delayed and distant future, a hope that is certainly secured in Jesus' death and resurrection but that is perpetually allusive in its mystery and ambiguity. As Martha makes sense of the resurrection based on her theological framework, Jesus must challenge her resurrection theology just in time for her to be a witness to what is about to take place.

To anticipate and locate the promises of the resurrection *only* in a future life with God is counterintuitive to the Fourth Gospel. This is why Jesus must interpret the final sign before it actually happens, lest persons even as close to him as Martha maintain only one mind-set for what resurrection can mean. This Gospel wants us to know that another way to imagine the resurrection is to make it synonymous with life here and now. Jesus' revelation that he is the resurrection *and* the life upends any and all expectations of our future lives as heaven or hell, some sort of get-out-of-jail-free card, or postponed grace. Rather, the consequences of this final sign for the Fourth Gospel are that resurrection lays claim on our lives today. This particular construal of the resurrection is often described as "realized eschatology" in the fourth evangelist's theology. The assurances of life after death are available now in the present. This theological assumption is not necessarily unique to John. The Synoptic Gospels also present a vision of realized eschatology in their portraits of Jesus, especially in the concept of the kingdom of God or the kingdom of heaven. At the same time, the specific ways in which each Gospel writer construes the particularity of God's eschatological promise attained in the present are essential to understanding their interpretation of God's activity in Jesus. While John's supposition is not categorically different, there is a palpable relentlessness in the Fourth Gospel when it comes to making sure that abundant life with God is experienced now. The elemental surmise at work for John is the incarnation. To know the ramifications of God's dwelling in the flesh requires that the fullest expression of God's love be experienced now.

In the history of Johannine scholarship, textual evidence indicates that even the Gospel's earliest interpreters assumed that "and the life" in this specific

"I AM" statement must be a duplication on Jesus' part (11:25) so that the clause is omitted in even reliable manuscripts. Surely Jesus must be repeating himself, thought the scribes, so that the term "life" is synonymous with "eternal life." When Jesus says "and the life," the entirety of abundant life because of Jesus is in view. Reading further in the story, beyond the boundaries of the chapter, we will find Lazarus reclining on Jesus and eating dinner (12:2). This post-resurrection picture of Lazarus's existence after the tomb validates the implications of "and the life." The immediacy of life here and now as promise and possibility of resurrected life is portrayed in a seemingly ordinary scene of a meal among friends. Of course, there will be nothing ordinary about this dinner for Jesus, where Mary will anoint Jesus for his impending burial. The anointing of Jesus must inform interpretation of the raising of Lazarus. Twice in the next scene (12:1–11) Lazarus is described as the one whom Jesus "raised from the dead" (12:1, 9), yet there he is, eating and drinking and hosting a meal at his house. The fact that we find the man who was formerly dead now having dinner with friends has every bit to do with what "life" here and now entails. Life with Jesus, life because of Jesus, means what is needed to sustain life is provided. The next meal Jesus will have will be his last, shared with his disciples. This sharing of a meal with Jesus is part of what discipleship looks like and what life with Jesus promises. Presumably, the disciples also attend the dinner hosted by Mary, Martha, and Lazarus since Judas is mentioned in 12:4. For the disciples, gathered around a table with Jesus the night before his arrest, they would remember not only the raising of Lazarus but where Lazarus ended up after being unbound.

JOHN 11:1-6
SETTING THE STAGE: THE ILLNESS OF LAZARUS

The opening verses that set the stage for the last sign are an unfolding of information, every detail causing a reevaluation of what has been revealed up to that point and an expectation of what is to come. The effect is to create a mood of anticipation, which is more than appropriate for this final public display of Jesus' power, identity, and love. Our preaching on the raising of Lazarus might fashion a similar suspense rather than arriving at what we know as the finish too quickly. At first, we know only that Lazarus of Bethany is ill, Bethany being the hometown of Mary and her sister Martha. Whether these sisters are the same as those described in Luke 10:38–42 is not essential for interpreting this event, but the differences in how John introduces the sisters can be a helpful lens through which to view the evolving tale. If there is an association with Luke's characters and if John's readers have that recollection or awareness, what then follows in the chapter will be full of surprises. A preacher might even play on assumptions or previous knowledge of Mary and Martha to set up the marked differences in John's account.

The next verse (11:2) provides two more important details: Lazarus (and once again we hear that he is ill) is the brother of the sisters, thereby emphasizing the intimacy of this sign, and this is the Mary who anointed Jesus. The anointing, however, will not happen until chapter 12. Why this proleptic note here, an entire chapter ahead? It has two functions. First, the purpose is again to generate a sense of anticipation. When will this anointing take place? What does it have to do with Lazarus being sick? As it turns out, the anointing will have a great deal to do with the illness of Lazarus. Second, it connects Lazarus and Jesus—what happens to Lazarus will happen to Jesus. The raising of Lazarus is replete with connections to Jesus' own death and resurrection.

Verse 3 establishes the close relationship between Jesus and Lazarus. Chapter 11 is the first time that Lazarus appears in the Gospel, but that Jesus loves him assumes a relationship over these last few years, no doubt longer. Jesus has likely been to their home numerous times, not just for Lazarus's post-resurrection dinner. For the third time in just three verses we are told that Lazarus is ill, providing emphasis to the potential gravity of his situation, but also anticipating the repetition of "who was raised from the dead" in chapter 12. The sisters summon Jesus, whom they must trust to be able help in some way. Their display of conviction is a curious detail. Why should they ask for Jesus? The story does not indicate that they have witnessed Jesus performing miraculous signs in the past. There is no reason given for them sending a message to Jesus except that they have a relationship with Jesus and thereby know of his love for Lazarus. At the same time, their trust in Jesus in this last sign mirrors the trust of Jesus' mother at his first sign. These three women see something in Jesus. In placing their confidence in Jesus they demonstrate the dependence demanded of discipleship, but more so, they demonstrate what it means to see, truly, who Jesus is.

Jesus' response to their news about Lazarus is similar to the question posed by the disciples in 9:4. It is cryptic and in fact is an untruth because Lazarus does die. A careful reading of Jesus' words, however, will observe that Jesus says Lazarus's illness will not lead to death but rather to life. The death of Lazarus will necessitate a return to Jesus' words and a need for reinterpreting what Jesus could have meant. That Lazarus's death and resurrection will result in the glorification of God and the Son of God makes another connection to Jesus' own death, where he is glorified (11:4).

Verses 5 and 6 initially make little sense. Jesus loves Mary and Martha and Lazarus, but instead of going immediately to them, he stays behind two days longer. The reason for the delay will be understood only in retrospect. One pressing and even disturbing issue when it comes to preaching this passage is the unnerving feeling that Lazarus is being used for the sake of the wider purposes of Jesus' ministry. In fact, we have asked this question of a number of characters who encounter Jesus in this Gospel. The conversations and happenstances with Jesus have an immediate impression of mere surface dialogue, as if those who come into contact with Jesus are being "played." Moreover, the christological portrait in the Fourth Gospel tends to display an ultra-divine Christ manipulating situations toward a larger theological purpose of which we are unaware. The evidence, however, that argues against such interpretation is exactly the Gospel's larger theological goals. Because of its radical commitment to the incarnation, to the Word made flesh, nothing can be what it first seems. For the human to contain the divine necessitates a constant invitation to imagination beyond our earthly constraints. At stake theologically for the Fourth Gospel is the firm belief that God is human in the life and ministry of Jesus. As a result, there is a constant pushing beyond the immediate and obvious confines of daily human expectations.

JOHN 11:7-10
GETTING CLOSER TO THE HOUR

Verses 7-10 are similar in tone and meaning to the opening verses of chapter 9. The travel to Judea indicates that we are getting closer to Jesus' final visit to Jerusalem. By the end of the chapter, not even stoning Jesus will be a satisfactory consequence of Jesus' actions. Raising Lazarus from the dead will be the impetus for wanting Jesus dead (11:53), not the cleansing of the temple. The reference to stoning this early in the chapter creates an added sense of suspense, even fear and the stakes seem to be higher than for the other signs Jesus has performed. Jesus' response to the disciples (11:9) needs to be interpreted against this backdrop. Jesus' presence as the light of the world has a limited duration and that presence is soon coming to completion. At the same time, there is a subtle promise that the shining of the light will not be limited to Jesus' ministry, recalling 1:5. Those who believe are able to see the light and do not stumble. "To stumble" calls to mind that which creates too much of an impediment for some to move forward (6:66). It functions as a synonym of other similar expressions and underscores the difficulty of Jesus' words and even Jesus' presence. Jesus also promises, however, that those who believe are not only able to see the light, but have the light in them. That they will have the light in them foreshadows the witness to which the disciples will be called.

JOHN 11:11-16
THE NECESSITY OF MISUNDERSTANDING

Confusion about Lazarus's actual situation abounds in verses 11-16. The disciples are in good company with likes of Nicodemus and the Samaritan woman at the well and interpret Jesus' words literally, that Lazarus is asleep. Our contemporary challenge when interpreting biblical texts is to remember that we have read or heard these texts multiple times. It is impossible to replicate a first-time reading of any biblical passage given the millennia of hearings and interpretations. At the same time, to recall that the disciples are hearing Jesus' words for the first time without knowing the ending of the story, as we do, might preach how this conversation is working, generating suspense and anticipation. Verse 14 is a rare moment of plain speech in this Gospel, and yet still the disciples do not comprehend the truth of Lazarus's demise. Thomas's statement is puzzling at the least (11:16). Once again, to believe is not an assent to faith in the resurrection of the dead, but knowledge that life and relationship with Jesus extend beyond the boundaries of death. Thomas can see only the reality of death and rightly so. To craft a sermon that captures a sense of Thomas's same puzzlement and assumptions would add to the misunderstanding of Martha later in the story. Listening deeply to the interactions and responses of the characters in the dialogue leading up to Lazarus's exit from the tomb would attend to the very real human feelings and confusion that surround death. We know this to be true when death is anticipated. Tending the questions, the miscommunications, the misunderstandings, the denial that precede an expected death would be imperative in a sermon on the raising of Lazarus. The narrative space given to the human feelings surrounding Lazarus's sickness and then his death intimate that these feelings are worth preaching.

JOHN 11:17-37
"I AM THE RESURRECTION AND THE LIFE"

If we thought that Jesus was too late to the scene because Lazarus is already dead, verse 17 provides absolute confirmation that there is no hope for this situation. Lazarus has been dead and buried four days. That Lazarus has been in the tomb four days secures that Lazarus is really dead. Jews believed that the soul left the body after three days so that what will happen with Lazarus is no mere resuscitation. For readers unfamiliar with the geography of ancient Palestine, we now discover just how close Jesus is to Jerusalem, only two miles away. Jerusalem is getting closer and closer, as are Jesus' arrest, trial, and death. This is another instance whereby the deaths of Lazarus and Jesus are juxtaposed in the narrative.

Mary and Martha have been consoled in the loss of their brother, one more detail that accentuates Lazarus's actual death and the very truthful human condition of grief and loss (11:19). Lazarus is referred to as "brother" three times (11:19-23), emphasizing the relationship, the intimacy, and sheer bereavement. When Martha hears that Jesus is near, she goes to him in trust and assurance that his presence prevents death (11:20). What she thinks Jesus could have done is unclear and perhaps not necessary to know when it comes to making sense of this conversation. In the end, she connects Jesus with life. As discussed earlier in this chapter, the interchange here between Jesus and Martha is the primary reason for changing the structure of sign, dialogue, discourse as used for the previous signs. Martha's response to Jesus' words, "your brother will rise again," is indicative of the general belief in a final resurrection. Jesus' correction of Martha's conviction is the theological center of this chapter. In the statement, "I am the resurrection *and* the life" (11:25), Jesus makes clear that the raising of Lazarus will not be a postponed event but will happen right here and right now. Jesus absolutely assures life with him in our future, about which he will say much more in the Farewell Discourse, but his presence as the Word made flesh, as the incarnation of God, as the divine becoming human demands the concern with and importance of life here and now. Were we to in any way set aside the full implications of what it means to be human, including the reality and even fear of death, we would overlook what God wants to reveal about God's self—God's absolute commitment to know and be us.

Martha's response to Jesus' question, "Do you believe this?," recognizes several truths about Jesus. He is certainly "Messiah" and "Son of God." Her statement, "the one coming into the world" is in the present tense, however, which highlights the importance of the presence of Jesus here and now. Mary is then summoned to meet Jesus, delaying further Jesus' arrival at the tomb of Lazarus. The people who were comforting Mary follow her to Jesus, so that now there is a crowd around Jesus to witness the sign. Mary makes the same statement as Martha, essentially, "Jesus, where were you? You should have been here." Undoubtedly we have uttered the same cry in our own moments of loss, in our own prayers to God. Remarkable about Mary's declaration is the simultaneity of anger and trust. While Mary expresses her grief at Jesus' absence, at the same time she confesses her certainty that Jesus could very well have prevented this from happening. This verse alone is worth exploring in a sermon. Jesus sees Mary crying (11:33) as well as those who had followed her. Is Jesus sad? Angry? Irritated? The first verb means literally "to groan," the second, "to be disturbed, agitated"; Jesus then joins them in their weeping. "Come and see" are the same words used by Jesus to the first disciples and by the Samaritan woman at the well to her townspeople, inviting them to come and see Jesus. Could it be that Jesus himself needs to have his own encounter with the grave that will soon entomb him? The multiple parallels between the death and raising of Lazarus and that of Jesus suggest that this is not simply a comparison of interest. To what extent, in this moment, is Jesus being asked to face his own mortality? Are his tears for Lazarus and for those who loved him also for himself? There is a sense that this moment is Jesus' "agony in the garden" which is absent in the Fourth Gospel. Preaching this passage would consider the kinds of emotions intimated in these verbs. How *would* Jesus respond? The theological commitments of this Gospel have made for a portrait of Jesus unlike that in the other three Gospels, a Jesus who is clearly God in the flesh. If we take the divinity of Jesus as seriously as the fourth evangelist does, then interpretation of Jesus' emotions at this point must honor both his humanity and his divinity. Since he is the Word made flesh, he is fully aware of his pending reality. It is virtually impossible for us to understand completely how this Gospel holds together simultaneously that Jesus is fully human and fully divine, yet this is precisely what many Christians confess in the creeds of the church. These confessions of faith are contextual responses to convictions about Jesus that circulated in the early years of Christianity. Forced to make some kind of stand for certain doctrinal tenets, the church articulates its fundamental beliefs about Jesus. For preaching, however, doctrine is rarely motivating speech. Presented with biblical texts that support these claims about Jesus, the better preaching is to preach the way in which a particular text expresses such specific claims about Jesus. In other words, do not preach the fact that the church believes Jesus is fully divine and fully human. Rather, preach *how* this is the case—What does this mean? Where do we see it? And what difference does it make? The difference it makes in this case is to engage the ways in which Jesus' awareness of his divinity had an impact on his understanding of his humanity and vice versa. Here is a moment when the divine and human collide, Jesus' knowledge of his fate and the very human corollary to that reality. In fact, those witnessing Jesus' response name exactly this truth. Some name Jesus' reaction as the emotion of losing a loved one, tears of grief and sorrow (11:36). Others name the truth of Jesus' power (11:37). If Jesus could heal a man blind from birth, a feat never accomplished in the history of the world, why could he not have kept Lazarus from dying?

JOHN 11:38-44
JESUS RAISES LAZARUS TO LIFE

After thirty-seven verses, we finally arrive at the tomb, and at this point the suspense should be flagrant. The deliberateness with which the next scene is reported slows the action, narrating the events in real time. A preacher should think about how best to allow the story to unfold so that every detail, every step, weighs heavily on the listener, increasing the almost unbearable expectation. Twice in these verses Lazarus is described as "the dead man," underscoring that he is, indeed, categorically dead. Jesus commands the stone to be removed from the tomb, to which Martha complains that the stench will be unbearable. Lazarus will "stinketh" (KJV) not simply because Lazarus is dead but because he has been dead four days. As discussed above, in Jewish belief, the soul was thought to leave the body after three days. Lazarus is really dead. This is not a resuscitation but a resurrection. How bad it will smell when the stone is rolled away also stresses how long Lazarus has been dead. We know that smell. Preach that smell—the smell of certain death from which God is able to provide life abundant. In verse 40 Jesus makes the connection between believing and the glory of God that provides the lens through which to witness the next moments. In doing so, Jesus foreshadows how his own death and resurrection need to be interpreted. Jesus' prayer to God at this moment, which all those present overhear, foreshadows his prayer in chapter 17. This intercession is powerful in its brevity, essentially summarizing the main theological claim of the Gospel. Jesus thanks the Father for hearing him, which will be the sensorial response of Lazarus to Jesus that raises him from the dead and recalls the ability of the sheep to hear the voice of their shepherd. Lazarus will hear his name being called and will come out of the tomb. Hearing is believing as are seeing, tasting, smelling, and touching. For the sake of those listening, Jesus reiterates the truth of his origin, the promise of 1:1, that he is from God. The prayer also functions to set up the correct interpretation of the sign. There is only one reason why Jesus is able to perform a sign such as this and that is because he is from God and is God.

The actual raising of Lazarus finally occurs in verse 43. Like man ill for thirty-eight years, like the man blind from birth, Lazarus hears and does what Jesus says. That Jesus calls Lazarus by name creates multiple narrative reverberations within the Gospel that should be brought to bear in the interpretation and preaching of this passage. This verse alone, this moment alone, is enough good news for one sermon. In the previous chapter, the Good Shepherd knows his sheep by name. Lazarus, then, is not only a dear friend but also a disciple, a follower, a believer, a sheep of Jesus' own fold who knows the voice of his shepherd and follows. This moment also makes a connection to Jesus' words in the Farewell Discourse, "I no longer call you servants, but call you friends." When Jesus calls his disciples friends, Lazarus provides the model and template of what friendship with Jesus looks like. The connection between one's name being called and resurrected life will be made again in Jesus' first resurrection appearance. It is only when Mary hears Jesus calling her name that she recognizes him. The final sign in John is yet another embodied narration of grace upon grace (1:16). What does grace upon grace sound like? It sounds like when you are deader than dead and you hear your name being called, by the shepherd who knows you and loves you, and you are then able to walk out of that tomb, unbound to rest at the bosom of Jesus.

"The dead man" walks out of the tomb, the description of the strips of cloth around Lazarus's hands, feet, and face are the same as will be for Jesus (20:6-7), making another connection between the resurrection of Lazarus, the resurrection of Jesus, and the promise of resurrection for all who are in a relationship with Jesus. "Unbind him, and let him go" invites multiple possibilities for preaching. From what is Lazarus unbound? From what does he need to be released? To what extant does John 8:31-32 come to mind at this point? The discernible answer of Lazarus's freedom is the tomb and death. The larger narrative and theological implications, however, suggest life and existence without God. While we regularly confess that not even death can separate us from the love of God, it is John's Gospel that makes that abundantly clear, and clear in such a way that such a confession is not simply a theoretical or even hopeful assertion. It is given meaning and truth in the embodied reality of Lazarus's own life and death and resurrected life. We would do well at this point to remember the community for whom this Gospel was written. To hear that not even death, which they have, in part, experienced by expulsion from the synagogue, can separate them from God's reach would indeed be a moment of grace upon grace.

JOHN 11:45-57
LIFE MEANS DEATH

The response to this final sign mirrors the reactions to past signs that Jesus has performed. There is belief, but it is belief in a sign, which is not enough according to this Gospel. Believing in Jesus means being in a relationship with Jesus, not just a hoped-for result after witnessing a miracle. The other retort is disbelief and Jesus' name is taken to the Pharisees. Verses 47-48 offer a rare glimpse into the political and religious realities of first-century Judaism, but more so into the portrait of Jesus as a political and religious challenger. The Jewish authorities have every right to be concerned that Jesus' acts will bring attention from Rome, attention that could, and did (as this Gospel is written after the destruction of the temple in 70 c.e.) cause Rome to suppress any uprisings against its power. As post-70 c.e. documents, the four Gospels are literature shaped by the devastation of the temple and Jerusalem and are attempts to make sense of these events in light of Jesus' ministry and God's faithfulness. Each of the Gospel writers engages these issues in a different way, and paying attention to each one's unique interpretation of the purpose of Jesus' life and death is essential for preaching. At the same time, the religious authorities give voice to the kinds of thoughts that continue to precipitate our predilection for anyone or anything that might deter loyalty or challenge authority, "If we let him go on like this, everyone will believe in him" (11:48). An entire sermon could be based on this one verse, the ways in which our human propensity for power seeks to dislodge and disavow that which would threaten the standing and perception of power.

The next scene in the narration of this last sign provides another viewpoint of the religious and political consequences of Jesus' ministry. The role of Caiaphas and his prophetic declarations necessitate interpretation through the lens of the Fourth Gospel's theological commitments, particularly the incarnation. Caiaphas states the truth—that Jesus' death could very well deter attention from the Roman authorities. At the same time, his truth is couched in the larger truth of God's action. Caiaphas does not say this on his own but functions as a prophet. Jesus' death, however, is not a sacrifice to save the nation. The nation has already been compromised at the time of the writing of the Fourth Gospel. Nor is Jesus' death a ransom or an exchange for the sake of Israel or for its, or our, salvation. The death of Jesus has a very different function in this Gospel, indicated in verse 52, "and not for the nation only, but to gather into one the dispersed children of God." The phrase "the dispersed children of God" has multiple meanings in the context of the Fourth Gospel. Historically, the promise of God to restore Israel after the exile clearly lies behind this claim. The community for which this Gospel was written has experienced its own dispersion, expelled from the synagogue, of which they were members, for following Jesus. Narratively, two previous verses also inform any understanding of this phrase. First, "children of God" recalls 1:12, "but to all who received him, who believed in his name, he gave power to become children of God." This assurance from the Prologue is restated and reimagined now here through the meaning and function of Jesus' death. Second, the role of Jesus' death here foreshadows the scattering of believers about which Jesus' will speak in the Farewell Discourse (16:32) and to which he has already referred in the Shepherd Discourse, "I have other sheep that do not belong to this fold. I must bring them also, and they will listen to my voice. So there will be one flock, one shepherd" (10:16).

The conclusion to the story of the raising of Lazarus provides three significant details that indicate the importance of where we are in the Gospel thus far. John 11:53 summarizes the ultimate function of this unique sign, that the raising of Lazarus serves as the impetus for the desire for Jesus' death. In the commentary on chapter 2, we noted that, in the Gospel of John, the temple incident has been moved from Jesus' entry into Jerusalem to the very beginning of his ministry. As a result, this event is not that which causes the need to put Jesus to death. It is raising Lazarus to life that will effect Jesus' death. The irony here is worth exploring in a sermon on this passage. The rejection of the provision of life, that it will be in Jesus' death that life abundant is possible, that in death there is life, these are the promises in which we have hope. At the same time, it is at the moment of Lazarus being raised from the dead that the irony of the Christian faith takes on flesh and blood.

We are also told in these final verses of the chapter that the Passover is near (11:55). Narratively speaking, this is the third and final Passover celebration. Twice before, Jesus has come to Jerusalem for the celebration of Passover. This will be his final visit to Jerusalem. The third detail to note is related to Passover itself, the question of whether Jesus will actually attend the festival this time, given the political and religious situations he faces. English translations of the question posed by those in the temple for purification do not quite capture the Greek grammatical construction used. The strong future denial construction would imply something like the following, "surely, he will never, not ever, come to the festival," which recalls the similar questioning of whether or not Jesus would travel to Jerusalem for the Festival of Booths in chapter 7. There appears to be little debate among those asking about Jesus. The expectation, confirmed by verse 54, is that Jesus is fully aware of the dangers that await him in Jerusalem and will not enter the city or the temple for the required festival rites and sacrifices. Jesus is completely cognizant of the perils that he faces, and this is partly what is being emphasized in this questioning. Moreover, in the very next chapter, Jesus will indeed enter Jerusalem and it will be a only a matter of time before he will be arrested, tried, and crucified. The anticipation of this certainty creates a mood of suspense. When will Jesus be arrested, especially if the temple incident is not in its proper place? When will the Jewish leaders discover his presence in the city? Who will be the one to follow the directives given in the final verse of the chapter, "Now the chief priests and the Pharisees had given orders that anyone who knew where Jesus was should let them know, so that they might arrest him" (11:57). As a result, the six chapters that follow which fashion the narrative delay of Jesus' actual arrest and the events of the passion, should be almost unbearable when it comes to any kind of resolution of the plot set in motion.

This anticipation and expectation also contribute in an important way to understanding the function of chapter 12 in the Fourth Gospel. Chapter 12 is typically assessed as a mere transition chapter between the Book of Signs and the Book of Glory, or simply summative of Jesus' public ministry. When it is viewed, however, through the lens of the narrative suspense generated at the end of chapter 11, we are invited to view Jesus' words in chapter 12, his last public discourse before the events of the hour, as interpreting the last three years and the next three days. Rather than regard this as a chapter easily passed over of more of the same, the reader must be attentive to the ways in which Jesus reflects on his ministry, recasts the reality of the incarnation, and reimagines what his arrest, trial, and death will mean for the world.

CONNECTIONS TO THE LECTIONARY

The raising of Lazarus is assigned to Lent 5 in Year A. It is the last text from John in a four-Sunday series in this lectionary year beginning with Nicodemus (3:1-17), the Samaritan Woman at the Well (4:1-42), and the Healing of the Man Blind from Birth (9:1-41). As the culminating passage to this four-part series from John and as the final Sunday in Lent before Palm/Passion Sunday, the raising of Lazarus plays an even bigger role than its own monumental testimony to the fact that Jesus does indeed promise resurrected life for every believer. A preacher could explore the juxtaposition between the raising of Lazarus and the death of Jesus, but that also looks forward to Jesus' own resurrection. The narrative positioning of the raising of Lazarus also presents a homiletic clue, that on this final Sunday before Jesus' passion it is his giving life that will cause his death. The other portion of the raising of Lazarus that appears in the lectionary is 11:32-44 for All Saints' Sunday in Year B. The liturgical positioning of this passage from John might very well present the preacher with some exegetical promise. The raising of Lazarus at the end of Lent and for the celebration of All Saints' Sunday could be a place of homiletical dialogue and discernment, how each passage is heard and might mean given these ecclesial locations. On the precipice of Easter and on that Sunday which commemorates those who have died, the lectionary invites the preacher to think about how this last sign speaks into each of these occasions in our lives of faith. The preacher might take a cue from these ecclesial decisions to hear not only *what* the raising of Lazarus says about resurrection but also *how* the story functions to provide comfort and hope in the midst of death.

JOHN 12
THE ANOINTING, THE ENTRY INTO JERUSALEM, AND THE LAST PUBLIC DISCOURSE OF JESUS

Chapter 12 narrates three major episodes in the ministry of Jesus: his anointing by Mary (12:1-11), the entry into Jerusalem (12:12-19), and his final public address before the events of the hour (12:20-50), which begins in chapter 13. While Mary's anointing is the primary focus of the first eleven verses of the chapter, there are actually two other significant proceedings being told at the same time, with in fact four characters in play. This is, therefore, no simple anointing, but an occasion surrounded by other happenings that give meaning to each other when it comes to interpreting this passage.

JOHN 12:1-11
THE ANOINTING OF JESUS

The anointing takes place at the home of Lazarus, Mary, and Martha. We are told yet again that Lazarus was the one whom Jesus raised from the dead, emphasizing the importance of the last sign but also suggesting that the last sign is essential for interpreting the anointing. It is six days before Jesus' final trip to Jerusalem to celebrate Passover. He is once again in Bethany, where the raising of Lazarus took place. We know from 11:18 that Bethany is near Jerusalem, about two miles away to the east. Not only is Passover near, but Jesus' proximity to Jerusalem is also noted.

The setting of the anointing, therefore, is extremely intimate. This is no random house of a Pharisee (Luke 7:36-50), nor is the woman who anoints him a stranger (Matthew 26:1-13; Mark 14:1-9). Mary, Martha, and Lazarus, as we know, are people to whom Jesus is exceptionally close. He loves all three (11:5). This intimacy establishes the tone for the entire chapter, and Mary's act will demonstrate what it looks like to be in an intimate relationship with Jesus, a reciprocal love, a love that is mutual and equal and a love that Jesus will ask his followers to show others in chapter 13. The intimacy between Mary and Jesus also elicits a stark contrast between Judas and Jesus, especially when Judas is one of Jesus' disciples.

Mary, Martha, and Lazarus are hosting a dinner for Jesus, and Jesus will host a meal for his disciples in the very next chapter. The location of Lazarus, at the table reclining with Jesus, recalls the place of Jesus at the bosom of the Father in 1:18 and foreshadows the introduction of the Beloved Disciple in 13:23, where the disciple whom Jesus loves reclines on the bosom of Jesus. As noted in the commentary on chapter 11, these opening verses in chapter 12 in which Lazarus is present recall the promises made in chapter 11. Before Lazarus experiences the resurrection on the last day, he experiences Jesus as the resurrection right now, because Jesus is the resurrection *and* the life. Life with Jesus is not postponed to future existence but is presence with Jesus. The first two verses of this chapter provide a picture of resurrected life, life that is both relationship with Jesus during his ministry on earth, and life that he prepares for us after his ascension. We can imagine that what ascended life looks like for us is what Lazarus experiences in these opening verses of chapter 12.

Like previous events in the Gospel of John, particularly the signs, the actual anointing is narrated with only one verse, signaling that the meaning of the anointing lies beyond the act itself. The description of Mary's actions foreshadows the foot washing only a chapter later, inviting a direct comparison between Mary's act for Jesus and Jesus' act for his disciples. As a result, the foot washing will need to be interpreted in light of Mary's devotion and expression of love. The same verb that is used for Mary's wiping of Jesus' feet (12:3) is used for Jesus' washing of the disciples feet in 13:5.

First and foremost, the anointing of Jesus should be experienced as an act of abundance. Every detail in the verse points to an expression of profuse love. A pound of ointment, costly perfume, pure nard, the fragrance filling the entire house, which exceeds any and all expectations, like the wedding at Cana. The perfume is expensive, but we do not find out just how expensive until Judas's reaction in verse 5, three hundred denarii. This is a ridiculous, absurd cost, when one day's wage was one denarii. Mary spends almost a year's salary on this display of affection and love for Jesus. The perfume is made of pure nard, very expensive, reserved to anoint only people of honor, nard originating from the *Nardostachys jatamansi* plant, indigenous to India. The distance from India to Palestine added to its value. Moreover, the nard is pure, not spliced with other ingredients to water down its potency. It is important to note that this is not just Mary's way of thanking Jesus for raising her brother from the dead. To simplify her act as one of only gratitude overlooks the connection to the foot washing in chapter 13 and discounts the larger theme of abundance throughout the Gospel as a whole. Mary's act foreshadows Jesus' act, and his recalls hers. The proximity of these two displays of abundant love demonstrates the extraordinary reciprocity that is assumed between Jesus and the believer, between the believer and Jesus, which Jesus will articulate in its fullest expression in the Farewell Discourse. That the fragrance of the perfume permeates the entire house calls to mind both the stench of death, of Lazarus and of Jesus, and the smell of abundant grace. A preacher might build on this detail, the way in which a smell can literally seep into every nook and cranny of a house, into your clothes, into your skin. Mary's extravagance does not erase the smell of death but matches it, a metaphorical depiction of how the life that God provides will be present even in the reality of death. Death cannot be erased or even overcome in its inevitability. To do so would be to disavow the truth of the incarnation. The incarnation means death and not even resurrected life can take that reality away. At the same time, the exaggerated fragrance is yet another way the Fourth Gospel seeks to create experiences of abundant grace. Grace upon grace smells like an absurd amount of the most expensive and lovely perfume, the fragrance of which when released from the bottle soaks into every possible crevice. There is no place in the space where the abundance of the perfume cannot be detected.

Verses 4-6 bring back the character of Judas, first mentioned in the Gospel in 6:64, "But among you there are some who do not believe. For Jesus knew from the first who were the ones that did not believe, and who was the one that would betray him." The first time that Judas is introduced is not by his name, but by what he will do, betray Jesus. This future active participle masculine nominative singular of *paradidōmi* will be that which designates Judas again in 6:71; 13:2, 11, 21; 18:2, 5; and here in 12:4. The commentary on chapter 6 discussed the very different understanding of what betrayal is in the Gospel of John. How the character of Judas is portrayed previously in the Gospel is essential to get at the full extent of the role of Judas here in the story of Jesus' anointing and his future position outside of the garden at Jesus' arrest. A first glance presents Judas as having feigned concern about the amount of money seemingly wasted by Mary's act. Judas is a thief, we discover. Yet this information about Judas as a thief has little, if anything, to do with money or with his reputation as a petty penny-pincher. He is a nonbeliever, whereas Mary is a believer. Mary believes in Jesus, and to believe in Jesus means to be in a relationship with Jesus. With the anointing, Mary demonstrates her love and how much her relationship with Jesus means. She acts out the essential premise of reciprocity in relationship. Judas reveals how distant he is from Jesus even though he one of Jesus' disciples.

The reference to Judas as a thief recalls the activity of the thief in the Shepherd discourse, the only other time the term "thief" is used in the Gospel of John. The thief comes to steal and kill and destroy. The thief tries to enter the sheepfold by some way other than through the gate or the shepherd. It will be this "thief" who comes to the garden at the arrest of Jesus with other bandits to try to enter the garden, to get at the sheep that the shepherd protects, that the door keeps safe. This thief, who once was in the garden, in the sheep pen, in the fold as a disciple is now standing outside of it, outside of life. As a result, both chapter 10 and chapter 18 must inform the activity of Judas here in chapter 12, especially as he is compared to Mary's act of belief. The presence of Judas in the middle of Jesus' anointing should be heartbreaking. It reminds us of the duality of discipleship in this Gospel and the contrast between abundant grace and disbelief.

Jesus' response to Judas interprets Mary's devotion (12:7-8). Jesus is the focus of the act of abundant love because the end of the incarnation is becoming more immanent. Mary's act of love must be directed to him because he will soon depart, but also because it is what Jesus will act out in the foot washing and what he will explain in the Farewell Discourse. The Farewell Discourse will be Jesus' final words to his disciples but at the same time will describe what believing in Jesus must look like in his absence. One of the most crucial aspects of the anointing in the Gospel of John is that it is an act of reciprocity and mutuality.

The closing verses of the anointing return to Lazarus, who thus brackets the entire episode. The prominent presence of Lazarus intimates that the anointing of Jesus is about more than it appears (12:9). Lazarus is here, in part, to foreshadow what will happen to Jesus. Even though the anointing is for Jesus' death, the fact that Lazarus surrounds the anointing suggests that life will surround Jesus as well. Lazarus, having been raised from the dead, has as much attention as Jesus. Because of this attention, yet another parallel is drawn between Jesus and Lazarus, that they are both the object of death threats. For the raising of Lazarus from the dead, the Jewish leaders want Jesus dead, and now they want any evidence of the miracle eliminated as well. The abundance of life is matched by an abundance of death. It is the Gospel's cosmology that makes this observation all the more potent. The fourth evangelist situates these kinds of theological claims within the larger framework of the battle between good and evil, God and Satan—that the response to the entry of God into this world will be hate, albeit in various forms and expressions. Preaching this text will mean facing head-on this reality of what it means to be human. This Gospel will not let this truth slide, nor should we. Resistance to good, the want to eradicate competition, the desire to purge that which would call our own power into question is at the heart of the human condition. Here is a moment to call out the truth of who we are when it comes God's abundance, and then preach that Jesus will wash your feet regardless.

CONNECTIONS TO THE LECTIONARY

As the reading for Holy Monday in all three lectionary years, the only time the people in the pews will hear the anointing of Jesus according to John is if they all show up on the Monday of Holy Week—were we to hold a worship service. This is clearly undesirable in that the anointing in John has its own peculiarities and possibilities when compared to the Synoptic Gospels (Matt 26:6-13; Mark 14:3-9; Luke 7:36-50). Yet it is also regrettable because it is essential to the interpretation of and preaching on the foot washing, which will also hold together the juxtaposition of true and false discipleship. With this in mind, the preacher should seek to bring Mary's act of abundance into other sermons on John, and even a sermon on John 13. Her demonstration of love that foreshadows Jesus' display of love in the foot washing is worth a sermon or at least mention when other events of abundance are witnessed.

JOHN 12:12-19
ENTRY INTO JERUSALEM

The triumphal entry into Jerusalem in the Fourth Gospel is a far less monumental event than the version told by the Synoptic Gospels. John's account appears in the lectionary only as an alternate reading for Palm/Passion Sunday in Year B. Clearly, the author of the Fourth Gospel is aware of this occasion in the life of Jesus, yet its purpose for John is entirely different than it is for Matthew, Mark, and Luke (cf. Matt. 21:1-9; Mark 11:1-10; Luke 19:28-40). For the first three Gospels, the entry into Jerusalem is the means by which Jesus gets to Jerusalem. Jesus' entire ministry has been in Galilee, and the events of the passion are all in Jerusalem. For John, Jerusalem has been present from the very beginning of this Gospel. In John, the less than triumphal entry into Jerusalem functions in two ways. First, it reiterates that even here, Jesus in control of the situation, finding his own colt on which to sit. Verse 16 parallels other instances in the Gospel of a lack of understanding of Jesus' words, but after the events of the crucifixion and resurrection Jesus' words gain more clarity.

Second, it primarily sets out significant themes that Jesus will take up in his last public discourse. Verses 18-20 call attention once again to Jesus' last sign, the raising of Lazarus. The crowd who witnessed the sign continues to testify, and there is a crowd of people who have heard of the sign who want to meet Jesus. The importance of the last of Jesus' signs continues to have an impact on the unfolding of the narrative even now, particularly as the story moves into the events of the hour. The response of the Pharisees to the reaction of the crowds points to the reason for the incarnation, that God so loves the world, "the world has gone after him." The remark of the Pharisees also sets up the third section of chapter 12, Jesus' last public discourse. The next characters introduced in the Gospel will represent the world.

CONNECTIONS TO THE LECTIONARY

John's version of Jesus' entry into Jerusalem takes a liturgical back seat to that of the Synoptic Gospels. It is the alternate reading only for Palm Sunday (12:12-16) in Year B. One reason for its peripheral status is that, in John, Jesus' entry into Jerusalem is not followed by the temple incident. Perhaps there is little that can be done to alter the course of ecclesial impulse but at the very least, the preacher can have John's report in mind when preaching on the versions documented in the other three Gospels. At the same time, the themes restated in John's account of Palm Sunday should inform and enliven other preaching of John's Gospel. That Jesus secures his own colt reinforces his identity and therefore his control of the events of the hour. The entry into Jerusalem highlights once again the importance of the raising of Lazarus (12:17). Lazarus continues to be present in the narrative, even though the event of his resurrection concluded a while back. Why is Lazarus still mentioned? It is a narrative reinforcement of Lazarus's certain

> life. In case we wonder whether or not he was really raised from the dead, he really was.

JOHN 12:20-50
JESUS' FINAL DISCOURSE FOR THE WORLD

The opening verses of this last large section of chapter 12 set the stage for how to view this final public speech of Jesus. Greeks arrive on the scene, find Philip, and make one of the most extraordinary requests of the entire Gospel, "Sir, we wish to see Jesus." Ironically, it is the Pharisees who set up this monumental moment in John's Gospel, "The Pharisees then said to one another, 'You see, you can do nothing. Look, the world has gone after him!'" (12:19) Jesus' last public discourse is, in part, a response to this request. If you wish to see Jesus, then this is what you will and must see. There is a reason 12:21 finds itself carved or engraved on pulpits around the world. It is a summative theology of preaching, but more so, the homiletical premise of the Fourth Gospel. Any sermon on the Gospel of John has this as its goal, creating the very real presence of Jesus for all to see so that God can be seen and known (1:18).

JOHN 12:23-33
THE SON OF MAN IS GLORIFIED

Jesus responds to the request of the Greeks, announcing that the hour has come. In many respects, what follows is an interpretation of the hour for the world to hear. One way to view Jesus' last public discourse is as an interpretation of the "final" sign in the Gospel, Jesus' crucifixion, resurrection, and ascension. What will also become clear is that this discourse introduces themes and images that will be picked up and developed in the Farewell Discourse. As a result, we will note toward what these images look forward in the Farewell Discourse and imagine mutual interpretive possibilities between chapter 12, Jesus' final public discourse, and chapters 13-17, Jesus' final private discourse for the disciples. Both this discourse and the Farewell Discourse are based on the fact that the hour is here. These two discourses share that perspective, shaping what Jesus will say and how he will say it.

An immediate example of how Jesus' last public words foreshadow his personal words to the disciples is the image offered in 12:24. The metaphor of bearing fruit will receive fuller treatment in the image of the vine and the branches in chapter 15. Verse 25 is further commentary on the agricultural metaphor presented in verse 24 but, viewed through the lens of the Farewell Discourse, has less to do with the function of Jesus' death than with the possibility of what the disciples will do when Jesus is gone. They will do greater works than these (14:12) because Jesus is returning to the Father. So much of these last discourses of Jesus, both public and private, is about discipleship. To serve Jesus (13:16) is to follow Jesus, and to follow Jesus is to do the works that he did, to feed and tend his sheep (13:36-37; 21:15-19), to testify on his behalf (15:27).

Verse 27 is demonstrative of how different the portrait of Jesus is in the Gospel of John. John's Jesus would never ask for this cup to pass (18:11); as the Good Shepherd (10:17-18) he willingly lays down his life in the events that are to come (18:4). Verses 28-30 should be reminiscent of both the baptism of Jesus and the event of the Transfiguration in the Synoptic Gospels (Matt. 17:1-9; Mark 9:2-10; Luke 9:28-36). The latter is omitted from the Fourth Gospel, and the former, the baptism of Jesus, does not include the words from heaven, neither for the benefit of the crowd nor for Jesus. In the Gospel of John, Jesus does not need confirmation of who he is (12:30). He is perfectly aware of his origin, his relationship with God, and his identity (1:1). The voice from heaven does not confirm Jesus' origin, his relationship to God, or his identity, but rather offers testimony to the fact that in Jesus, God's name has been glorified (12:28-30).

Verses 31-33 are the moment of judgment, because this is the last time the "world" will hear Jesus' words. To listen to Jesus is to believe in him, and this, for all intents and purposes, is the ultimate chance. The ruler of this world will be cast out, which will be acted out in the next chapter, with the departure of Judas to the dark side (13:27-30). This is another example by which one can know that what Jesus says is true in that what he says here comes to fruition only verses later. Verses 32-33 at first glance seem to foreshadow the crucifixion. At the same time, literally, "what sort of death he was about to die" suggests that the "the sort of death" includes also that death leads to his resurrection and ascension. When Jesus is lifted up from the earth to draw all people to himself, that lifting up is simultaneously all three events, crucifixion, resurrection, and ascension. The Farewell Discourse provides confirmation of this in that Jesus' parting words are not just in anticipation of his death but in anticipation of his ascension, perhaps a far more difficult truth than his inevitability in a tomb. To what extent is the ascension even harder theologically because of the resurrection? Jesus must prepare his disciples for his twofold departure, his death *and* his ascension.

JOHN 12:34-36A
THE LIGHT SHINES IN THE DARKNESS

Inasmuch as Jesus is the Messiah, he is more than the Messiah, he is the Word made flesh. This is the moment of judgment; the crowd still is only able to see that Jesus could be the Messiah and nothing more. Jesus at this point has said nothing about the "Son of Man" being lifted up, but he did in 3:14 and 8:28. Verses 35–36 revisit the theme of light and darkness. Jesus as the light of the world is here only a little while longer. Narratively, this is also true. Here and in 12:46 are the last occurrences of "light," and of Jesus as the light in the Gospel. The light will no longer shine come chapter 13. In the statement "If you walk in the darkness, you do not know where you are going," there is nothing conditional about the construction in Greek. Literally, this verse reads, "the one who walks in darkness is not able to know where he/she is going." This is a moment of judgment. While the darkness does not overcome the light (1:5), Jesus' presence as the light of the world here and now is coming to an end. There is still, in this final discourse for the world, a call to respond to the light, to believe in the revelation of God as the Word made flesh.

Where Jesus is going will be a major theme of the Farewell Discourse, especially its opening verses, "'And you know the way to the place where I am going.' Thomas said to him, 'Lord, we do not know where you are going. How can we know the way?' Jesus said to him, 'I am the way, and the truth, and the life. No one comes to the Father except through me'" (14:4–6). John 12:36a recalls 1:13, that Jesus presence in the world as the Word made flesh is to make it possible for all who believe to be children of God (1:12; 11:52). It is significant to note here that Jesus now connects being children of God and the concept of light, "While you have the light, believe in the light, so that you may become children of light." This connection communicates an important aspect of discipleship that will become more clear for the disciples in the Farewell Discourse. As the light of the world will no longer be present in the world, the disciples, as children of God, are children of light. They will now need to be the presence of the light in the world since Jesus is returning to the Father.

JOHN 12:36B-43
THE WITNESS OF THE PROPHETS

Explaining, understanding, making sense of why some were not able to believe in Jesus is the focus of these comments before Jesus' final words that close his public discourse. These are touching words, as if the fourth evangelist is trying to work this out, contemplating for himself why this disbelief is possible. A primary answer was offered, the presence of evil/the devil, but why is it that people cannot see? It is a rare glimpse into the very real struggles of the Gospel authors, who write for their audiences but also from a personal place of faith, commitment, and theological confusion. There are no fewer than four possible reasons for disbelief, almost as if the fourth evangelist is grasping for those proverbial straws. Before listing the possible answers, it is necessary to pause and ask the same question, especially here and now, and perhaps that is exactly what this narrative interlude demands. Before we go any further, we need to wrestle with the same issue. Perhaps we ask the question in a sermon. Why are some able to believe and some not? There will not be another chance for an encounter with Jesus after this point, why can't you see? Preaching this passage will invite those listening to answer these questions for themselves. What reasons would you give? Where would you have gone back? (6:66). Many in our congregations struggle with this issue on a daily basis, why some believe and some do not, especially with regard with persons closest to them. At the same time, we might also be the ones about whom the questions are asked. Why do you believe in Jesus? What difference does it make? So real for us are parents whose children have abandoned faith, siblings who do not believe, or friends to whom it seems you have to justify your faith. This text provides an opportunity to name these difficulties, the kinds of questions this issue raises, and how we might find some peace or comfort in our uncertainty about others and even about ourselves.

The fourth evangelist offers four possible answers. First, for whatever reason, the crowd (the world) is not able to believe in the signs he performed (12:37). While the crowd is the direct audience of Jesus' discourse, the question of the Greeks concludes that this is the final discourse for the *world* God loves. Of course, believing in the signs is not enough; yet should there have been some sense of who Jesus was, some realization of his power, some understanding of where he came from? Second, perhaps the world's inability to believe is a fulfillment of prophecy, "Lord, who has believed our message, and to whom has the arm of the Lord been revealed?" (12:38; cf. Isa. 6:10). History has shown that God's prophets were less than appreciated and often rejected for their message from God. Third, it could be that a specific prophecy is at work among those Jesus encountered and yet they did not believe, their hearts were hardened: "He has blinded their eyes and hardened their heart, so that they might not look with their eyes, and understand with their heart and turn—and I would heal them" (12:40; cf. Isa. 53:1). Finally, while the world may have believed, they did not confess, in part because of their fear of being put out of the synagogue, but maybe because "they loved human glory more than the glory that comes from God" (12:43). Every single one of these reasons might be entertained in a sermon on this text, not only from the perspective of "why didn't they," but also from the viewpoint of "why didn't I?"

JOHN 12:44-50
THE LAST CRY

The concluding words of Jesus' last public address should resonate as both heroic and yet heartbreaking. While there is certainly an aura of Jesus' confidence in his identity, his source of power, and his relationship with God, that Jesus "cries out" intimates some level of despair. There is an analogous sense in and thematic connections to chapter 7, where Jesus cries out with similar pleas (7:28; 37). There is also a foreboding in that a very real moment of judgment looms closer as Judas goes out into the darkness (13:30). Much in these concluding expressions in Jesus' final discourse for the world is a reworking of the Prologue. Verses 44-45 encapsulate 1:18. Jesus is sent by God to reveal God to the world. What you see in Jesus is who God is, and who God is, is what you see in Jesus. Jesus was sent, sent as the Word made flesh, to make God known. That has been the central point of the incarnation. That the incarnation is coming to an end makes this claim all the more urgent. Once again, we are reminded that the light of the world will be extinguished. This will be the last time that Jesus is described this way in the Gospel of John (12:46; cf. 12:35, 36). Narratively and within the overall plot, "the light [that] shines in the darkness" as the first articulation of the incarnation will be snuffed out. Verses 47-48 return to the theme of judgment because this is the last moment of judgment for the world. Jesus did not come to judge, but his presence in the world means judgment, that which causes a moment of crisis for those who encounter the light. Jesus' own words serve as judge. That is, it will be his words by which one will come to believe (20:30-31). Verses 49-50 introduce for the first time in the Gospel the concept of commandment. While the term will appear only twice in the Farewell Discourse (13:34; 15:12), it is critically in the context of the language of love, "I give you a new commandment, that you love one another. Just as I have loved you, you also should love one another" (13:34). The commandment about what to say and what to speak (12:49) is about love, and not just any love but the kind of love that God has shown that God has for the world; the kind of love that has been revealed in the grace upon grace embodied in Jesus' signs and Jesus' words and Jesus' life; the kind of love that means abiding at the bosom of the Father forever, "and I know that his commandment is eternal life" (12:50). Jesus' last few words may seem inconsequential. "What I speak, therefore, I speak just as the Father has told me." After all, Jesus has been saying this all along, hasn't he? Yet, if we remember and imagine that the Word became flesh and that the incarnation is coming to its end, then for Jesus to connect his words with what the Father told him brings the Word made flesh full circle. Nothing that Jesus has said, nothing he could have been as the Word made flesh would be possible without the outrageous promise of 1:1, "In the beginning was the Word, and the Word was with God, and the Word was God." Jesus is the Word, God's words, and the Word made flesh. Word and words mean everything for this Gospel and mean everything for the last words from Jesus that the world is able to hear.

CONNECTIONS TO THE LECTIONARY

The only portions of Jesus' final public discourse from John 12 that appear in the lectionary are 12:20-33 for Lent 5, Year B, and 12:20-36 for Holy Tuesday in all three lectionary years. John 12:34-50 never occurs in the lectionary. That 12:20-33 is positioned as the final Gospel reading before the events of the passion sets in motion numerous trajectories for preaching moving into Palm/Passion Sunday and Holy Week. The preacher could imagine using the request of the Greeks, "Sir, we wish to see Jesus," as the guiding perspective for the events that lie ahead. Jesus' confidence and control might come as a surprise for many and could offer an alternative view of the events of Jesus' passion. Regardless of its relative absence in the lectionary, Jesus' final discourse should inform and influence the interpretation of the whole of the Gospel. These final public words of Jesus are a culmination of the themes presented in the Prologue situated in the real event of a request of the world (the Greeks) to see. How Jesus languages these themes for the world before retreating to the intimacy of time with his disciples is worth attention. Furthermore, this final public discourse of Jesus presents a unique moment in Jesus' ministry. While Jesus is the Word become flesh for the sake of the world God loves, this very public discourse should call to mind the many private conversations Jesus has had with distinctive characters. The collocation of communal and personal encounters with Jesus solidifies, at this critical juncture, God's love of the world but also the necessity of an individual encounter with the Word made flesh, essential for relationship and intimacy.

8

———————————

The Foot Washing, the Last Meal, and the Farewell Discourse (John 13–17)

Chapters 13-17 in the Fourth Gospel are classically designated as the Farewell Discourse and for good reason. These are Jesus' final words to his disciples, only for his disciples, where he quite literally tells them good-bye. This observation alone is essential for preaching any portion of this section of the Gospel. The preacher needs to realize the tenderness of this place in the narrative and ask how each pericope communicates the pathos of this last night shared between the disciples and Jesus. It is Jesus at his most pastoral. This is Jesus as pastor, friend, mentor, teacher, lover, and speaking to every emotion that accompanies such relationships. Sermons on the Farewell Discourse will recognize the spectrum of these emotions and seek to create an experience of them, capturing the affection and compassion. It is also important to note that these five chapters occur within only one night. This is a striking contrast to chapters 2–12, which take place over the span of three years.

These chapters in the Gospel of John can be divided into three separate events. Chapter 13 recounts the foot washing as the primary act of Jesus in contrast to the meal highlighted in the Synoptic Gospels. Chapters 14–16 are the substance of Jesus' words of farewell, with the central focus being the promise of the Holy Spirit. Chapter 17 narrates what is known as the "high priestly prayer," Jesus' prayer to God for his disciples before his arrest.

CHAPTER 13

THE FOOT WASHING

The event of the foot washing is unique to the Fourth Gospel and takes center stage as Jesus' final act before his arrest. In many respects, the sign and the ensuing dialogue and discourse should function as the prologue to the Farewell

Discourse, that is, an introduction to the tone and themes that will unfold in the following chapters. We have noted in past chapters that a central structural pattern for the Fourth Gospel is that Jesus performs a sign, which is followed by a dialogue, and then a discourse by Jesus that interprets the sign. Although there are seven labeled signs of a somewhat miraculous nature in the Gospel, a "sign" that Jesus performs does not necessarily have to be a full-fledged miracle to warrant Jesus' comment and interpretation. The foot washing holds to this same pattern.

JOHN 13:1-11
THE HOUR HAS COME

Passover is near and is the reason that Jesus is in Jerusalem, but this is not a Passover meal that Jesus and his disciples will celebrate. The events of the foot washing at the meal take place on the night before the Day of Preparation for Passover. As discussed in chapter 2, Jesus is crucified on the Day of Preparation, not on Passover. The Passover meal is shared at the feeding of the five thousand. It is important to note that the foot washing is not a separate act from the meal but takes place "during supper" (13:2). The foot washing will have connections to expectations of hospitality when hosting a meal. Since the foot washing is not an isolated incident from the context of the meal being shared this should shape its liturgical function in our Maundy Thursday observances.

The hour has finally come, which was first introduced at the wedding at Cana, and it is specifically described as the time when Jesus is to depart and return to the Father. Once again, the hour in the Gospel of John includes the crucifixion, the resurrection, and the ascension. The foot washing comes from love, the love that Jesus has for his own (cf. 10:14). "He loved them to the end" foreshadows Jesus' last words on the cross, "it is finished." It is the same Greek root, *telos*, both here and in 19:30 and has a sense of something arriving at its goal, to completion, perhaps here, to the end, or to the uttermost end. That this is an act of love of this kind of completion and magnitude should give preachers pause if there is any urge to say "go and do likewise."

In the midst of this demonstration of ultimate love, foreboding enters in the form of Judas's impending betrayal. That Judas is introduced at the very beginning of the chapter (13:2) stands in contrast to Jesus' love. The presence of Judas this early on in the foot washing narrative should cause reflection on the nature and purpose of foot washings in our current liturgical contexts. Can we replicate in that ritual the element of betrayal and evil that are clearly present? We now know that something is going to happen with Judas. The question is when and where. Verse 3 is a remarkable moment of introspection, as if in a single verse one could view the past three years in one glimpse, a looking back to the moment of the incarnation and a looking forward to its end. The end of the incarnation is front and center in this act of love. Loving his disciples to the end does not mean only the crucifixion, his death. It means the entirety of his life, the whole witness of the Word made flesh.

The actual washing of feet is relatively short and is narrated in real time. That is, the details are told with a step-by-step pacing so that we are able to visualize and experience what Jesus is doing. By not summarizing the act, it is given narrative space to indicate its importance. It is an act performed by Jesus with his full knowledge of who he is and what is to come. Preaching might explore what the disciples could be thinking at Jesus' every move. As discussed in the commentary on the anointing in chapter 12, there are many connections between the anointing and the foot washing. Both take place at a dinner, both are the washing of feet, and both single out the act of wiping (*ekmassō*) the feet. As Mary's act was an anointing for Jesus' burial, Jesus' act is an anointing in full awareness of what is to come, so that each act of love is situated in the full knowledge of impending death.

As happens with the other signs in the Gospel, the sign is misinterpreted. Peter is astonished that Jesus is going to wash his feet, that a master would be washing the feet of a disciple, or a host washing the feet of a guest when it should be a servant's job. Jesus' response, "You do not know now what I am doing, but later you will understand" (13:7), foreshadows Jesus' words of love, discipleship, servanthood, and friendship that will be taken up in the Farewell Discourse (cf. 15:15). Peter cannot fathom that Jesus would wash his feet, and his statement is emphatic in a strong future denial construction in Greek, literally, "you will never wash my feet . . . into eternity!" Jesus' response makes a subtle yet important shift from washing feet to, "unless I wash *you*," indicating that there is more to this washing than standard hospitality practices for dusty feet in the ancient world. The symbolism of washing here is more complicated than we tend to imagine, particularly in our preaching and in our ritual enacting. What does being washed mean? To be washed clean? This is perhaps Peter's meaning in his response to Jesus. To be washed clean makes some interpretive sense looking ahead to the increased tension of Judas's betrayal and the prediction of Peter's denial. At the same time, we have to ask, washed from what, for what? Can one really be washed clean? Is that really what Jesus is doing here, given the very palpable presence of evil in the room? The only other time the term "wash" is used in the Gospel of John is for the healing of the man blind from birth (9:7, 11, 15). He healing happens by washing in the Pool of Siloam. The washing restores his sight, but also makes possible his ability to recognize who Jesus is. While it is true that the act of washing heals the man's blindness, the washing also enables him to see where Jesus comes from, and, in the end, he is brought into the fold of the Good Shepherd. The healing of the man born blind is also a sign that exposes those who do not believe. The foot washing in chapter 13 has similar connotations. It is a washing to be made clean if the sense is washing away that which would prevent full recognition of who Jesus is and what is about to happen. It exposes Judas. The washing makes possible having a share with Jesus, being in relationship with him, in his community, in the fold, as opposed to being cast out, like the blind man or going out, like Judas. Preaching this passage will take time to reflect on what washing in this context symbolizes. Like the other signs in the Gospel thus far, Jesus is performing a sign that has implications beyond its obviousness. Peter's reaction to Jesus' pronouncement intimates a response similar to that of Nicodemus and that of the Samaritan Woman at the well and points to why it is necessary to consider the inferences of washing. Upon hearing what Jesus will do, Peter interprets Jesus' act as literal washing. "Don't just stop with my feet, Jesus! Give me a bath!" Jesus will have to make sense of this sign so that the disciples, and we, do not reduce the meaning to an act that can be easily replicated. In verse 10 Jesus acknowledges Peter's exuberance and realizes his misunderstanding. Jesus uses the language of being clean because this is how Peter is making sense of Jesus' act, and justifiably so. To be made clean or to be clean in this situation, however, must be understood in the context of what Jesus says about Judas (13:10-11). Judas is not clean because he does not believe.

JOHN 13:12-20
AN EXAMPLE OF LOVE

Jesus now interprets the foot washing for the disciples. His question, "Do you know what I have done to you?," is one that might be asked in a sermon on this passage. Do we have any idea what Jesus has done—not just here but in his entire ministry as the Word made flesh? Verses 13-15 address the prevailing misunderstanding even by the disciples. How is it that someone like Jesus, their teacher and Lord, could wash their feet? And so Jesus starts there, where the disciples are in their understanding, or lack thereof. Jesus is upending the social customs, bending down, literally, to our level, yet a careful reading of Jesus' words reveals that there is more going on than shared equality. "Example" can also be translated "model" or "pattern" (13:15). To what extent might Jesus be referencing the entirety of his ministry here? That is, Jesus as the Word made flesh, has established a pattern of being, God fully present, witnessing to God's presence in the world, that the disciples will now need to take on. The foot washing is somewhat of a microcosm of God becoming flesh, God dwelling with us, now no greater than we are. Reading forward in the Farewell Discourse, Jesus will insist that the disciples will do greater works than these (14:12). This is possible because "servants are not greater than their master, nor are messengers greater than the one who sent them" (13:16). The disciples need to begin to realize that Jesus is returning to the Father. As such, the ongoing revelation of God in the world, making God known (1:18), will now be up to them.

Furthermore, Jesus even washed the feet of the one who would betray him, Judas. Jesus will also share bread with Judas. For the disciples, and for the community to whom this Gospel was written—the people who are the closest to them, whose feet they may wash, with whom they may have shared countless meals, may not believe and leave the fold. We are asked to wash the feet of our betrayers. Our church communities today experience similar feelings when members leave, or even when we leave. Preaching on this portion of the foot washing would tend the emotions felt in these moments of separation and perhaps abandonment and consider the ways in which Jesus' actions and words in the foot washing and in the Farewell Discourse provide a theological response to our questioning.

Verse 19 is the only absolute "I AM" in the Farewell Discourse, and its placement is not only significant for interpretation of the foot washing but also helps to assist in clarifying the verses that surround the "I AM" statement. To what does the "it" refer in verse 19? An initial answer might assume the betrayal of Judas, especially after verse 18. Why do the disciples need to believe in Jesus' identity at the moment of Judas's betrayal? They need to know just what power is at work, especially with Jesus' departure becoming more and more certain. Moreover, it is essential that the disciples believe all that Jesus as the "I AM" signifies because it is to this that they will give witness in the world. The "it" in verse 19 is also the events of the hour, Jesus' crucifixion, resurrection, and ascension. Given that the hour has arrived, more so than ever the disciples necessitate this last revelation of Jesus' identity as the "I AM" in the world. The disciples need to be assured that the betrayal of one does not mean the betrayal of others, or even of Jesus himself.

JOHN 13:21-30
THE DEPARTURE OF JUDAS TO THE DARK SIDE

These nine verses narrate the penultimate appearance of Judas until his return outside the garden at the arrest of Jesus. Jesus' soul is "troubled," which can also be translated as "stirred up, disturbed, or thrown into confusion." The same verb occurs in 14:1, "Do not let your hearts be troubled. Believe in God, believe also in me" (14:1; cf. 12:27; 14:27). This is a disturbing time, a troubling time, made even more so now by the prospect of one of Jesus' own, who has been with them for three years, one of the Twelve, betraying Jesus. The disciples look around at one another, wondering who it could be. Who could it be, indeed? Verse 22 merits attention in our preaching on this passage, especially in the context of the verse that follows that mentions, for the first time, the disciple whom Jesus loved. Verse 22 confirms that, when the disciples look around at each other, they are also looking at themselves, as should we. Why Judas? Why not Judas? Why not me? It is essential to situate this moment in the Gospel within the commentary on Judas in chapter 6 and in chapter 18. Betrayal in the Gospel of John is not believing in Jesus. It is not an act of greed or handing Jesus over directly to the authorities. It is the very real and frightening truth that not everyone will believe who Jesus is, and the reason for that disbelieving appears to be nothing short of the presence of evil itself. There is no easy answer to "why not me?" It could be any one of us and perhaps it has been, several times, when we consider the history of our lives of faith.

Verse 23 is the first appearance in the Gospel of the disciple whom Jesus loves. He is described as reclining on the bosom of Jesus, the very intimate location of Jesus in 1:18, and reclining just like Lazarus in 12:2, and again in 13:25, emphasizing how close he is to Jesus. Much interpretive energy in the history of Johannine scholarship has attempted to determine the identity of the Beloved Disciple. Typically he is pinpointed as the author of the Gospel—presumably, John the son of Zebedee—but as noted in Introduction, there is no proof for this conclusion. Moreover, if he is the author, where has he been for the last twelve chapters? What is more persuasive especially with the Gospel's purpose in mind (20:30-31) is that the Beloved Disciple is the one who hears and reads this story; it is every disciple, it is you, it is I. He is introduced here in a marked contrast to Judas, who does not believe. The Beloved Disciple is one who believes, meaning that he is in relationship with Jesus, which is intimated by his closeness to Jesus, the very place Jesus is with the Father. This is what believing looks like, reclining on the bosom of Jesus. Perhaps Judas cannot bear such closeness, such intimacy. True intimacy necessitates vulnerability, and for some sitting in our pews this is a terrifying proposal. Exposure of this kind is too much for many This means that Jesus is awfully close and it may be that our operating christologies would resist a Jesus in such cozy proximity. We may be more comfortable with a Jesus we can keep at a little bit of a distance, at arm's length. Who knows what Jesus might see? What do we not want Jesus to see? While the intimate relationship with Jesus presented in the Fourth Gospel may be good news for most, there will certainly be those who would rather have Jesus a little farther away. Preaching this passage should name our human fears of and discomfort with intimacy and vulnerability.

The suspense around the identity of the betrayer increases in verses 23-25. Who could it be? The revelation of Judas as the betrayer happens in real time: the disciples look around at each other, which one is it?; the disciple whom Jesus loves is introduced; Peter asks the beloved disciple to ask Jesus; and then the disciple whom Jesus loves asks Jesus, "Lord, who is it?" "Tell us already! The suspense is killing us." The expectancy has the dual purpose of both wondering who it could be and could it be me. Jesus finally says, "It is the one to whom I give this piece of bread when I have dipped it in the dish" (13:26). Jesus dips the bread in the dish, and . . . gives the bread to Judas. The protracted nature of this scene emphasizes the experience of the disciples in verse 22 and can be an experience that a preacher might create in a sermon. It is, in many respects, a moment of crisis for the disciples, and for the hearers of this Gospel.

Verses 27-30 are devoted to Judas's departure, but the disciples do not know that this is what betrayal will mean. Once again, the narrative is drawn out to fashion a feeling of anticipation. We now know who it is that will betray Jesus, but we still do not know what this actually involves—at least the disciples do not. The reason for Judas's disbelief is Satan entering into him, an acute divergence to what will be given to the disciples, the Spirit (20:22). What Judas will now do, about which there is confusion among the disciples (13:28-29), is leave the fold. Judas went out. "And it was night." For all intents and purposes, this is when the scene should end and the curtain should come down. These last two details—that he went out and that it was night—are meant to have dramatic effect. Judas has left the fold. The next time Judas will appear in the Gospel will be standing *outside* the fold, outside the garden that he often visited with Jesus and the other disciples. "And it was night" should bear the entire weight of what darkness symbolizes in the Gospel of John. Judas has entered the darkness. He has gone to the dark side. The pathos of this moment is worth a sermon alone. What is our response in hearing, "and it was night," especially when we know what the dark signifies for this Gospel? Fear? Foreboding? Sadness? Grief? Confusion? For whom? Even for ourselves?

JOHN 13:31-38
THE LOVE COMMANDMENT

When we return to the narrative, reminded that Judas has gone out, imagine
what the disciples need to hear. What does Jesus need to say to them? Jesus'
first words after Judas's departure have to do with his glory, and perhaps that is
exactly what the disciples yearn for in this instant. Not a pep talk, but to know
that there is something bigger, something beyond, this moment of disorder
and dismay. Here really begins the Farewell Discourse and not at 14:1. John
13:31 is the true start to Jesus' words of farewell, and they refer back to how
chapter 13 began, the recognition that that hour is here. While it appears that
Judas's departure set in motion the events of the hour, Jesus has. "Little children"
is a touching address on the part of Jesus, especially in view of the words
that follow. Verse 33 is the Farewell Discourse in summary: "I am with you
only a little longer. You will look for me; and as I said to the Jews so now
I say to you, 'Where I am going, you cannot come'" (13:33). Into the midst
of these difficult words Jesus inserts the commandment of love. It is critical
for the interpretation of this commandment to recognize that it follows Jesus'
very direct statement about his departure. As a result, this is not a general,
generic claim to love one another; it is, rather, an essential injunction for the
disciples to know and feel Jesus' presence when he is gone. To love one another
is for the sake of remembering the feeling of how Jesus loved them. Love is
a mark of discipleship, for the outside world to see, but it is also necessary
for them to show each other. To be sustained in their believing (20:31), they
need to practice the love toward one another that they themselves experienced
from Jesus. The last three verses of the chapter predict Peter's denial, but it is
important when interpreting these verses not to end the pericope at the end of
the chapter. Peter has just heard that he will deny Jesus. He will need to hear
Jesus' next words, "do not let your hearts be troubled." These words are as much
addressed to Peter individually as they are to the disciples altogether.

There are several key textual issues when it comes to interpreting verses
36-38 for preaching. First, the repetition of "to follow" no fewer than three
times recalls the calling of the disciples in chapter 1 (1:43) and looks forward to
Peter's conversation with Jesus on the shore of the Sea of Galilee in 21:15-19.
While the disciples cannot follow Jesus to the cross—and Jesus is specific in
saying so—they can follow afterward, and Peter will be asked to do so. What
does it mean, then, to follow Jesus? Looking forward, it will require feeding
and tending Jesus' sheep in his absence. It will entail following Jesus in the
abiding places that he prepares for us (14:2). Peter cannot follow now because
he cannot go where Jesus is about to go. He will be able to follow later, in

part because he will have the presence of the Paraclete, the Advocate, the Spirit, which Jesus will breathe into the disciples in 20:22. At this point, Peter does not know what it means to lay down one's life for Jesus, and Jesus is not asking him to do so now. In fact, Jesus' will ask his disciples to lay down their lives for their *friends*, not for him (15:13). He does not need that. He is the Word made flesh. As Peter's denial is predicted here, it is important to allow the specifics of the denial of Peter to weigh in on the interpretation of these last verses of chapter 13. Peter's denial is not of Jesus but of his own discipleship. The term for denial is found also in the questioning of John's identity, "He confessed and did not deny it, but confessed, 'I am not the Messiah'" (1:20). The interrogation of John is similar to that of Peter, with both John and Peter responding to questions about *their* identity, not that of Jesus, with "I am not" (cf. 18:17, 25). A preacher might consider exploring different translations for "denial" in this context, given the interpretive weight that the denial of Jesus carries in our imaginations, particularly for Peter. For John the Baptist, the question posed to him is whether he is the Messiah, Elijah, or the prophet; for Peter, it is if he is one of Jesus' disciples. Both John and Peter "reject, refute, negate, rebuff," the claims: in the case of John, because his identity is as a witness; in the case of Peter, because he cannot yet realize his own discipleship.

CONNECTIONS TO THE LECTIONARY

Chapter 13 in the Gospel of John occurs three times in the lectionary: 13:1-17, 31b-35 for Maundy Thursday in Years A, B, and C; 13:21-32 for Holy Wednesday in Years A, B, and C; and 13:31-35 for Easter 5 in Year C. While it makes sense that this is the chosen Gospel text for Maundy Thursday, the preacher is left with a potential predicament about what to preach, the Lord's Supper or the foot washing or both. The particular challenge with the foot washing is that it is frequently performed in worship on Maundy Thursday without an accompanying sermon To have a foot washing without a sermon that should function to mirror Jesus' discourse interpreting his actions is to rely on the sign alone for what it means. As a result, the act taken on its own will communicate that Jesus' command to love one another as I have loved you is to wash one another's feet. The lectionary exacerbates this diminution by omitting 13:18-30. The love commandment is directly connected to the foot washing when there has been an interlude of twelve verses that speak directly about betrayal.

Furthermore, 13:2 makes little sense with with 13:18-30. The significance of the foot washing is not only the act itself, but what it communicates about Jesus. The self-sacrifice of Jesus' love cannot be replicated any more than God's love for the world can be matched by ours. Moreover, the foot washing is an expression of love that acknowledges the difficulty of love, which is narrated in the excluded verses in the lectionary. To enact or preach on this "ritual" without recognizing this element of Jesus' act is not only to misinterpret the foot washing but to suggest implications that are fundamentally incorrect.

Fundamentally, "as I have loved you" does not refer to the foot washing alone. In its cumulative place in the story, in the Farewell Discourse, it is representative of Jesus' entire earthly ministry, the multiple ways in which Jesus has shown love for his disciples, or put another way, grace upon grace for his believers. This is a summative statement on Jesus' part, not a demonstrative one. Moreover, it looks forward to acts of love not yet narrated, "no greater love than to lay down one's life for one's friends," that foresee Jesus' giving up of himself at his arrest, his willing death on the cross, his taking up his life again at the resurrection and the ascension, and that even imagine possibilities beyond the confines of the narrative itself.

That our congregations will only hear Judas's exit into the darkness if they choose to read the story on Holy Wednesday begs the preacher to incorporate this event in any preaching on this chapter of John or when preaching on the character of Judas. John 13:31 makes little sense without 13:30, and yet 13:31-35 is the Gospel lesson for a Sunday after Easter. To some extent we do not serve our parishioners well by glossing over past unpleasantries for the sake of a glorious Easter season. Preaching on the resurrection and during the season of Easter needs to come to terms with a resurrection reality. That is, preaching the resurrection that is not a glorious end but a deserved end, and one that nevertheless takes seriously the perils of our future.

John 14
The Farewell Discourse Continues

14:1-6
Abiding Places

Chapter 14 picks up with direct words from Jesus to his disciples about his impending departure, words that continue after the prediction of Peter's denial at the end of chapter 13. The words that open chapter 14 are words of comfort and hope, promise and plain speech. They are words that both Peter and the disciples need to hear, not only because of Jesus' pending departure, but because of what they have just experienced in Judas's departure.

Jesus' farewell words to his disciples in this discourse anticipate and assume the events that lie ahead: the crucifixion, the resurrection, and the ascension. Each one of these realities is the result of the primary theological event in the Gospel of John, the incarnation. The disciples are going to be faced with the end of the incarnation, the end of Jesus' presence on earth as God. Jesus needs them to know that there is more beyond the crucifixion which, for John, is the inevitable outcome of being human. At the same time, the resurrection and then the ascension are the next promises in store, for Jesus and for his believers. Not even the resurrection is the end. The resurrection presumes that there is something even beyond itself, the ascension. The beginning of chapter 14—in fact, a good portion of the Farewell Discourse as a whole—describes not *resurrected* life but *ascended* life with God. Just as Jesus will ascend to the Father, so also will Jesus' believers; he goes to prepare an abiding place for them. It is from this particular theological perspective that we need to hear and interpret these introductory statements of the Farewell Discourse.

"Believe in God, believe also in me" are critical at this juncture, as the disciples have just witnessed both Judas's departure and the prediction of Peter's denial. They need to hear what is central to the entire ministry of Jesus, believing in him. It is that belief, that relationship, that is the premise on which everything Jesus says going forward is based.

Most people in the pews will hear the words from 14:2 and think they are attending a funeral or memorial service. For many, the image is of a great mansion in the sky for the recently departed deceased. A quick perusal of translations will show where people get the idea of houses or rooms that Jesus is preparing for those who have died. Yet these "dwelling places" (NRSV) are really no "place" at all unless the words mean being in the intimate presence of God, or better yet, being at the bosom of the Father. The root of the term is *menō* ("abide"), John's favorite and most often used word to describe being in a relationship with Jesus. Ascended life, toward which the resurrection looks, is with God, with Jesus, sharing in their intimate bond and all that that intimacy entails. Where Jesus is, there we will be (14:3).

Like most of the characters in John's Gospel, Thomas hears Jesus' promise of place on a literal level. "Where are you going, Jesus? We need a map, a diagram, something like that to get us to the right location." In this regard, the Farewell Discourse is no different than the other dialogues and discourses in the Gospel. There is always movement from misunderstanding to recognition of who Jesus is revealing himself to be, yet here the stakes are higher. The Farewell Discourse is not only parting words for comfort but clarification of what is to come, lest the disciples misinterpret the events of the passion narrative. This could easily be the case, given Martha's mistaken perception of the soon-to-be resurrection of her brother (11:24-25). Against this misunderstanding Jesus offers one of the more well-known and ill-used "I AM" statements in John's Gospel, "I am the way, the truth, and the life." The predicate nominative "I AM" statements in the Fourth Gospel make known Jesus as the source of life, abundant grace, and, seen in connection with the absolute "I AM" statements, they signal the very presence of God. Yet, removed from the conversation between Jesus and Thomas, and from the situation of Jesus' last alone time with his disciples before his arrest and crucifixion, this particular "I AM" statement in the Gospel of John has turned into evidence for and proof of Jesus as the sole means of salvation, no matter how salvation seems to be defined. The identifiable problem of being extracted from its narrative setting is one issue, but an additional glaring misappropriation of this "I AM" statement is that it then stands as contradictory to every other "I AM" statement in the Fourth Gospel. "I AM the way, the truth, and the life" becomes an indication of God's judgment, exclusion, and absence. "No one comes to the Father except through me"—rather than a word of promise—becomes a declaration of prohibition. What difference does this make for preaching? Sometimes preaching necessitates correction of interpretation history that has gone amiss. In this case, preaching this powerful "I AM" statement for its promise and not its discrimination will "save" many in that very moment. Truly.

JOHN 14:7-14
THE PRESENCE OF THE FATHER

Reading beyond verse 6, we realize that the Father has already come, is already present, in the life and ministry of Jesus. "If you know me" is a condition of fact, "if you know me, *and you do.*" These are words of comfort, not condition, for the disciples. There is nothing uncertain for their present or their future because of their relationship with Jesus. In that, Jesus wants them to be secure. The misunderstanding continues with Philip's request to see the Father, eliciting Jesus' most unambiguous claims about his identity and his relationship with God (1:1). In verses 10-11, the relationship that Jesus has with the Father becomes the basis for how Jesus will talk about the promise of believers being brought into this union in the rest of the Discourse. This is crucial. These words that seek to reiterate his relationship with the Father are meant for the disciples to imagine themselves in that same relationship, which has become more evident after the introduction of the Beloved Disciple in 13:23. The relationship that Jesus has with the Father is the very one the believer has with Jesus and the Father (14:20). So many of the images that follow in the Farewell Discourse assume this oneness, particularly looking forward to chapter 15 and the image of the vine and the branches. This is made exceedingly clear by the use of *menō* in 14:10, "The words that I say to you I do not speak on my own; but the Father who dwells (abides) in me does his works." Jesus' words to Philip, "Have I been with you all this time, Philip, and you still do not know me? Whoever has seen me has seen the Father. How can you say, 'Show us the Father'?" (14:9), are a summary of 1:18. The essential reason for the Word made flesh is to make God known, to declare God, to reveal God, to bring God out so that God can be known and seen and touched.

The works to which Jesus refers in 14:11 mean believing, and to believe in Jesus is to witness in the world to his presence so that others might have their own encounter by which then to believe in Jesus. Verse 12 is an astonishing claim, to imagine that the disciples are capable of doing greater works than these, considering all that Jesus has done during the three years of his public ministry. How is this possible? That which Jesus has done, his primary work, is to be the presence of God in the world, the "I AM." Every sign, every encounter, every conversation has been with that sole purpose in mind, to make God known (1:18) so that a moment of believing might happen. In these works, the disciples are invited to participate. Their participation here and now is essential for three reasons. First, Jesus is returning to the Father and will no longer be the Word made flesh in the world. Second, because the sending of the disciples (20:21) and discipleship itself are based on their witness. To be sent is to witness, to point and say, "Look, the Lamb of God who takes the sin of the world!" and to invite, "Come and see." Third, greater works will be possible and have to be because God loves *the world.* The entirety of the world has yet to know God's love (20:30-31), and so the disciples are charged with embodying

God's love and grace for the world to experience. Discipleship must show grace just as grace was shown in Jesus.

CONNECTIONS TO THE LECTIONARY

John 14:1-14 is the first of two Sundays in a row from the fourteenth chapter of John, Easter 5 and Easter 6, Year A. It should seem just a little odd, or feel like an itching burr under our liturgical saddles, that a chapter in which Jesus offers his formal good-byes to the disciples is heard in the Sundays after Easter, when he is, well, for lack of a better term, back. Taking the literary context seriously when interpreting this text, however, gets at a critical theological claim for the Fourth Gospel and, particularly, for what resurrection means for the fourth evangelist. To be clear, this is not to suggest a sermon on reading the mind of the author of the Fourth Gospel and then telling your congregation an interpretation of the resurrection. It proposes that the specificity with which this text speaks to the function and meaning of resurrection might frame how we construe the promise of the resurrection beyond the Seventh Sunday of Easter. As discussed in the commentary above, most persons in church listening to this text will connect it with a funeral. One of the challenges of preaching this passage will be to acknowledge its words of comfort and at the same time hear them as a post-resurrection promise.

JOHN 14:15-21
THE SPIRIT AS PARACLETE

While the lectionary divides 14:1-21 into two separate sections, Jesus never stopped talking at 14:14. Maintaining a fluidity between this false dissection of the chapter is essential for its interpretation and preaching. In order to make sense of the language about commandments here and what it means in the larger context of John's Gospel, it is helpful to refer to the first location where the term is used, at the very end of chapter 12, Jesus' last public discourse, "for I have not spoken on my own, but the Father who sent me has himself given me a commandment about what to say and what to speak. And I know that his commandment is eternal life. What I speak, therefore, I speak just as the Father has told me" (12:49-50).

God has one commandment, and that is eternal life. Chapter 13 summarizes the foot washing and the meal with commandment language, "I give you a new commandment, that you love one another. Just as I have loved you, you also should love one another" (13:34). Bringing both of these references forward to 14:15 gives substance to the commandments to which Jesus is referring, "If you love me, you will keep my commandments." In the context of what has come before, the commandments of which Jesus speaks are love and life. God has one commandment, eternal life, and the disciples are asked to love one another as a demonstration of their love for Jesus and to make possible eternal life for others not of this fold. In the Greek syntax, their love for Jesus is not certain (14:15). The condition is contingent, with their love in question, calling attention to the events of the previous chapter in the betrayal of Judas and of Peter's denial. The commandment language here also looks forward to 14:21, "They who have my commandments and keep them are those who love me; and those who love me will be loved by my Father, and I will love them and reveal myself to them" (14:21).

This section of chapter 14 first introduces the Advocate, who is the Holy Spirit, in John's Gospel. It is important to note that a sustained discussion of the Holy Spirit first occurs at this juncture in the Gospel and not earlier in the narrative. While there have been references to the Spirit up until this point, a more substantive portrayal of the Holy Spirit is reserved for the Farewell Discourse. Why? As a reminder, the Farewell Discourse, or chapters 13–17, is Jesus' words of good-bye to his disciples; he is aware of his imminent arrest but, more so, sets forth the larger theological trajectory of his crucifixion, resurrection, and ascension.

One entry into preaching this text would ask, what is it that the disciples need to hear from Jesus about the function and purpose of the Holy Spirit in this moment? Answering this question will get at the heart of any kind of meaningful understanding of what difference the Holy Spirit actually makes for the lives of the disciples, particularly going forward in Jesus' absence, and even for our lives now. First and foremost, John's specific term for the Holy Spirit is *parakletos*, translated variously as "advocate, comforter, helper, intercessor." It is a compound word merging the preposition *para*, which means "with" or "alongside," with the verb *kaleo*, "to call." The Holy Spirit, according to John, is the one who is called to be alongside us. This unique interpretation of the Spirit alone is worth a sermon or ten. In the face of Jesus' departure, this concept of the Spirit is critical. The disciples will not be orphaned because the Spirit will now accompany them. In the commentary on specific passages that follows, rather than offering a translation of *Paraclete*, will use *Paraclete* consistently. How the term is translated in each circumstance has everything to do with the function of the Paraclete in that moment.

Another interesting feature about the Holy Spirit in the Farewell Discourse is that, rather than a lengthy development of the Spirit concentrated in one passage or one chapter, the Spirit is interspersed throughout the Farewell Discourse. There are two important aspects to consider in this regard. First, narratively, the Paraclete does indeed accompany the disciples in the midst of Jesus' farewell words. The presence of the Paraclete is consistent; in each chapter it will be present and reveal something new about its purpose. Second, where the Paraclete surfaces invites attention. That is, what does it follow? Why interject the Paraclete here and now? What have the disciples heard from Jesus such that they need the Helper, the Intercessor, the Comforter to be present? What will they hear next that they need the Paraclete to accompany them?

In hindsight, the work of the Paraclete makes sense of how Jesus can say what he did in the opening verses of this chapter. John 14:12 should seem virtually impossible unless the Holy Spirit was and is present. In fact, verse 12 foreshadows how Jesus first describes the Holy Spirit as "another advocate." If the Holy Spirit is *another* Advocate, then that means there has been an Advocate already, Jesus. As a result, we are invited to conceive of the fact that one way of understanding the role of the Holy Spirit is to reread the Gospel up to this point and notice what Jesus has done. To have seen Jesus at work is to anticipate the work of the Holy Spirit. That the imagination for the presentation of the Holy Spirit is first grounded in the experiences of and encounters with Jesus provides a foundation and tangibility to what is otherwise a rather ethereal tenet of Trinitarian belief. There are reasons why we rarely hear sermons on the Holy Spirit unless it is Pentecost Sunday or there is direct mention of the third person of the Trinity in the text itself. If we are honest, preacher and layperson alike, many of us have a rather dysfunctional pneumatology. We do not quite know what to do with or think about the "shy member" of the Trinity.

Our views of and preaching on the Holy Spirit are also deeply affected by the lectionary and the liturgical year. With one Sunday dedicated to the Feast of Pentecost and with a selection of texts that offers different portraits of the Spirit, too many of our sermons are an intermingled mess of texts and ideas that are no more than doctrinal arguments for the existence of the Holy Spirit. The role of the Holy Spirit in the Gospel of John provides a unique presentation of who and why the Holy Spirit is. As a result, one possible preaching perspective on this particular section of the Farewell Discourse is to acquaint us with the Holy Spirit, as it is presented here, but to use the other passages where John develops his pneumatology as a means by which to flesh out in the sermon the purpose of the Holy Spirit. These other passages include 14:25-27; 15:26-27; 16:4b-11; and 20:22. Each passage contains new details to add to the character development of the Spirit, and each feature pulls in multiple themes from the entirety of the Gospel.

In the case of 14:15-17 specifically, there are several important aspects of what the Paraclete does that gain a fuller meaning when the larger context of the Fourth Gospel is in view. First, this is the Spirit of truth. Jesus has just revealed himself as the way, the truth, and the life (14:6), and in the trial before Pilate, the concept of truth will play a major role (18:37-38). In the trial narrative, the truth is that to which Jesus testifies and "everyone who belongs to the truth listens to my voice." The truth is synonymous with Jesus. Jesus is the truth. Later in the Farewell Discourse, Jesus promises, "When the Spirit of truth comes, he will guide you into all the truth (16:13). Second, the disciples "know" the Paraclete, and to "know" in the Gospel of John is to be in relationship (14:17). The Paraclete abides with you and will be in you; abiding also means relationship in the Fourth Gospel (14:17). The Paraclete will also be in you, a foreshadowing of Jesus breathing into the disciples the Spirit in 20:22 (14:17). In only one verse, the disciples hear that they know the Paraclete, the Paraclete *abides* in them, and the Paraclete is *in* them, the primary terminology by which intimacy and relationship are described in the Fourth Gospel. Third, the coming of the Paraclete, the promise of the Paraclete, means that the disciples will not be orphaned (14:18), a particularly poignant claim. This specific assurance of not being abandoned, without a parent, calls to mind the strong parental theme across the entirety of this Gospel, between Jesus and the Father, but also between the Father and those who believe. The Prologue asserts that "all who received him, who believed in his name, he gave power to become children of God" (1:12). In this section of chapter 14 we find the fulfillment of that promise.

CONNECTIONS TO THE LECTIONARY

John 14:15-21 is the lectionary reading for Easter 6, Year A. What if you preach the coming gift of the Holy Spirit before Pentecost, just as this passage from John anticipates that you will? Lay the groundwork for Pentecost rather than putting the entirety of the Spirit into one Sunday, as if that were even possible. And when you get to the Day of Pentecost, preach John's Spirit. In other words, start suggesting that there is life beyond

Easter Sunday and it has everything to do with the Spirit. That this text is located in the Sundays after Easter promises that the presence and power of Jesus will extend beyond the empty tomb, beyond Easter, and well into this next season we call Pentecost. All too often, the resurrection is preached as a culmination rather than an inauguration, the believer's ultimate reality rather than the penultimate promise, especially for the Gospel of John. A primary theological assumption throughout the Farewell Discourse is that there is more to being a child of God than being raised from the dead. The crucifixion will indeed bring to an end the incarnation, but the resurrection is not the end-all of eternal life. For the Gospel of John, the ascension is the final surety that secures every single claim about abundant life.

To preach the promise of the Spirit and the assurance of Jesus' ascension in the middle of the Easter season may very well get us out of our resurrection ruts, that the resurrection is all that God has in store for us. In fact, it is not and it could very well sound like an empty platitude. There will be people in the pews asking, "So what exactly am I supposed to do with Easter anyway? I'm still here." So get them ready for Pentecost. Preach that there's Christian life beyond a discovery of an empty tomb. Help them imagine that resurrection is a matter of death and life, even life right here and now.

John 14:8-17 (25-27) is the determined Gospel lection for Pentecost Sunday, Year C. Preachers should immediately be suspicious concerning why there are verses in parentheses, especially when these verses offer a precise and powerful portrait of the Paraclete according to John. Preaching John in the midst of powerhouse Spirit passages such as Acts 2:1-21; Genesis 11:1-9; Psalm 104:24-34, 35b; and Romans 8:14-17 demands that the preacher pick a Spirit. In other words, preach John's Spirit for all its worth this Sunday, or choose another text on which to focus your attention. To offer the listeners an amalgamation of Spirit texts for the sake of some sort of unified presentation of the Spirit's work will only serve to confuse and confound any sense of why the Spirit actually matters for a life of faith. At the same time, this passage should inform any moment in the Gospel of John when the Spirit is referenced or preached. It does not have to be limited to Pentecost Sunday but can help imagine the importance of the Spirit as it is presented throughout the entire Gospel.

JOHN 14:22-31
THE ABIDING OF THE FATHER AND THE SON

Verses 22-23 reiterate that the intention of the Father and the Son is to make their abiding with us, "make our home with them" (NRSV). The term translated as "home" again comes from the root, *menō*, so that literally, "we will make our abode with them." Verse 24 confirms that what Jesus says and who Jesus is are one and the same and come from the Father. The importance of Jesus' words is threefold (14:24). First, he is the Word made flesh. John 1:1 established Jesus' identity as the Word who was in the beginning with God. However we determine the source of John's imagery here with regard to the Word—as wisdom, Greek influence, or an extant poem—the narrative, textual clue to the meaning of Jesus as Word comes from "in the beginning." To begin the Gospel with the same words as the book of Genesis calls to mind that God's Word is that which creates and gives life. Jesus embodies this characteristic of God. The Word made flesh is life. God's one commandment is eternal life. Second, so much of who Jesus is, what Jesus means, is predicated on his words that interpret signs, that engage in conversation, that deliver sermons of comfort. Very little would be known about Jesus in this Gospel were knowing Jesus to rely only on what he did. Third, what will make possible that God loves *the world* is that others will hear these words and come to believe (20:30-31). Verses 25-27 introduce additional characteristics of the Paraclete, particularly in the context of the importance of hearing the words of Jesus. "I have said these things to you while I am still with you" (14:25), but now Jesus will be gone. Three more aspects of the Paraclete are brought together in these verses. First and second, the Paraclete will teach and remind. Jesus as Word and his words will no longer be present in human form, but the Father will send the Advocate who "will teach you everything, and remind you of all that I have said to you" (14:26). This characteristic of the Paraclete foreshadows Mary's moment of recognition in the resurrection garden, "Rabbouni" (20:16). Jesus is teacher. The disciples will still need their teacher, and the Paraclete will function in that role for them in Jesus' absence. Third, the Paraclete is connected to peace and will bring peace to the troubled and afraid hearts of the disciples. This recalls how the chapter opened, "Do not let your hearts be troubled" (14:1). In addition, this promise of the Paraclete as a bringer of peace anticipates the giving of the Spirit in the second resurrection appearance: "Jesus said to them again, 'Peace be with you. As the Father has sent me, so I send you.' When he had said this, he breathed on them and said to them, 'Receive the Holy Spirit'" (20:21-22). The order of Jesus' words in his appearance to the disciples and the emphasis on peace here in 14:15-27 suggest that when the disciples hear "peace, be with you," they might know that the Spirit will follow. Preaching might explore how the disciples need to hear words of peace and promise before they can comprehend the Spirit's presence, especially breathed into them.

At first glance, in John 14:28-31 Jesus seems to be repeating himself. At the same time, "I am going to the Father," "I have told you this before it occurs," and "I will no longer talk much with you" are perhaps some of the more direct statements from Jesus in the entire discourse about his departure. There is a pattern of relatively clear and precise sentences from Jesus as to what is about to take place, followed by additional words of comfort and imagery that situate what Jesus has just said in a context in which it may actually be heard. In this case, what will follow will be the lengthy image of the vine and the branches.

CONNECTIONS TO THE LECTIONARY

Year C, Easter 6, the lectionary offers John 14:23-29 as an alternate reading. The preacher should ask how these verses might be heard differently in the midst of the Easter season compared with Pentecost. What role does the Spirit play in the season of Easter? Is that a question we have ever asked in our preaching? Moreover, the grouping of verses 27-29 with the previous verses about keeping Jesus' words suggests the possibility of actually following through with Jesus' request.

CHAPTER 15
THE IMAGE OF THE VINE

Chapter 15 introduces a new metaphor by which the disciples might view their relationship with Jesus even in the face of his absence. When chapters and verses were added to biblical texts, clearly this new image dictated a new chapter for the Gospel of John, much like the break between chapters 9 and 10. We will see, however, that the image of the vine answers the question intimated in 14:31—what commandment? Like the rest of John, Chapter 15 resists manageable pericopes for preaching. Since this is a lectionary commentary, the discussion below is structured based on the textual parameters established by the lectionary. At the same time, the progression through the chapter will demand a forward and backward motion of interpretation and commentary as the narrative of this chapter seeks to underscore its primary theological claim of abiding and union.

JOHN 15:1-8
"I AM THE TRUE VINE"

The image of the vine introduces the last "I AM" statement with a predicate nominative. Twice Jesus will identify himself as the vine, first, as the true vine (15:1) and then as "I AM the vine" (15:5). The vine imagery follows on the heels of "do as the Father commanded me" (14:31). The disciples are surely wondering, what might that be and how do we do it? The commandment is first and primarily to bear fruit but at the same time, the image of the vine offers a picture by which the disciples may see themselves as able to do as commanded because of their connection to the vine. The image begins as a way for Jesus to describe *his* relationship with the Father. Jesus first unpacks this image as it describes his relationship with his Father before he moves to how the image might portray his relationship with the disciples. This is key for the mutual abiding at stake between Jesus, the Father, and the disciples. Jesus is the vine; "my Father" is the vine grower. Like any good vine grower, the Father tends the vines with care, pruning where necessary so that they bear as much fruit as possible (15:16). At the forefront of this image is the theme of mutual dependence. The vine needs the vine grower as much as the vine grower needs the vine. The vine needs the vine grower for its optimal growth and production, even its abundance. It will produce more fruit, fruit in abundance, if cared for. The vine grower needs the vine to produce, to make abundance possible for sustenance and life. There is a mutuality in this image critical at this point in the narrative. It is the last "I AM" of its kind in the Gospel and focuses on mutuality and dependence.

Verse 4 then calls upon the language already used in the Gospel to describe relationship—to abide. Throughout the Gospel thus far, *menō* has been the central concept to describe a relationship with Jesus. The image of the vine affords another means by which the concept of abiding might be understood. As a result, all previous references to abiding in Jesus, and the results of that abiding, should be fully present in the interpretation of the image of the vine. The reason for the breadth of imagery in the Fourth Gospel, particularly in the predicate nominative "I AM" statements, is to provide accessible common pictures meant to relay a fundamentally complicated theological truth. How can we make sense of what it means to abide in Jesus? The imagery assists in this understanding. Furthermore, that the images are directly connected to Jesus himself by the use of the predicate nominative "I AM" statements undergirds their primary premise of denoting relationship, intimacy, and dependence. We might compare Jesus' means of communicating in the Synoptic Gospels, for example, "the kingdom of heaven is like." For the Fourth Gospel, everything is predicated on relationship so that a third person description of what God is up to in Jesus will not suffice. Moreover, Jesus does not only offer multiple images to make known God's revelation, but connects them directly, in the first person predicate nominative "I AM" statements, to himself.

Jesus first describes his own relationship with God (1:18) by concentrating on the vine grower and the vine; now it is time to add the branches. The entirety of this image is meant to offer a way for the disciples to understand the intimacy between the Father, Jesus, and the disciples. It is frequently at this point that a preacher begins to wonder how many times and in how many ways does this idea of intimacy need repeating—and how many sermons can I really preach on the same topic? First, it bears repeating because of the location in the story. This is a pastoral moment. This is the hour, and everything will change for the disciples shortly. Second, the repetition of this theme of the unity of the Father, Son, and believer is meant to be a narrative way to emphasize what is being said theologically. That is, if it were only stated once or twice, would one really believe that this is important, that this is central, to who Jesus is? The repetition undergirds the theological truth. Third, the community for whom this was written, who have been thrown out of their synagogue for believing in Jesus, who have been separated from their community and everything community means, now hear of an intimacy with God that they thought they had lost, a relationship that extends beyond the bounds of human relationships they have known.

Verses 4-6 underscore the dependent relationship of the branches on the vine, which has two possible meanings for the disciples. First, as noted above, their connection to the vine makes following Jesus' commandments conceivable and probable. In a related way, greater works than these are possible because the disciples are not alone and rely on both the vine and the vine grower (14:12). Second, this image pulls together the themes of dependence, provision, and sustenance that have been present throughout the Gospel and that are rooted in 1:18. Verse 6 is not a verse of condemnation because that is not what Jesus came to do. Rather, it is a statement of life. Without connection to a life source, abundant life is not possible. Verses 7-8, rather than sounding like "ask and it will be done for you," should be heard within the framework of the dependent relationship already established. The disciples may ask for whatever they wish. That is, Jesus knows that they will have many needs, requests, and wants in his absence. This is an invitation to ask. It is an assumption of reliance and dependence. This is not any wish, but those wishes and needs grounded in relationship.

JOHN 15:9-17
ABIDING IN LOVE

This section of the chapter focuses on love, that abiding in the vine is the same as abiding in love. But what does this really mean? There are two critical referents. The first is chapter 13 and how love is articulated in the act of the foot washing. The second is that God loves the world (3:16). Love is not an abstract concept in this Gospel but is deeply grounded in God's decision to dwell as Jesus in the world. The entirety of the Gospel has been not only Jesus revealing what God's abundant love is but creating experiences to feel this abundant love. John 15:10 returns to the language of commandment, but to keep God's commandments has everything to do with life and love. There may be subtle differences between Jesus and the Jewish authorities outlined especially in chapters 7-8, but the larger question is what it means to keep God's commandments. Jesus performed his healings on the Sabbath because both brought life. For the disciples, the litmus test for holding fast to God's commandments is life and love. If life and love become the test points for what it means to follow the commandments of God, then how the disciples are in the world after Jesus is gone is based on these principles.

Verse 11 seems misplaced in a passage that deals primarily with Jesus' departure and impending death. Yet, in the midst of this and because of this, joy is possible. Chapter 16 will also speak about joy being fulfilled, "Until now you have not asked for anything in my name. Ask and you will receive, so that your joy may be complete" (16:24). What is joy doing here? What is its place in the Gospel? Why now? Answering this question in preaching might recall that the Greek words for "grace" and "joy" share the same root. Joy may very well be a feeling of grace, the emotion of grace, even the response to grace. Joy is that indescribable sense when you find yourself experiencing abundant grace.

As discussed in chapter 13 concerning Peter's denial, Jesus does not ask the disciples to lay down their lives for him, but for each other. There is no servant and master but friends. This is the only time in the Gospel of John that Jesus calls the disciples friends. When familial relationships are severed, on whom can one rely, or on what social constructions do relationships come about? If the disciples, and those who heard and read this Gospel, are without family because of their situation of being thrown out of the synagogue, friendship is the next social structure that might embody the relationships that no longer exist. Like his mother and the Beloved Disciple at the foot of the cross, Jesus is showing on whom you can be dependent when everything on which you were dependent has abandoned you. Friendship still demands accountability and responsibility, a trusted dependence. Jesus is setting up a framework for relying on each other in his absence.

"You did not choose me but I chose you" (15:16) is regularly lifted out of its Gospel setting to justify various theological systems that typically have little to do with the literary situation of this verse. While we might be eager to conjecture that Jesus chooses us to be his disciples, one has to put this verse in the larger context of the theme of judgment, or "crisis," that exists for everyone who encounters Jesus. How a preacher negotiates language of choice when it comes to believing in Jesus is usually dependent on denominational loyalties. Jesus' words here are actually a restatement of the same promise made back in chapter 6, "Did I not choose you, the twelve?" In both cases, chapter 6 and here in chapter 15, the disciples need to hear Jesus' commitment to them, his reassurance that the relationship is firm and sound. In the case of chapter 6, the disciples had just learned that one of them will betray Jesus. In the case of chapter 15, that betrayer has just left them; Jesus will leave them—What words of comfort do they need to hear? I did choose you, friends. "You are here. With me. Now is not the time to wonder whether or not you should be here, are meant to be here, are worthy to be here." "You are here" might be a way to paraphrase what is behind this assurance here and now. In other words, the language of choice is language of promise in this moment of loss and fear rather than theological doctrine justifying systems of confessions.

CONNECTIONS TO THE LECTIONARY

While the lectionary separates the first section of chapter 15 into two separate Sundays, 15:1-8 Easter 5, Year B, and 15:9-17 Easter 6, Year B, the preacher would benefit from having the full picture of this passage in view when preaching one or the other. Like other passages in John, the progression helps to make sense of what comes before and after. With the larger section in mind, the preacher would be able to single out particular themes on which to focus in preaching and use the entirety of the section to preach that theme. A preacher might also envisage a two part sermon series that creatively explores the unique image of the vine and the branches, really working this image, not only theologically, but as a means by which people realize its many facets of meaning.

JOHN 15:18-27
THE HATRED OF THE WORLD

The language of choice, that Jesus chose the disciples, precedes the situation for the disciples outlined in the last section of this chapter. Before Jesus says, "If the world hates you, be aware that it hated me before it hated you" (15:18), the disciples need to know their chosenness. The disciples have to hear they are chosen before learning that they will be hated. That indeed the disciples will be hated by the world is not in question. A better translation here would be "since the world hates you." Furthermore, their mutual love for one another will bring comfort in the face of antagonism (15:17). As Jesus' believers and particularly in his absence, the disciples will face certain hardships, resistances, and hatred. It is one thing to know of these realities when Jesus is still around. It is quite another circumstance to conceive of these privations when you are on your own. The truth of the pending adversity calls to mind the healing of the man blind from birth, who testified to what Jesus did for him and believed in Jesus with Jesus ever present. The disciples will now meet this same reality, yet without Jesus around. They will need to know that Jesus chose them when they confront hatred and persecution (15:20). Jesus came and spoke to the world, but the world did not listen and now remains in sin or unbelief (15:22).

The Paraclete's return in 15:26 is a direct response to Jesus' words in 15:25, "They hated me without a cause." The Paraclete will give testimony about Jesus, as must the disciples, in the face of the world that hates Jesus and hates them. The disciples will have to be witnesses, like John the Baptist, like the Samaritan woman at the well, like the man blind from birth, to who Jesus is and what Jesus has done. They are not alone in that act of testimony, as the preceding list proves, and because of the Paraclete. To witness is a primary characteristic of discipleship according to the Gospel of John, and it means witnessing in the face of anticipated resistance and rejection.

The disciples have had examples of what it means to give testimony to Jesus and now, at this point, they need to draw on and remember those models. The mention of testimony at this point also looks forward to the topics in the next chapter, when there will be more plain speech about what the disciples must anticipate in Jesus' absence. The brief reference to "the beginning" in 15:27 can be interpreted at the literal level of the disciples having been called before the advent of Jesus' public ministry. At the same time, it is a reminder of where this Gospel started, "in the beginning." The disciples must remember this as well because it is to this fact that they will give testimony, that Jesus was in the beginning with God, comes from God, and is God (1:1).

CONNECTIONS TO THE LECTIONARY

John 15:18-25 never appear in the lectionary but should inform any preaching on the Farewell Discourse. That is, the Farewell Discourse is not only Jesus speaking to his imminent departure, but also addressing the resistances the disciples will face just as he encountered when he was in the world. The Farewell Discourse anticipates Jesus' absence, but at the same time addresses the disciples's remaining presence in the world. The last three verses of chapter 15 in the Gospel of John are grouped with 16:4b-15 to make up the Gospel lesson for Pentecost Sunday in Year B. In other words, the lectionary is pulling together verses from John to create a Gospel portrait of the Spirit. It is interesting to note that, for every Pentecost Sunday, the Gospel lesson comes from John. One could assume that this is due to John's supplemental status in the lectionary template as a whole. At the same time, however, it is also an acknowledgment that John's pneumatology is worthy of attention and is perhaps the most developed, with only the Gospel of Luke as an immediate rival. Preaching this collection of verses would consider the very specific claims about the role of the Spirit, perhaps even focusing on one characteristic that is then more fully explored and developed in a sermon.

CHAPTER 16
CONTINUING WORDS OF COMFORT

One of the challenges of preaching on the Farewell Discourse is determining manageable pericopes for preaching. The break between chapter 15 and chapter 16 is forced, and for the sake of interpreting chapter 16 in its true context, the commentary that follows picks up where chapter 15 left off with the opening verses of chapter 16 flowing immediately from Jesus' words about the Advocate and testimony in chapter 15.

JOHN 16:1-6
THEY WILL PUT YOU OUT OF THE SYNAGOGUES

To what "I have said these things to you" refers is a recurrent issue when it comes to interpreting the Gospel of John. While "these things" are certainly much of what Jesus has said thus far, they are also meant to call to mind the more immediate words of encouragement, bringing them forward into this very moment of what Jesus has to say. The most recent comments about the Paraclete in the closing verses of chapter 15 are also critical to hearing the first verses of chapter 16. Jesus has said these things, that is, these things about the Paraclete's role as witness, testifying on Jesus' behalf, a role that the disciples also will take on, that will be demanded of them, especially in the events of the hour. The disciples, however, will not be alone in their witnessing. The Paraclete walks alongside them and is also one who testifies about Jesus. This is what will keep them from stumbling, recalling Jesus' words in 6:61, "Does this offend (scandalize) you?"

For this testimony, the disciples will be put out of the synagogues, just as the parents of the blind man feared. Once again, the very certain situation of the community for which this Gospel was written is fully present. The use of the term *aposynagōgos* here in the Farewell Discourse makes a direct connection to the healing of the man blind from birth. Why that sign, here and now? To bring his story forward for the disciples to remember means that they must also remember what happened when the blind man was thrown out. Jesus found him, and the blind man worshiped him. Jesus and the blind man demonstrated for the disciples what it looks like for Jesus to be the shepherd of the sheep, what it looks like to be a sheep of Jesus' fold. Moreover, the blind man exhibited true worship, and those who will seek to kill the disciples will think that by doing so they are offering worship to God (16:2). Jesus as the Good Shepherd is not metaphorical but every bit true. Now, not only will the disciples be thrown out of their synagogues, they will also be killed. Bringing to mind the images of chapter 9 and 10 at this point in the discourse secures the promise of protection into the midst of danger. The imagery in chapters 9 and 10 here in the discourse also anticipate how these chapters will be "acted out" in the arrest scene in chapter 18. Those who want to expel the disciples and kill them do not know the Father or Jesus (16:3) in contrast to "I am the good shepherd. I know my own and my own know me" (10:14).

Verses 4-5 point to how difficult these words would be for the disciples to hear. Unlike the passion predictions that appear relatively early in the Synoptic

Gospels, Jesus' words about his impending death and departure and what the disciples will experience because of their belief in him are postponed to this point in the narrative. As a result, these predictions are surrounded by words of comfort and the promise of the Paraclete. In many respects, the Farewell Discourse is indicative of the pattern we find in the conversations between Jesus and those who encounter him—here is a gradual process of recognition, even belief, that happens in the dialogue. Neither the Samaritan woman at the well nor the man blind from birth had an immediate response of belief in Jesus. It was in dialogue and in having to give testimony to their own experience with Jesus that believing in Jesus happened. Furthermore, that which Jesus must reveal happens in gradual conversation (16:12), "I still have many things to say to you, but you cannot bear them now."

In 16:6 Jesus acknowledges how difficult this must be for the disciples to hear, not only the revelation of his own departure but also what they will confront in his leaving. This is one of those verses in the Gospel of John that works against the prevailing view of the Jesus of the Fourth Gospel, picturing him as unattainable, not understandable, distant, not human "like the other Gospels." Jesus is fully aware of the pain and grief that his disciples are experiencing and will face as the hours progress. Into this very real suffering Jesus interposes the last significant development of the Paraclete. As discussed in the commentary above, the interspersing of the Paraclete and the particular characteristics of the Paraclete throughout the discourse rather than assembling them together in one passage or chapter conveys the truth of who the Paraclete is: the Comforter, the Helper, the one who will walk alongside you.

JOHN 16:7-15
THE PRESENCE OF THE ADVOCATE

This last developed section about the characteristics and functions of the Paraclete focuses on the Paracletes's role as Advocate. We noted above that each appearance of the Paraclete will necessitate a decision as to how to translate *parakletos*. For this passage, Advocate seems fitting, as the Spirit "stands up" to prove the world wrong "about sin and righteousness and judgment" (16:8). The term *prove* can also be translated "expose, convict, convince, point out, and bring to light." It appears in the Gospel in Jesus' response to Nicodemus, notably when Jesus speaks of judgment, "For all who do evil hate the light and do not come to the light, so that their deeds may not be exposed" (3:20; cf. 8:46).

The Advocate will bring to light the world's sin "because they do not believe in me" (16:9), a succinct summary of the concept of sin in the Gospel of John. The Advocate will "convict the world about righteousness, because I am going to the Father and you will see me no longer" (16:10). Verses 8 and 10 are the only occurrences of the noun form of *righteousness* in the Gospel of John. The verb "to make righteous" is never used, only the adjective form (5:30; 7:24; 17:25). It is critical that we not import views and understandings of righteousness from other New Testament authors into John's Gospel. John uses the word only here and for a reason. Righteousness has something to do with Jesus going to the Father and that we are no longer able to see him. Then, what is righteousness exactly? It seems here best understood as a restatement of 1:18, that since Jesus is going to the Father, the disciples will no longer be able to see Jesus. Jesus has been in the world to make God known for before, we were not able to see God. Righteousness is both God's revelation of God's very self, but also the ability to witness this revelation. The Spirit's role will be to continue to bring to light what we have seen about God in Jesus. At the same time, reclaiming the translation "justice" for this term may be helpful in this circumstance, especially as Jesus invites manifestations of justice and condemnation in light of his own ministry. The Paraclete will convince the world about judgment, "because the ruler of this world has been condemned" (16:11). If the ruler of this world, presumably Satan, has been condemned, then what is judgment in this instance? The concept of judgment must be located in its wider discussion in the Gospel. While Satan has been condemned, Satan has been directly tied to unbelief in the character of Judas. The Paraclete's role will be to expose those who do not believe, or alternatively, will allow situations of their own judgment for not believing in Jesus.

The Paraclete is connected to truth, "When the Spirit of truth comes, he will guide you into all the truth; for he will not speak on his own, but will speak whatever he hears, and he will declare to you the things that are to come" (16:13). We know already that Jesus is the truth. The Paraclete will guide the disciples in knowing and living the truth that is Jesus which is especially critical when Jesus as the truth is no longer in this world. The Paraclete will glorify Jesus "because he will take what is mine and declare it to you" (16:14). All that Jesus has is what the Father has (16:15). In other words, everything that the Father is and who the Father is in Jesus they will be told, they will be reminded, even in Jesus' absence.

John 16:12-15 is the designated Gospel reading for Trinity Sunday in Year C. In addition to 16:4b-15, it is also the only passage from John 16 included in the lectionary. Festival Sundays are challenging to preach in that sermons on the background, purpose, and justification for liturgical festivals tend to be far less interesting than the texts presented to support them. Festival Sundays are baffling to our congregations, and sermons can easily digress into arguments of doctrine rather than imaginative speech about the ways in which the biblical texts provide possibilities for viewing God in new ways. With that said, the preacher would approach this section of John 16 not to prove the case for Trinity Sunday, or for the Trinity itself, but to invite creative and imaginative thought about what it means to confess a Triune God. The last thing our parishioners need is sermons that postulate preexistent dogma. What they want is a way into biblical imagination that shapes and forms how they might make sense of and give witness to believing in the Trinity. John 16:12-15 provides specificity to the actions of the Father, Son, and Spirit especially in their relationship to one another.

JOHN 16:16-24
THE POSSIBILITY OF JOY

In this section Jesus anticipates the events of the hour, particularly how they will be felt by the disciples. "A little while, and you will no longer see me, and again a little while, and you will see me" (16:16) refers to the tomb and then the resurrection appearances. The misunderstanding of the disciples and their confusion are warranted (16:17-19), and the desire for "plain speech" (16:25) from Jesus is coveted now more than ever. At the same time, 16:12 rings true, "I still have many things to say to you, but you cannot bear them now," which is why the Paraclete is so critical at this point in the Gospel narrative. The events of the hour are impossible to comprehend now and even in the near future, which is the reason for the focus on the Paraclete in the Farewell Discourse and the actual giving of the Holy Spirit from the *resurrected* Jesus. In verses 20-24 Jesus turns to another image by which to help the disciples anticipate and make sense of the crucifixion. The image that Jesus chooses is of a woman in labor who is about to give birth. The pain experienced in labor is real but is hardly remembered when replaced by "the joy of having brought a human being into the world" (16:21). This image invites imagination around preaching on several levels. It is a fitting image by which to describe the events of the hour because this is exactly what the disciples will experience. The NRSV translation is a very accurate one of the Greek, literally, "the joy of begetting or bearing a human being into the world." It is also important to notice that by using this image, Jesus is addressing the experience of the crucifixion *and* the resurrection, not the crucifixion alone. The image should also bring forward to this moment in the Gospel the themes of new life and creation. The image recalls the intimate relationship described in 1:18, with Jesus at the bosom of the Father. To what extent was this God's experience in the Word made flesh? God's very self knows what it means to bring a human being into the world. Finally, the image draws on the role of Jesus' mother in the Gospel of John and how important she is for him. As discussed in the commentary on chapter 2, she surrounds his ministry and is therefore ever present. It is this maternal familiarity of intimacy and relationship on which Jesus relies when describing how the events of the hour will be experienced.

JOHN 16:25-33
"I HAVE CONQUERED THE WORLD"

Coming off of this picture of childbearing, Jesus now emphasizes again, this time more plainly for the disciples, and much to their relief, that he has come from God. Indeed, this is one of the more direct statements about Jesus' origin in the Gospel: "I came from the Father and have come into the world; again, I am leaving the world and am going to the Father" (16:28). The emphasis on Jesus' origin at this point in the Farewell Discourse serves two purposes. First, it anticipates what will happen with the disciples. They will be scattered and will leave Jesus alone, perhaps not on their own account but because of the scattering. Jesus, however, will not be alone. Jesus acknowledges the grief and sadness of the disciples because of what they will not be able to do for Jesus in his hour. In contrast to the Synoptic Gospels, there is no chastisement of the disciples on the part of Jesus but a truth-telling that this is way it has to be. To be certain that Jesus comes from God is both peace and promise, realizing their abandonment of Jesus but also assurance that he is not alone.

Second, the emphasis on Jesus' origin assumes and anticipates the third event of the hour, the ascension. The disciples cannot be left with only the awareness or promise of the resurrection. Because Jesus came from the Father, he must return to the Father, and the disciples need to be aware of this promise as much as that of the promise of the resurrection. The last verse of chapter 16, while triumphal in tone, is a theophany, that is, the appearance of God in our midst. "Take courage" is rare in the New Testament, in Matthew, for example, "But immediately Jesus spoke to them and said, 'Take heart, it is I; do not be afraid'" (Matt. 14:27; cf. 9:2, 22), Mark, "But immediately he spoke to them and said, 'Take heart, it is I; do not be afraid'" (Mark 6:50; cf. 10:49), and in Acts 23:11. We should observe that in two of the instances the disciples are in a boat at sea in a storm. Here now are these same words, similar feelings of fear—of the very certain presence of chaos, into which Jesus speaks, "take courage and do not be afraid." "I have conquered" the world is the only time this verb is used in the Gospel of John and is in the perfect tense. It is a remarkable statement at this point in the Gospel, as Jesus' last words to his disciples before he turns to his Father in prayer. That Jesus has overcome the world looks forward to the events that follow, that what he will conquer will happen in his death, resurrection, and ascension. At the same time, he conquers every power that would stand in opposition to God, as the "world" makes evident. The verb is relatively infrequent in the New Testament, only used in those writings designated as Johannine literature (1 John and Revelation). In the context of this Gospel and its audience, for Jesus to claim his power over the powers of the world would be crucial. There are times and places when we need to know that the power of God's love has indeed overcome that which seeks to destroy it. The verb tense (perfect) is significant because it indicates that the act of conquering has already happened, with the effects of that happening ongoing in the present. When, then, did Jesus conquer the world? It will not be on the cross alone, or vanquishing death with the empty tomb. Jesus conquered the world at the incarnation, which by default then assumes the crucifixion, resurrection, and ascension. The last words from Jesus before he prays to the Father are a reminder to his disciples that his life, his ministry, and the grace upon grace it revealed, is that which has overcome the resistance of the world, particularly the resistance of the world to relationship with God.

CONNECTIONS TO THE LECTIONARY

As noted above in Connections to the Lectionary for chapter 16, only 16:4b-15 and 16:12-15 are included in the lectionary. By this time in the Farewell Discourse, perhaps Jesus has already said what he needed to say. The portions from chapter 16 selected by the Lectionary comment primarily on the Paraclete, so have a particular liturgical function. This leaves the rest of chapter 16 without a liturgical home. The goal of the commentary on John 16 was to suggest ways in which specific expressions of known themes in the Gospel might then inform, shape, and guide sermons on other parts of the Gospel. Particularly, some of the phrases in this chapter about joy, courage, and overcoming the world are worthy expressions to bring to bear in preaching the whole of the Gospel.

Chapter 17
Jesus' Prayer to the Father

The last chapter of the Farewell Discourse is Jesus' prayer to the Father. In this sense, it should not be included as part of the Farewell Discourse, because Jesus' attention is turned to God alone before his arrest. Moreover, "after these words" signals a shift in focus, much as in 18:1, "after he had spoken these words." At the same time, it is part of the Farewell Discourse because the disciples overhear this prayer, which essentially summarizes for them the Farewell Discourse. The act itself, that the last thing Jesus does before he takes the disciples to the garden is to pray is certainly a noteworthy point. That he commits the entirety of his life, his ministry, his disciples, and everything said in the discourse to the Father, which the disciples get to overhear, is quite another point altogether.

Jesus' final prayer in John presents a number of variances when positioned next to Matthew, Mark, and Luke. In the Fourth Gospel, when Jesus prays to the Father before his arrest in the garden, he is not off alone somewhere with clutched hands praying on a big rock while the disciples nap. He is sitting around a table, after a meal and an extended conversation, with the disciples hearing every single word that Jesus says. This aspect alone of Jesus' prayer may be all a preacher needs to get a sermon started. What difference does it make to overhear Jesus praying for us? How might we hear Jesus' words differently because we are able to hear them for ourselves? How might we understand prayer in a new way? It really is nothing short of astonishing to envisage this passage as a model for prayer. In the Gospel of John there is no request "Teach us how to pray," followed by the Lord's Prayer. We might imagine that this is the Lord's Prayer according to John. Prayer is seemingly scarce in the Gospel of John, especially compared to the role of prayer in the Gospel of Luke. The relationship with Jesus and the Father is so immediate that prayer seems somewhat superfluous. This is not the same thing as saying prayer is not important. It is to say, however, that this Gospel chooses to present the relationship with God and Jesus in such a way that prayer is not necessarily indicative of its intimacy. To make this claim, therefore, may suggest that that is exactly what prayer is, intimacy with God. Because Jesus knows God, is God, that intimacy is embodied more than it is demonstrated in the act of prayer. Moreover, it also suggests that prayer is more for the disciples than it is for Jesus, and how very true this frequently is of our own prayers to God. For preaching, this demands an intentional rigor on the part of the preacher not to fall back into surface claims about why we should pray, when we should pray, or that prayer is good for us, so do it. Nobody wants to hear a sermon about the blanket benefits of prayer. Instead, preach the specificity of *this* prayer, why it happens when it does, what it assumes, and who gets to hear it. Then maybe prayer will get a new lease on life. To gain a sense of the fullness of the prayer, the commentary that follows addresses the entirety the prayer, without delineating sections on which to comment. Essential for preaching on Jesus' prayer for his disciples in the Gospel of John is to go through it as the disciples would have experienced it. Reading and interpreting its totality might create for the preacher, and for our listeners, the same feeling of those first disciples—the incredible emotion of overhearing Jesus pray *for you.*

It is not often that we get a straightforward definition of eternal life, but here it is in Jesus' prayer, "And this is eternal life, that they may know you, the only true God, and Jesus Christ whom you have sent" (17:3). How many times have we heard this depiction of eternal life? Eternal life is to know God and Jesus. What if it is that simple? How would that change what we imagine in this life? How would it affect our thoughts about and beliefs in our future life with God? How does this alter even our picture of God? Of course, what it means to "know" God is key, and to know God in the Fourth Gospel has no connection to cognitive constructions, creedal consents, or specified knowledge about God. Rather, knowing God is synonymous with being in a relationship with God. The preacher is invited to use the entirety of John's Gospel to paint a picture of what being in a relationship with God looks like. In fact, the depiction should be multifaceted and multi-sensorial, especially given the narrative of Jesus' ministry up to this point and the fourth evangelist's theological center, the incarnation. Be specific. Use the details of the stories. Do not offer bland or general statements. The incarnation demands specificity and sensoria. At the end, the people in the pew should be able to feel, actually feel, what a relationship with God means. Let them taste it, smell it, hear it, see it. Anything less and the reality of relationship is reduced to mere acquaintance.

In the next verses, 17:6-10, the disciples hear a summary of who Jesus is and what Jesus came to do. John 1:18 rests behind these words, particularly that Jesus has made God known. Jesus has made God's name known as "I AM." Here, every single "I AM" statement can be recalled. Jesus has made God's name known in each of the "I AM" statements, both those with the predicate nominative and the absolute "I AM" statements. With the predicate nominative "I AM" claims, God is made known by that to which the "I AM is connected. With the absolute "I AM" statements God's very presence is made known and in very specific situations such as the Samaritan woman at the well. Jesus affirms what the disciples know and what they have done, which the disciples are allowed to overhear. While much of what Jesus says in verses 7-8 is restating what has already been said, the new context, in a prayer from Jesus to God, changes how these words should be heard. This is no longer Jesus telling the disciples what they know and what they have done. Jesus is telling his Father. Jesus is giving witness to the disciples, testifying about them to God. Imagine the disciples' possible reactions to this moment in the prayer, to hear both the promise of what you know and what you have done on behalf of Jesus in the world, but now to hear Jesus telling God all about it.

What Jesus is asking of the Father is made clear in the next two sections of the prayer. Jesus will ask the Father to protect the disciples (17:11-16) and to sanctify them (17:17-19). Jesus asks that the disciples be protected in the name of the Father, the power and presence of "I AM," and in that protection they will have unity. What is important about unity, that they will be one, here and now? Jesus has already talked about the possibility of their being scattered (16:32). They will testify on Jesus' behalf and be thrown out of their synagogues. To be one is what will give them community and identity. These verses in the prayer draw especially on the image of Jesus as door and shepherd in chapter 10. Protection because of the activity of the door and the shepherd makes possible the safety of the sheep in the fold as one flock (10:16). "Not one of them was lost" also resonates with the shepherd imagery, particularly when recalling the man born blind, thrown out, and then found by Jesus. Jesus will also show what this protection actually looks like in chapter 18. The disciples hear *about* protection in Jesus' prayer and then *are* protected during Jesus' arrest. In addition, Jesus will say again during the arrest scene, "This was to fulfill the word that he had spoken, 'I did not lose a single one of those whom you gave me'" (18:9). Jesus says these things so that his joy may be made complete in them. The verb is a perfect passive, that is, this has already happened, and the effects of the joy being made complete are ongoing in the present. Joy is a marked juxtaposition to the realities that the disciples face. Jesus recalls their discussion about joy in chapter 16 here. In verses 15-16, Jesus is clear that he is not asking the Father to remove them from the world. It is urgent that the disciples hear these words, because they will remain in the world and they will be sent into the world to testify to God's love for the world. Believing in Jesus is by no means escapism. Rather, as the last resurrection appearance will show, Jesus will rely on the disciples to be fully in the world when he is not. The prayer for protection from the evil one would remind the disciples that what happened to Judas can happen to any one of them. This connection made here anticipates the return of Judas in the next chapter. The disciples hear, however, that God will protect them and that protection comes from the intimate relationship they already have with God.

In John 17:17-19 there is a call to sanctification. The idea of being sanctified brought in at this point in the prayer, and in the Gospel, may seem odd until we remember that Jesus himself was sanctified by the Father, "Can you say that the one whom the Father has sanctified and sent into the world is blaspheming because I said, 'I am God's Son?'" (10:36), and that Jesus is himself holy (6:69). The disciples now overhear Jesus praying for them to be sanctified just as Jesus was, and they are reminded that it is a characteristic of who Jesus is. In addition, Jesus requests that they be sanctified "in truth" (17:19), that is, in him. To be sanctified has connotations of being set apart, dedicated, or consecrated. In this Gospel, it is directly connected to being sent into the world, for Jesus and now for the disciples. The language of sanctification surrounds Jesus' announcement, "As you have sent me into the world, so I have sent them into the world" (17:18). Sanctification is that which is essential to being sent into the world. Another way of imagining the meaning of sanctification in this context is that it is a synonym for protection.

In verse 20 Jesus prays now not only for his disciples but also for those new believers for whom the Gospel was also written (20:30-31), who are not yet of his fold (10:16), and whom God loves (3:16). That Jesus prays for believers yet to be suggests to the disciples that they are to do the same. This is not praying for unbelievers or for those to see the error of the ways and "come to Jesus." A careful reading of the text suggests otherwise, that this prayer is on behalf of those who "will believe in me through their word" (17:20). There will be believers because of the testimony of the disciples. They pray *for* these new believers and their new abundant life in Christ, not that they will come to believe. One critical aspect of this prayer is that those who do not yet believe are brought immediately into the prayer for those current believers, thereby reinforcing the unity of which Jesus speaks. The end goal is being one with the Father, relationship. These last verses of the prayer are the most clear and succinct statements about this unity in the entire Gospel which is especially consequential against the backdrop of a community that desperately needs to hear about unity and community. Their unity is not a made-up concept but is based on the unity between the Father and the Son. Answering the question of what this unity looks like gives us the definition of what unity is. For this Gospel, unity with God means making God known. It means being the "I AM" in the world. It means knowing that, in the midst of all that would seek to undermine that unity, you are at the bosom of the Father. These verses demand preaching on unity that is not generic or sensational aspirations of unity in the midst of diversity but that ground an image of unity in the Fourth Gospel itself.

The last verses of the prayer return the focus to the disciples. Jesus wishes that the disciples "may be with me where I am," which is how the Farewell Discourse began, Jesus preparing an abiding place for the disciples. While not the same syntactical construction as the other "I AM" statements in the Gospel, the "where I am" would certainly elicit resonances and reverberations with the purpose of the previous "I AM" statements. "Where I am," therefore, communicates not only Jesus' revelation of God in the absolute "I AM" statements, but also what Jesus provides in each of the predicate nominative "I AM" statements. Jesus wants them to see his glory, which they will witness in the crucifixion, resurrection, and ascension, but to know that they have already witnessed his glory in the incarnation. Verse 24 returns to the place where the Gospel began, in the beginning, before the world was created, before the "foundation" of the world. This is a reminder of where Jesus comes from but also a statement of where he is going, his return to the father. The disciples will witness the glory of the crucifixion and the resurrection, but the ascension is never narrated in the Gospel. Jesus therefore testifies to this moment of glory here, that he was loved by God in the beginning and it is to God that he must return. Verse 25 affirms once again that the disciples know that God sent Jesus, that Jesus comes from God and therefore must ascend to God. Verse 26 is a summary of Jesus' ministry, to make God's name known; and to make God's name known is to be the "I AM" in the world so as to create encounters that lead to an intimate relationship with God. Jesus will also continue to make God's name known. How will this be? This reference intimates the role of the Paraclete, the other Advocate, who will not only accompany the disciples as they are sent but will be breathed into them when they are sent (20:22). Calling to mind the Spirit here makes it possible to believe Jesus' final words in the prayer, "and I in them" (17:26). One final note about this last verse of Jesus' prayer is the mention of love, "so that the love with which you have loved me may be in them." Exploring the idea of how God loved Jesus will prevent nondescript sermons about love on this verse. How might we answer this question when the next chapter moves into the events of the passion? How has God loved Jesus up to this point? Answering these questions truthfully and with the whole of the Gospel in mind will perhaps be one's own experience of grace upon grace.

CONNECTIONS TO THE LECTIONARY

Jesus' prayer to the Father is spread out through all three lectionary years on the Seventh Sunday of Easter, 17:1-11; 17:6-19; and 17:20-26. It is worth considering that the entire seventeenth chapter of John is included in the Revised Common Lectionary and all on the final Sunday of the Easter season. As the seventh and last Sunday of Easter before the festival of Pentecost and the beginning of the long green season, Jesus' closing words, are more than a fitting finish. "And now I am no longer in the world, but they are in the world, and I am coming to you. Holy Father, protect them in your name that you have given me, so that they may be one, as we are one." What if this blessing was that which provided a theme for the entire season of Pentecost for your congregation? It is, perhaps, one of the most relevant and truthful definitions of what Pentecost is supposed to be for disciples of Christ. Jesus is no longer in the world. The incarnation is over. Jesus has been resurrected. He ascended to the Father from whence he came (1:1). But *we* are still in the world. Jesus' works are now in our hands (14:12), and Jesus is counting on us to be his presence in the wake of his absence (21:15-17). What if we imagined that the resurrection of Jesus was just the beginning and not the conclusion of the Gospel? That the promises of the resurrection are, in part, ours to fulfill? How would a life of discipleship, of witness, of love, between Pentecost and Advent, be different if we were to trust that Jesus meant what he said in 14:12, "Very truly, I tell you, the one who believes in me will also do the works that I do and, in fact, will do greater works than these, because I am going to the Father." *We* are in the world now, the world that God loves (3:16).

9

The Passion Narrative (John 18–19)

JOHN 18:1-13A
THE ARREST IN THE GARDEN

The passion narrative in the Fourth Gospel begins at 18:1, "After Jesus had spoken these words." As it turns out, "these words" refer to a lot of words, specifically, the entirety of the Farewell Discourse. Jesus and his disciples cross the Kidron Valley, the surprisingly small valley between the Mount of Olives and Jerusalem's west gate. John 18:1 is the only reference to the Kidron Valley in the entire New Testament. While it is true that the direct route to enter the city of Jerusalem from the Mount of Olives would be to cross the short valley of Kidron, we have noted throughout this commentary that geographical references are rarely, if ever, only about geography. Rather, they are freighted with theological meaning. In the Old Testament, the Kidron Valley is the place to which David fled from Absalom (2 Sam 15:23), and tradition describes it as the valley of judgment. John 18:1 signals that the narrative has shifted to Jesus' judgment and condemnation, but not Jesus' alone. Judgment will carry forward as a major theme for the passion narrative—judgment of Judas, of the world, the disciples, Peter, Pilate, and every bystander at Jesus' trial. Not one character will be spared examination when it comes to realizing who Jesus is in this particular moment in the story. Yet, as noted previously, this is not an act of judgment that comes from outside. This is not God's judgment on any of the characters at this point, but rather an individual brings judgment upon him- or herself in response to making sense of Jesus' arrest and crucifixion.

Jesus and his disciples enter a garden. While the commonplace knowledge of the location of Jesus' arrest is a garden, it is only the Gospel of John that provides this specific setting for Jesus' arrest. There will be no agony in the garden and there is no Garden of Gethsemane (cf. Matt. 26:36-56; Mark 14:32-51; Luke 22:39-53). Matthew and Mark locate Jesus' prayer and arrest in Gethsemane, Luke near the Mount of Olives. In John, Jesus and the disciples "enter" (NRSV) the garden, which is the second time in only two verses that a variation of *erchomai* is used. Jesus and his disciples "go out" of the place where they shared their last meal. They now "go into" another space of intimacy, a garden. This verb takes center stage in Jesus' arrest in the Gospel of John to indicate not only Jesus' action on behalf of the disciples, but also the location of disciples, believers, when it comes to Jesus' arrest.

Verse 2 narrates the return of Judas, who exited the story in 13:30. His reappearance in the narrative is first described in language of intimacy and relationship. Previous knowledge of Judas recalls the circumstances of his departure from the inner circle of disciples, and that personal relationship is what is highlighted before his actual act of betrayal. Judas's betrayal is noted in the past tense. His presence here and his stand with the soldiers to arrest Jesus are, in the end, not the moment of betrayal. That moment came in 13:30, when he went to the dark side, "going out" (*erchomai*), overcome by the forces of evil, the act of disbelief being that which removes us from relationship with Jesus. This distinction is critical to the events of the arrest because what causes Jesus' capture is Jesus himself and not Judas. The description of the location for this moment in the Gospel is also exceedingly intimate. Judas knows the place because he has often been there with Jesus and the other disciples. In other words, over the past three years, Jesus and his disciples frequented this garden. They talked. They wondered. A sermon on Jesus' arrest according to John should emphasize this intimacy, highlighted not only in the garden itself but the fact that this was a regular place of sharing and community between Jesus and his disciples. Furthermore, these details underscore the contrast between what Judas experienced before 13:30 and his situation at this point in the story. Judas knows to bring the enemy to this place because he has been here many times. If response to this moment is not filled with overwhelming sadness then the pathos has not been fully realized. The juxtaposition of this intimate location with what will occur next should elicit despair, grief, and sorrow. The contrast should be almost unbearable, that one so close to Jesus, as close as possible, would then be so far removed from Jesus.

In John, the only familiar or expected detail of the betrayal of Jesus by Judas comes in verse 3, that it is Judas who brings the arresting figures to Jesus' location. Most speculations about the number of persons present to arrest Jesus estimate somewhere between twenty-five and fifty, as a best and somewhat uninformed guess. For the Gospel of John, however, the number is clear. The term *cohort* depicts a Roman battalion approximating six hundred soldiers. The origin and the number are both significant. Present at the arrest of Jesus is the entire world, Romans and Jewish authorities. Theologically, it has been the world that will reject Jesus, and thus, at Jesus' arrest, the world is entirely represented. The number of soldiers underscores the power of the presence of Jesus that will manifest itself as the narrative unfolds. At the same time, not even the most formidable enemy on earth, Rome, and its militia, can defeat God (cf. 16:33), and, even when God makes the radical and unbelievable decision to become human.

The Roman soldiers, along with the police from the chief priests and the Pharisees, bring lanterns and torches and weapons. A number of English translations temper the arrival of the enemy by inserting commas, "lanterns, torches, and weapons," when the use of *kai* ("and") seeks to emphasize the presence and potency of the enemy. The use of *kai* in the Greek builds the suspense, "lanterns *and* torches *and* weapons"! The reference to lanterns and torches suggests a false light in contrast to the true light, Jesus, included in John's Gospel alone (cf. Matt. 26:47-56; Mark 14:43-51; Luke 22:47-53). The enemy brings fabricated light in a feeble attempt to overcome the true light. That weapons are assumed to have power over the presence of God in Jesus contributes to the irony of the scene. Six hundred soldiers with weapons are then virtually made powerless in Jesus' action to come out of the garden, his stepping forward of his own will as "I AM."

Jesus comes forward to initiate his own arrest. Any other act at this point would be counterintuitive to the Christology of the Gospel of John. The majority of translations interpret the impetus for Jesus' act as "knowing what will happen." While this translation is an adequate rendering of the Greek, and certainly captures the Christology of John of Jesus as God present and incarnated and all-knowing, the verb used plays again on the primary verb of the entire arrest scene of Jesus, *erchomai* ("to come"), literally, "knowing everything that was coming toward him." This verbal construction seeks to hold together the primary theological claim of this Gospel, that in Jesus, the human divinity and divine humanity are always present. Jesus *knows* what is coming and Jesus knows what is *coming*.

This knowledge propels Jesus to step out of the garden and face his enemy. Most translations render Jesus' action as "coming forward" but the verb here continues the verbal wordplay on *erchomai*—Jesus "comes out" of the garden. This location solidifies his act and his protection of the disciples. As noted in the commentary on chapter 10, this is Jesus being the gate, being the shepherd. He lays down his life for the sheep, here and now. Laying down his life is not isolated in the crucifixion. Rather, Jesus lays down his life, as both door and shepherd in this moment, coming out of the garden, the sheep pen, to face the thief, whom we already know as Judas (12:4; cf. 10:1, 8, 10), and the strangers, those who would threaten the sheep in any way. This is the instance where "I AM the door" gains its greater meaning. Jesus places himself between his disciples and those who have come to arrest him. He will not allow the hundreds of soldiers to enter the fold, to harm his sheep. He will not allow the thieves or bandits to enter the fold by some other way. No one enters the fold except through him.

His question, "Whom are you looking for?" recalls the calling of the disciples, when Jesus turns to those following him and asks, "What are you looking for?" (1:38). The difference here, of course, is the interrogative, who? And, in the end, this is the essential question for the Fourth Gospel, Whom are you looking for? Are you looking for God? If this is not the primary query, you will either experience non-recognition or you will come to a realization that this has been the wrong question all along. Who Jesus is, is the primary theological and christological claim at stake for the Fourth Gospel.

The response of the representatives standing outside the garden, who are both Roman and Jewish, is indicative of the theological issue at stake for the Fourth Gospel: "Jesus of Nazareth." Yes. And no. For the Gospel of John, Jesus is Jesus of Nazareth but Jesus is also from God. Jesus is the Word made flesh. As the world stands outside the garden to arrest Jesus, it is given one more chance to recognize who Jesus is. The answer of the world is a half-truth and in the end, not the right answer when it comes to Jesus' origin and identity.

The "I AM" statements in 18:5, 6, and 8 are the last "I AM" statements in the Gospel. They are absolute "I AM" statements, without a predicate nominative, and the pronoun "he" included in most English translations does not appear in the Greek text. As the last "I AM" statements in the narrative, every single previous "I AM" statement, absolute or with a predicate nominative, should be recalled and come into play when imagining the significance of this "I AM" at this moment. Theologically this final "I AM" statement bears the full weight of every "I AM" claim up to this point. This is especially true in view of the reaction of the detachment of soldiers to this particular "I AM" statement of Jesus. That they step back and fall to the ground is typical of a theophany (Ezek. 1:28; Dan. 10:9; Acts 9:3-4; Rev. 1:17). It is significant that this reaction to Jesus' revelation as "I AM" is recorded here and not earlier in the Gospel, as if all that Jesus has revealed himself to be is present here and now. The impact of Jesus' revelation in every single "I AM" statement is realized in this moment. No wonder a mass of 600 plus soldiers falls over. The reality of who Jesus is, 17 chapters later, has now reached its full theological weight.

Placed between these potent "I AM" statements is Judas, who stands not with Jesus or in the garden with Jesus' disciples but with the cohort to arrest Jesus. The reminder of the location of Judas as "with them" serves to emphasize just how far outside the fold he is, how much into the darkness he has gone. "With them" should be a detail that elicits an intermission, a need for serious reflection because it is the last time Judas will be mentioned in the Gospel of John. It is a detail that not only states where he is physically but also theologically. That Judas stands *with them* is his judgment. There will be no remorse, no suicide, no other acknowledgment of Judas's decision ever again (cf. Matt 27:3-5). This is the final verdict for Judas. The implications of this conclusion come devastatingly close to a sense of our own commitments and convictions when it comes to Jesus. If this can happen to Judas, one as close to Jesus as Judas was, then it can happen to any of us. The only reason we are given for Judas's disbelief is the presence and power of darkness, represented by Satan (13:27). There are no answers, at least no easy ones, for why some who encounter Jesus are not capable of belief. Preaching this aspect of Jesus' arrest in the Gospel of John continues to be an individual and communal question. For the audience of the Fourth Gospel, Judas also represents the community from which they were expelled. How is it that those they loved could not recognize what they saw in Jesus? It is a question for which there is no answer, only the cosmological claim that evil exists. Wrestling with this ever-present concern in the daily lives of our parishioners would give focus and direction to preaching on this passage.

Jesus asks the question again, "Whom are you looking for?" which draws the same answer from the crowd and from himself, "I told you that I AM". The repetition of the question and the answer underscores the importance of both. This is perhaps the central question and answer of the Gospel, and it is as much for the disciples to hear as it is for the soldiers and the police, especially at the moment when Jesus will be taken away. As the Good Shepherd, Jesus' essential concern is for his sheep. Jesus willingly hands over his own life so that the disciples remain safe, demonstrating the greater love of which he spoke in the Farewell Discourse, "No one has greater love than this, to lay down one's life for one's friends" (15:13). The verse to which Jesus refers in 18:9 has no direct referent in the Gospel and thereby evokes other possibilities of meaning than as a direct quotation. In many ways, "I did not lose a single one of those whom you gave me" functions as a summary of the Farewell Discourse as a whole, to fulfill the word that he had spoken. The entirety of the Farewell Discourse is Jesus saying to the disciples that they will not be alone, they will not be lost, they will not be orphaned, they will be protected. These promises are made true in Jesus' handing himself over, yet this first step in giving up his life for his friends calls to mind what lies beyond his death: his resurrection and ascension. All three events, the crucifixion, the resurrection, and the ascension assure us that what Jesus has said will be fulfilled.

Peter's act is usually explained by his impulsivity. Peter is hasty, as demonstrated by his response to the foot washing, his actions here, and his jump in the lake when he recognizes Jesus on the shore of the Sea of Galilee (21:7). Peter cannot help himself and frequently misreads the situation. In the larger context of the theological themes of the Fourth Gospel, however, there is more to making sense of Peter's behavior here than impetuousness. Peter's act foreshadows the nature of his denial of Jesus in the trial narrative. The very essence of discipleship is at stake. Before we judge Peter, we may want to acknowledge that we might very well respond in the same way. Why? In what do we hope and for what? What is it that we intend to accomplish? Peter's reaction cannot be dismissed as a character issue on his part. It has everything to do with our own reaction to the revelation of who Jesus is. Before we explain away Peter's actions with a particular character trait, we would do well to contemplate our own urges when we begin to recognize the end of the Word made flesh.

John's Gospel is the only one that provides the name of the slave whose ear is cut off, and there is no healing of the slave's ear as narrated by the Gospel of Luke (Luke 22:51). Providing the slave's name gives a certain veracity to the story, a concretizing of the event beyond its oral tradition. At the same time, it personalizes the incident and recalls the importance of names elsewhere in the Gospel (10:3; 11:43; and 20:16). Malchus is known and remembered, even though there will be nothing more about him in the Gospel with the exception of a passing reference in the story of Peter's denial (18:26). The purpose of the incident is to call attention to what discipleship means and to give opportunity for Jesus' response. Verse 11 should sound familiar yet somewhat out of place if the Synoptic Gospels are also in view. Jesus does not ask for the cup to be removed, as we find in the Synoptic Gospels (Matt. 26:42; Mark 14:36; Luke 22:42-44), but acknowledges the necessity of what lies ahead. A comparison of translations for verse 11 yields interesting contrasts as to the primary focus of the verse, whether "I/me" is that which receives emphasis, as in the NRSV, "Am I not to drink the cup that the Father has given me?" (18:11), or the cup, "the cup which the Father has given Me, shall I not drink it?" (18:11, New American Standard). The Greek syntax is better represented by the latter with the cup as the accentuated image. The prominence of the cup as the symbol of Jesus' death places the focus on the necessity of the crucifixion. For the Gospel of

John, this necessity is because of the reality and importance of the incarnation and not because Jesus must suffer. There is no "agony in the garden" for John, and Jesus' death is not salvific in and of itself. For John's portrait of Jesus, it makes no logical sense for any kind of questioning of suffering on Jesus' part, since Jesus is the "I AM" in the world. As a result, the cup is given prominence and not the experience of Jesus himself. This is not necessarily to dismiss what Jesus is experiencing, particularly Jesus as a human being, but rather intends to locate the attention on Jesus as Good Shepherd. At stake at this point in the narrative is Jesus' promises made in chapter 10. The arrest of Jesus demonstrates and fulfills what Jesus meant in his revelation, "I AM the door" and "I AM the good shepherd." Jesus is then bound and brought to Annas, the high priest.

JOHN 18:13B–19:16A
THE TRIAL NARRATIVES

Several features of the trial narrative in the Gospel of John are important to note at the start of commentary on this major section in John. First, the trial narrative in the Gospel of John is simultaneously that of Jesus and of Peter. Jesus is on trial before Pilate, but Peter's verdict is also hangs in the balance. Peter's denial is interspersed throughout Jesus' trial. As in the other three Gospels, distinctive themes presented throughout John's narrative are central to interpreting the trial narrative. For the Fourth Gospel, these will include the themes of witness, truth, and one's response to the revelation of God in a personal encounter with Jesus. Peter's denial will not be narrated in a succinct passage but will be interposed with Jesus' interrogation. The simultaneity of Jesus' and Peter's trials serves to emphasize the intimacy and mutuality of Jesus and his disciples. While Jesus does indeed endure his examination on his own, nevertheless Peter is still narratively present. This should clue us in that Peter's denial will be of a different nature in the Gospel of John.

JOHN 18:13B-18
JESUS AND PETER COME BEFORE THE "AUTHORITIES"

Jesus is first brought to Annas, the father-in-law of the high priest Caiaphas to whom we were introduced at the end of chapter 11. It was Caiaphas who suggested that Jesus be put to death (11:49-53). In other words, Annas has no official role in this trial. In fact, in John, Jesus' trial is before Pilate, who represents "the world" as the Roman procurator, and not before any Jewish authorities (Matt. 26:57-68; Mark 14:55-65; Luke 22:66—23:2). There is an immediate segue to Peter, who, with another disciple, follows Jesus. Peter's place and role in the trial narrative are therefore established from the very beginning, so that the dual focus on Jesus and Peter is brought into focus. For the Gospel of John, the trial narrative is better articulated as the trial narratives because of Peter's concurrent tribunal.

Peter and the other disciple *follow* Jesus as he is led to the interrogation by Annas, recalling the following of the shepherd by the sheep (10:4) and the following that is characteristic of discipleship outlined in chapter 1. Because the other disciple is one "known" to the high priest, he is allowed entry into the "courtyard" of the high priest, the same term as "sheepfold" in 10:1, 16, the only occurrences of this word in the Gospel. Peter is not allowed in the fold and is left to stand outside at the door. Verses 16-17 also mention the "woman who guarded the gate," which is the feminine form of the doorkeeper in the Shepherd discourse. In both cases (one masculine, one feminine), it is that person who guards the entrance. In both cases, this doorkeeper has moments of recognition: in the discourse in response to the healing of the blind man (10:3) he recognizes the shepherd; the maid recognizes Peter as one of the disciples, for indeed Peter has *followed* Jesus (18:15). In the position at the entry to the fold, the doorkeeper plays a part in creating the imagery for the understanding of relationship: being inside and outside, being in the fold, and the concepts of "knowing" and "recognition." The recurrence of the doorkeeper also complicates the search for a direct referent for the doorkeeper in 10:3. Her question to Peter prompts his negative "I am not," which he repeats in 18:25.

What follows is typically described as Peter's denial, which is assumed, because of John's Synoptic counterparts, to be a denial of Jesus. This is certainly true in Matthew, Mark, and Luke where Peter is asked whether he "knows" Jesus. Peter's response is that he does not know the man (Matt. 26:69-75; Mark 14:66-72; Luke 22:54-62). In the Gospel of John, however, Peter's denial is not of Jesus but of his own discipleship. Peter's response to the woman, "I am not," should make a connection to Jesus' "I AM" statements in the Gospel. To deny discipleship is to deny one's relationship with Jesus and the intimacy that makes Jesus and his followers virtually inseparable. Peter does not deny Jesus, but denies being a disciple. The setting provided in 18:18 further emphasizes the fact that Peter's trial is not necessarily about his loyalty to Jesus, but rather it has to do with his identity as disciple. The charcoal fire foreshadows the charcoal fire on the shore of the Sea of Galilee in chapter 21, where Jesus and the disciples have breakfast and around which Jesus and Peter will have a conversation about what discipleship really means. Rereading Peter's denial in the trial narrative through the perspective of the dialogue between Peter and Jesus in chapter 21 raises the stakes of what discipleship means for this Gospel. While Peter has yet to learn what fully constitutes discipleship, his denial of that identity here signals its complexity and magnitude. Peter has no idea what discipleship will demand. There is no "take up your cross" in John, but you will be hated, put out of the synagogue. An interpretation of Peter's denial from the viewpoint of the fourth resurrection appearance suggests that what it means to be a disciple merits consideration, hesitation, and may very well occasion flat out rejection of being a disciple.

JOHN 18:19-24
JESUS BEFORE THE HIGH PRIEST

Verse 19 reiterates that Jesus' trial is about more than his acts of ministry. Jesus is first questioned about his disciples, just as Peter himself is questioned about his discipleship. Jesus' answer to interrogation about his disciples reveals what it means to be a disciple. A primary mark of discipleship is listening, hearing Jesus' words and recognizing Jesus' voice. "They know what I said" is a critical sentence. To know what Jesus has said, particularly at this juncture, is to know so much, to have heard so much, and it is synonymous with having a relationship with Jesus. Verses 23-24 are about right and wrong speech. What is the offense? Jesus is then sent to Caiaphas. We have a sense of how this will go, given the pronouncement of Caiaphas in chapter 11.

JOHN 18:25-27
THE INTERROGATION OF PETER, PART 2

In 18:25 the scene switches back to Peter, who is warming himself at the charcoal fire. Again Peter is questioned about his discipleship, to which he offers the same response as before, "I am not." Verse 26 articulates the pathos of this moment for Peter and for every listener and reader of this Gospel. The verse takes us back to the garden, reminding us of everything that the garden conveys. Even Peter's act in the garden is recalled. To refer back to the garden at this point calls attention to where Peter must now locate himself. Is he a disciple or not? His third response is a decided "no." He was not in the garden. To say that he was not in the garden is an additional denial of his identity as disciple. To be in the garden with Jesus communicates discipleship, relationship, and the intimacy that Jesus expressed in the Farewell Discourse, all of which Peter denies in this moment.

JOHN 18:28-19:16A
JESUS' TRIAL BEFORE PILATE

Verse 28 returns to Jesus' trial, and in particular, his trial before Pilate. The demarcation of the trial narrative before Pilate is typically 18:28—19:16a, with most scholars adopting an organizational structure for this section of text much like chapter 9, as a drama in seven scenes (18:28-32; 18:33-38a; 18:38b-40; 19:1-3; 19:4-8; 19:8-11; 19:12-16), and on two stages (outside/inside). "Preaching" this text as it occurs on Good Friday would create a means by which this "drama" might be viewed and thus the text would preach itself. Jesus is taken from Caiaphas to Pilate, early in the morning. The first conversation between Pilate and the Jewish leaders focuses on the charge against Jesus and who should really be handling his trial. The Jewish leaders state only that Jesus is a criminal, guilty of a crime that they do not name, and that Jesus should be put to death.

Scene 2 (18:33-38a) narrates the first conversation between Pilate and Jesus, which centers on the identity of Jesus as king and the actual charge against Jesus. Pilate's question comes as a surprise (18:33). Why would his first question to Jesus be "Are you the king of the Jews?" The pairing of "listening" and "voice" in Jesus' interaction with Pilate in verse 37 recalls the Shepherd discourse as the only other place in the Gospel that these two words are found together. Listening to Jesus' voice is representative of being in relationship with Jesus, but by the end of his encounter with Jesus, Pilate does not hear Jesus, but hears the Jewish leaders (19:15-16). Pilate's question, "What is truth?," is one of the most critical moments in the entire Gospel. Of course, the question for this Gospel is not "what" is truth? but "who" is truth? This is what Pilate is unable see. We know that Jesus is the truth, "I am the way, the truth, and the life." The irony here is the prominent discussion of the concept of truth in the midst of a trial.

The third scene (18:38b-40) is marked by Pilate's exit from his headquarters to confer a second time with the Jewish leaders (18:38b) because he finds no compelling case for why Jesus should be sentenced to death. That Barabbas is described as a "bandit" in 18:40 recalls the Shepherd discourse (10:1, 8), the only other time this term "bandit" is used in the Gospel. Pilate does not give the Jewish leaders a choice of Jesus *or* Barabbas, because there is only one Good Shepherd. The Jewish leaders come up with Barabbas all on their own, choosing the robber, the one outside the fold who tries to get in by some other way, over the Good Shepherd.

The fourth scene in the trial narrative (19:1-3) emphasizes Jesus as king. When comparing the versions of the Passion Narratives in the four Gospels, the Gospel of John locates the presentation of Jesus as king of the Jews most densely in the trial narrative itself and not during the crucifixion. Reflection on the theological implications of this difference on the part of the fourth evangelist would suggest that there is something critical about connecting Jesus' kingship with the events of the trial or even the nature of the trial in general. Part of what is at issue in the trial narrative for the Fourth Gospel is its resonances with the theme of judgment presented in this Gospel. The encounter with Nicodemus and Jesus' response to Nicodemus's confusion and misunderstanding first develop the meaning of judgment in the Fourth Gospel. Judgment in the Gospel of John is that which individuals bring upon themselves as a result of their reaction to Jesus' revelation. God does not judge or condemn and neither does Jesus. Rather, judgment is the result of a lack of recognition of who Jesus is. Judgment also finds expression in the related theme of witness or testifying in the Gospel. The trial narrative for the Gospel of John functions as a summary of these themes in the Gospel, centralizing the concepts of judgment and witness in this critical moment for Jesus, the disciples, the Jewish leaders, Pilate, and for all who "witness" the last "event" of the incarnation. Everyone is on trial and in jeopardy of recognizing who Jesus is.

A related probe of inquiry might ask why the presentation of Jesus as king is not predominantly present in the crucifixion according to John. Theologically, to present Jesus as king in the moment of the crucifixion makes little sense in the mind of the fourth evangelist. Jesus as king is an incarnational reality and not justified by his death. Moreover, Jesus' kingship cannot rely on the crucifixion for validation. Jesus is king because he is the presence of God in the world. To argue for the reign of Christ because of the cross makes little sense for John. The reign of Christ, Jesus as king, should have been known and realized from 1:1.

The fifth scene (19:4–8) has Pilate again convening with the Jewish leaders about the actual charge being brought against Jesus. His words, "Look, I am bringing him out to you to let you know that I find no case against him" are directed to every hearer of this Gospel. Pilate's words restate the meaning and moment of judgment in the Fourth Gospel. Pilate's back-and-forth between consultation with the Jewish leaders and his own interrogation of Jesus has less to do with his own vacillation about Jesus than with calling attention to the exact nature of what judgment means at this point in the narrative. Furthermore, more than likely, Pilate is more interested in saving his own reputation before Rome. All persons present in this particular point in the story will be asked to make a decision, to make a choice as to what they are willing to claim about Jesus. In this scene, Pilate brings Jesus out for display and again asks the Jewish authorities for the charge that they have against Jesus. The juxtaposition of Pilate's introduction of Jesus, "Here is the man," and the revelation of the indictment, that Jesus has claimed to be the Son of God again points to one of the essential themes of the Gospel of John, that in Jesus the human and divine are fully present. The irony here, of course, is that Jesus is both human and divine, not one or the other. The reason for Pilate's fear is very well a dawning realization of what he will ask Jesus in the next scene: Where is Jesus from? What is the origin or source of his power?

In scene 6 (19:8-11) Pilate returns to his headquarters and asks Jesus one of the central questions of the Gospel, where Jesus comes from, his origin. This is, in fact, the opening question introduced in the Gospel, in the very first sentence of the Prologue, "In the beginning was the Word." Pilate's concern for the origin of Jesus' power is exactly the question at stake. Pilate, in the end, has no power compared to the origin of Jesus' power. That Pilate raises the issue of power indicates his concern and intimates the reason for his fear. It is Pilate's very power that is on the line and how that power will be perceived. Pilate's anxiety about his perceived power recalls that same alarm of the authorities 11:48 (cf. 12:48). Pilate is yet another example of how those in power are threatened by Jesus' power. The irony, of course, is a complete ignorance of the precise power Jesus has.

Jesus' response to Pilate provides the specificity toward which the narrative has been moving and for which we have been waiting. Jesus' power comes from above. The Greek term here *anōthen* is the same as in chapter 3: "unless you are born again, from above, anew." The use of the term here again in the trial narrative connects the trial narrative and chapter 3, thereby emphasizing the themes of judgment and witness. Jesus' statement that the one who handed him over to Pilate is guilty of the greater sin seems to refer to Judas, but the meaning of greater sin for Pilate is certainly at stake for Pilate and any who are witnesses of this trial. The mention of sin here calls attention to what is really at risk, and what, in the end, matters for Jesus' trial. It is not Jesus who is on trial. It is those who sit in the audience or the witness stands. Jesus knows the results of his court case, but do we know ours? The response of the witnesses present, but more so those for whom the Gospel is written and now who hear its truth, is on the line. That Peter has already been on the witness stand means that everyone who hears this Gospel will end up there as well. The trial narratives are exactly this—that of Jesus, but in the end, and more importantly so, the trial of every potential believer.

The last scene (19:12-16) in the trial narrative according to John is a poignant glimpse into the political and religious realities of occupied Palestine in the first century. Pilate keeps trying to release Jesus, but the Jewish leadership ups the ante for Pilate with reference to the emperor. To call attention to the emperor, that Jesus' very presence is a threat, not only to Pilate's power but to that of the Roman emperor, is at the same time politically true yet theologically false. There is pretext to Pilate's political standing. If word got back to Rome about this, Pilate's own political future is in danger. In one final act of mockery, Jesus is placed on the judgment seat with Pilate's announcement, "Here is your king." Pilate's words are a haunting recollection of the witness of John the Baptist, using the same word in Greek "here, look, behold." Literally, Pilate says, "Here, your king" which has a very different intonation than that which includes "is." The reminder that this is the Day of Preparation for Passover calls attention to the difference in chronology for Jesus' death in John from that of the Synoptic Gospels. Jesus will die on the Day of Preparation, at the same time that the Passover lambs will be slaughtered for the festival. Pilate's final jeer of the trial, "Shall I crucify your king?," pushes the Jewish leaders to utter perhaps the most devastating testimony in the entire Gospel, "We have no king but the emperor." Tragically, their declaration stands as opposite of the true confession urged by the Gospel of John, that Jesus is king, but actually God. In Jesus, God has even reevaluated kingship. God's people do not need a new king—they need God.

Of course, how Pilate's question is voiced determines its interpretation. To view Pilate as on the fence in these proceedings will communicate a sincerity in Pilate's query, as if Pilate is really torn as to what to do. In the end, Pilate represents the world, and the Gospel has already communicated to us that the world stands against God. A different tone, one of sarcasm or parody, would indicate a significant truth of this entire episode, that there is no reason to imagine in what sense Pilate would find himself wondering whether or not he believes in Jesus. Rather, Pilate functions to bring out the shattering claim of the Jews. This is as much a commentary by the fourth evangelist on the community that rejected the audience to whom he writes. The inside/outside motif is less about Pilate's waffling decision than about firmly situating the Jewish leaders on the outside of the presence of God, outside of the sheep pen, outside of the fold, deeply and decidedly in the darkness, in sin. The final verdict, or judgment, for the Jewish leaders they end up bringing upon themselves. Their words are not only a rejection of Jesus but simultaneously a rejection of God. Their descent into the dark side is complete, with God pushed away as far as possible. What we find in the trial narrative of Jesus in the Gospel of John is that everyone is on trial in this moment: Jesus, Peter, the disciples, the Jewish leaders, Pilate, and with the presence of the power of Rome, the world itself.

John 19:16b-42
The Crucifixion of Jesus

One of the striking features of the story of Jesus recorded in the four Gospels is the remarkable similarity between the passion narratives irrespective of each Gospel's unique inclusions. This cohesiveness at this point in Jesus' ministry demonstrates the extent to which it was necessary to make sense of this unexpected outcome of Jesus' presence on earth. As a result, consideration of the distinctiveness of each Gospel's account of Jesus' passion reveals that there was no uniform interpretation of the crucifixion. Such differences demand preaching the meaning of Jesus' death that invites one's own entry into theological interpretation of the meaning of the crucifixion. Too often our preaching offers answers rather than inviting questions and contemplation. In the case of the crucifixion, to create a sense of exploration of its multiple meanings rather than to provide absolutes about atonement theory might make for a Holy Week experience that will have an effect on belief after Easter. In the commentary that follows, focused attention will be given to those features in the crucifixion narrative unique to the Gospel of John and to the significance of such features for preaching the Fourth Gospel and for a life of faith.

John 19:16b-25a
Jesus Is Crucified

The first difference between John and the Synoptic Gospels in the passion narrative comes immediately, that Jesus carries his own cross. There is no Simon of Cyrene compelled to assist a Jesus too weak from flogging by carrying the crossbar to the crucifixion site. The passion narrative in the Gospel of John will present a Jesus who is in total control. Jesus is crucified between the two criminals. The inscription on the sign above Jesus' head (19:20) represents the entirety of the world (cf. Matt 27:37). The comparable wealth of detail given about the sign points to two major themes in the Gospel, the reaction of the Jews and the object of God's love, the world. The fact that many of the Jews would read the description intimates the focus in this Gospel on "coming to believe" (20:31). The three languages represent the whole of the world at that time, emphasizing that the entirety of Jesus' ministry is directed to the world that God loves. Verse 21 reiterates the response of the Jewish leaders to Jesus' kingship, mincing grammar so as not to give Jesus the title "King of the Jews." Important to note in this first section of the crucifixion account in John is how briefly the event itself is narrated, "when the soldiers had crucified Jesus" (19:23). In the overall context of the Fourth Gospel, the brevity with which Jesus' crucifixion is described is like that of Jesus' signs. This suggests, of course, that the sign, the crucifixion itself, is not the primary focus but what happens around it, the details and the dialogue.

JOHN 19:26B-30
JESUS' LAST WORDS

The scene at the foot of the cross between Jesus, his mother, his mother's sister, and the Beloved Disciple introduces the first "last word" in the Gospel of John. Three of the seven last words attributed to Jesus on the cross during the crucifixion are from John's Gospel, and each one functions as a summation of a number of themes present throughout the narrative. As discussed in the commentary on chapter 2, the only other time the mother of Jesus appears in the Gospel of John besides the wedding at Cana is at Jesus' death. The mother of Jesus brackets the life of Jesus, underscoring his humanity and the need for her presence. Without Jesus, she would be alone, so that Jesus makes sure she is cared for by the disciple whom he loves. Without her, Jesus would be alone. He will not cry to his father from the cross. But he will need his mother, who has been there for him and with him, abiding with him, since the first sign. Some commentaries advise that in this moment, the fourth evangelist is imagining new paradigms for what it means to be family. In such an interpretation, the family would represent the community for whom this Gospel was written, a community that has lost its immediate family because of choosing to follow Jesus. Another avenue for preaching the presence of the mother of Jesus and the disciple whom he loved together at the foot of the cross presents an image of mutual care. The mutual care between Jesus' mother and the Beloved Disciple models the relationship between God and Jesus, between us and Jesus, between the believer and God. The mother of Jesus and the Beloved Disciple display the relationship that Jesus has described throughout the Gospel. She is not only representative of a new family but takes on the significant role of parent, as God is Father to Jesus. She is the parental figure during Jesus' ministry, a shared parenthood with God. It is the nurture of a mother, being at the bosom of a mother that provides the primary image of intimacy on which the rest of the Gospel draws to describe the relationship between Jesus and God, Jesus and the believer, God and the believer. While the implication of a new family unit made possible at the foot of the cross is certainly a meaningful way to understand the presence of Jesus' mother here and now, so also is the way in which the mother of Jesus is an essential figure for revealing the closeness of relationship Jesus has reiterated throughout the Gospel.

At the same time, the Beloved Disciple also models the reciprocity of discipleship assumed in the Gospel of John. There he is, at the moment of Jesus' death when his first moment with Jesus was at Jesus' bosom. Like Jesus' mother, his presence signifies that discipleship is first and foremost about abiding, about relationship. To that end, it is the mother of Jesus that provides the elemental portrait of what abiding looks like. In other words, the mother of Jesus is the Gospel's embodiment of what abiding means and looks like. It is about being there. Really being there, showing up, abiding, being in relationship, at the beginning and at the end of life. Anything short of that presence is theologically insufficient for the Gospel of John.

The second word from the cross in the Gospel of John initiates the offer to Jesus of something to drink, unlike in Matthew, Mark, and Luke (Matt. 27:48; Mark 15:36; Luke 23:36), where the offer comes to Jesus first. "I thirst," is another illustration of the Jesus who is in control of even this last day, this last moment, of his earthly life. As Jesus has revealed himself to be the living water and provides water it would make no sense for him to wait to be extended something to drink. At the same time, it is also an acknowledgment of his humanity. Jesus utters a basic human need yet one also that he is able to fulfill. In this simple request for a drink, this Gospel holds together theologically Jesus' humanity and Jesus' divinity. The reason for Jesus' request is also prompted by his awareness that the events of the hour are coming to completion. "When Jesus knew that all was now finished" (19:28) foreshadows the final word from Jesus in 19:30, "It is finished." The verb used here *teleō* has the sense of everything being brought to its intended goal, or that everything has been completed. It is not finished in the sense of coming to an end, but that the end point, the *telos*, has been reached. Consequently, the "it" in "it is finished" demands translation or interpretation. To what is Jesus referring in this statement? Said from the cross, "it" in this context, is the incarnation, Jesus' earthly ministry. That it alludes to the totality of Jesus' purpose as making God known is premature because the resurrection and the ascension have yet to occur. The sum of the theological event in the Gospel of John includes all four aspects of Jesus as the Word made flesh: incarnation, crucifixion, resurrection, and ascension. At this point, it is the incarnation that has arrived at its expected completion. Jesus "hands over" his spirit, the same verb that is used to describe the action of Judas. The Good Shepherd lays down his own life. No one takes it from him (10:18).

JOHN 19:31-37
BETWEEN DEATH AND BURIAL

The period between Jesus' actual death and his burial is curiously long compared to the Synoptic Gospels and is full of symbolism that draws on many of the themes presented already in John. We are reminded again of the timing of Jesus' death, on the Day of Preparation for Passover. Breaking the legs of the crucified would accelerate death, as the body would no longer be able to hold itself up, collapsing into asphyxiation. The soldiers break the legs of the criminals crucified with Jesus, but they find Jesus already dead. This was to fulfill Scripture, "None of his bones shall be broken." This detail calls to mind that Jesus is the Lamb of God who takes away the sin of the world (1:35). Directions for the Passover meal instructed that for the lamb, "you shall not break any of its bones" (Exod. 12:46). That Jesus is already dead and that the soldiers do not need to break his legs also confirm that Jesus has been in control of his own death.

In piercing Jesus' side Scripture is fulfilled again, this time Zechariah 12:10, "when they look on the one whom they have pierced, they shall mourn for him, as one mourns for an only child, and weep bitterly over him, as one weeps over a firstborn." The allusions to Jesus as the firstborn of God as well as the witness of the evangelist (19:35) highlight the human pathos of the scene. The blood and water that come out of Jesus' side recall the encounter with Nicodemus and rebirth (9:5), the Bread of Life discourse (6:53-56), and that Jesus is the source of living water (4:10; 7:37-38). Even in his death, Jesus gives life and provides life. The end of the incarnation cannot bring to an end grace upon grace. These verses between Jesus' death and burial anticipate the signs of abundance that will be witnessed in the resurrection appearances. The resurrection and the ascension have yet to come.

JOHN 19:38-42
THE BURIAL OF JESUS

Two persons are charged with tending Jesus' body and his burial, Joseph of Arimathea and Nicodemus. The former is a secret disciple for fear of the Jews, recalling the response of the parents of the man born blind to the questioning of the Pharisees and the reason the disciples are locked up after Jesus' crucifixion. Joseph of Arimathea has every right to be afraid, given what we have already been told about what happens to persons who are found to believe in or follow Jesus. This is Joseph of Arimathea's only appearance in the Gospel of John, here to care for Jesus' body and secure his burial, but it is clearly a tradition of which all four Gospel writers were aware since it is this character who is charged with the burial of Jesus in all four accounts (Matt. 27:57; Mark 15:43; Luke 23:50-52). Only the fourth evangelist describes him as a secret disciple who feared the Jews. This detail functions to underscore the plight of the Johannine community and foreshadows the next appearance of the disciples, behind locked doors for fear of the Jewish leaders. Moreover, only the Gospel of John pairs Joseph of Arimathea with Nicodemus in the burial of Jesus. As discussed in chapter 3, this is the third appearance of Nicodemus in the Gospel. There are three details that contribute to how we might resolve the character of Nicodemus and whether or not he ends up coming to believe in Jesus at his third occurrence in the narrative. First, Nicodemus is with Joseph. While it seems that Joseph is a disciple, he nonetheless is not the kind of disciple that this Gospel demands. It is not enough to be a believer, because a significant aspect of believing in Jesus is being a witness. Witnessing, by definition, requires a public act, a public accounting of one's beliefs, whether by invitation, like the Samaritan woman at the well, or by open confession, such as the man blind from birth, or Thomas. Metaphorically, to be a disciple means to be in the light, to be seen. Nicodemus is associated with a secret, fearful disciple which recalls the way in which Nicodemus first approached Jesus, by night.

Second, we are then prompted that Nicodemus came to Jesus by night. To repeat this detail would not be necessary unless darkness and that which it symbolizes were not essential both for interpreting Nicodemus's character and this scene. Burying Jesus does not automatically vindicate Nicodemus or validate his belief. He remains an ambiguous figure at best, which is really not an option for discipleship in the Gospel of John. Third, the amount of spices, myrrh, and aloes—seventy-five Roman pounds—that Nicodemus brings with him is enough to bury approximately seventy-five bodies. Even if Nicodemus is aware of Jesus' promises of the resurrection and Jesus' interpretation of the raising of Lazarus, his actions suggest that he has no real belief in Jesus as the resurrection and the life. At the same time, however, while the amount of spices seems to indicate the absolute veracity of Jesus' death, it also alludes to abundance, so that Nicodemus's actions here are comparable to Mary's act of excess in chapter 12

Even though the motives and meanings behind the behaviors of Joseph and Nicodemus are not easily determined, there is a poignancy to this scene that is deserving of notice. The devotion of these two clandestine disciples does indeed demonstrate love and abundance, much like Jesus' anointing by Mary (12:1-11). It may even be the fourth evangelist's way of communicating to the community for which this Gospel was written that abundance can still be received and displayed in the secrecy of their own fear. There is an extravagance that invites multiple levels of meaning. The great care for Jesus, particularly his body, and an intentional consideration of his body calls attention to the importance of the incarnation. That there are two persons tending to Jesus' burial emphasizes both the presence of the incarnation and its end. There is a sense that this is a real body, needing burial, which necessitates the same provisions as any other death. It may seem odd that the burial of Jesus serves to emphasize his death, but theologically this is critical. The function of Jesus' death is primarily to bring the expected end of the incarnation. To assign any other meaning to the crucifixion of Jesus would call into question the theological meaning of the incarnation. The incarnation is undermined if Jesus' death and burial were less than what is inevitable when it comes to the reality of being human.

The setting for Jesus' burial tomb is unique to the Gospel of John, a garden (19:41), which was the scene of Jesus' arrest and now will be the setting for the first resurrection appearance to Mary. This setting, of course, explains why Mary presumes, at first, that Jesus is the gardener. A garden is the setting for the arrest, crucifixion, burial, and resurrection of Jesus, thereby uniting all four of these events. The setting of the garden for the resurrection and its implications of new life, protection, and new creation are then applicable for what the garden means for Jesus' death and burial, that in death there is life. The garden and its presumptions of new creation stand in contrast to both Jesus' death and his burial. While death and life, incarnation and ascension, humanity and divinity are held tightly together, the conquering of life is made true by the promise of 1:5, "The light shines in the darkness, and the darkness did not overcome it." That it is a tomb in which no one has ever been laid has two narrative implications, the sense of newness, of new creation, and that Jesus' stature is worthy of such an honor. The latter points to his kingship highlighted in the trial, but also, clearly, his identity as the "I AM" in the world.

Verse 42 reiterates the chronology of the Fourth Gospel, that the death of Jesus happens on the Day of Preparation for Passover and not on the day of the festival itself thereby recalling the witness of John, "Behold the Lamb of God who takes away the sin of the world" (1:35). The death of Jesus is not the salvific sacrifice for sin but the expected end of the life of Jesus. Of course, to locate Jesus' death on the Day of Preparation for Passover most certainly has theological implications. While Jesus' death is the anticipated conclusion to his incarnation, to say that that alone provides meaning to the crucifixion would ignore the chronological shift made by the fourth evangelist. What are we to make of this alteration of time and the acknowledgment of incarnated time? John's particular witness to Jesus' presence must have theological significance.

Jesus is the Lamb of God and foreshadows the time of Jesus' death, unique to John. Is Jesus the sacrificial lamb? The atoning sacrifice? The blood exchange necessary for Passover? Yes. To argue otherwise is to dismiss the clear thoughtfulness of the fourth evangelist to record the death of Jesus in this way. That Jesus is the sacrificial lamb connected to Passover perhaps has less to do with the sacrifice per se than with the implications of whether or not the sacrifice happened. In other words, the origination of this festival has to do with God sparing God's people from the annihilation of their firstborn. That Jesus is the Lamb of God secures the promise of God's people, even beyond Abraham.

That is, to identify Jesus as the Lamb of God in this circumstance is not about the sacrifice required but indicates the promise that secures God's blessing to God's people. God promised Abraham that his blessings would be more numerous than the stars. For God to make good on that promise necessitates an imagination on God's part beyond the immediacy of Abraham. The Gospel writers get this, which is, in part, why Matthew traces Jesus back to Abraham, suggesting that God's Abrahamic promise extends into the presence of Jesus.

Theologically, this means that 1:12-13 and 10:16 are actually true. A central claim of the Fourth Gospel is the absolute assurance that to believe in God is to be a child of God. A less-articulated theological theme of the Passover is the importance of progeny. To be children of God is not just a nice thought, a guarantee, or a metaphor hoping to have an impact. Taking the theology of this Gospel seriously requires that there be a profound literalness in what it means to be a child of God. As such, the Passover meaning confirms this theological claim. In other words, that Passover marks the presence and protection of God, not in general but for the firstborn, suggests that Jesus as the Passover lamb is not only sacrifice but also emphatic of the centrality of the festival in this particularized location. Jesus as the lamb who was slain embodies the essence of Passover itself, never about atonement but having everything to do with God's promise and provision.

CONNECTIONS TO THE LECTIONARY

Selections from the passion narrative according to John occur at three different points in the lectionary. The entirety of John's passion is the designated Gospel lection for Good Friday in every year of the Revised Common Lectionary. That John's passion narrative is allowed a hearing only on Good Friday should be both problematic for the preacher but also inspired in that the Lectionary determines John's Passion Narrative as the primary lens through which to understand the events of Good Friday. A preacher might decide to use John's passion on Palm/Passion Sunday one year. The liturgical reality or irony is, of course, that what happens on Good Friday in our churches has very little to do with John's interpretation of the events. Many Good Friday services include all seven last words. Might we imagine that a truthful depiction of Jesus' last words from the cross, or a dedication to a unique Gospel voice, could cast Holy Week and Easter in a new and different light? Rather than preachers perpetuating the harmonization of the Gospels, particularly when it comes to Good Friday, might we take the church's clue to heart and preach John for all its worth this night? A preacher might focus on only the three last words according to John, or even one, and build an entire service around that one word that the Word made flesh spoke. Certainly there is a cultural, liturgical, and ecclesial commitment to what John decided to include. To take that seriously, and homiletically, is to invite thoughtful imagination about and attention to any preaching of this period in the history of Jesus. At the same time, imagination around and attention to how the different Gospels describe these last words of Jesus will be indicative of the meaning and function of the crucifixion.

In other words, the three last words of Jesus according to John need to be addressed on their own terms, with their own senses of meaning and their own contribution to our ongoing understanding of Jesus' salvific action for the sake of God in the world. It is rare in our liturgical rituals that we seem free to dream up a sermon and service that would preach, teach, and envisage only one word from the cross. To situate John's passion narrative as *the* text for every Good Friday service demands an intentionality as to how the specificity of John's presentation of Jesus' crucifixion helps us imagine the significance of Good Friday. This would include, then, the last three words of Jesus before his death and how they are both indicative of John's soteriology and representative of the church's wider and general expression of God's salvation. Anything less, as argued above, would reduce Jesus' death to a mere contemplation of that which is divine.

Two other portions of John's passion narrative occur in the lectionary. The first is 18:33–37 for Reign of Christ or Christ the King Sunday in Year B. Situating these verses within the larger context of John's passion narrative and the themes of the Gospel outlined in the commentary above would be essential for delving into how these verses inform and imagine this festival

Sunday. An understanding of Jesus as king, Jesus' kingdom, Jesus' reign are all better served by the particularity of a specific Gospel rather than general claims about Jesus' sovereignty. Broad claims about Jesus' rule or supremacy will only push the relevance of the Christian faith even further out than it already is. To unpack the reign of Christ according to John and its insistence on the humanity of Jesus might very well invite "new kingdom speak" for the sake of discipleship in the world God loves.

The second reading from John's passion narrative that occurs in the lectionary is Jesus' burial, John 19:38-42 as the alternate Gospel reading for Holy Saturday to Matthew 27:57-66 in all three lectionary years. The preacher, given the commentary above, would need to envisage where and when John's version of Jesus' burial might shape how to interpret, make sense of, and preach Jesus' burial. For the Fourth Gospel, that Nicodemus appears again at this point in the story mandates that the preacher have this appearance of Nicodemus in view when preaching his other appearances in the Gospel.

10

The Resurrection Appearances (John 20–21)

The resurrection appearances in the Fourth Gospel include four distinct stories, each unique in its presentation of how Jesus' resurrection matters for those who believe in him. One of the most interesting features of the resurrection stories in the Gospel of John is the focus on individual characters, Mary Magdalene, Thomas, and Peter. By specifying a single person around which the appearance revolves, John once again emphasizes the importance of the individual encounter with Jesus as central to believing who he is. The necessity of the singular encounter with Jesus recalls the first such meeting in the narrative, between Nicodemus and Jesus, as well as the individuality of the calling of the disciples in chapter 1. It is the means by which the fourth evangelist reiterates two theological themes that are intricately related to each other. To put each believer alone in the abiding presence of Jesus calls to mind the inimitability of the incarnation itself. The Prologue states that Jesus as the Word made flesh is this unique, or one and only, revelation of God in the world. This theological commitment, therefore, must address seriously the distinctiveness of each believer. God becoming human takes on all of the exceptionality and specificity of human expression. The incarnation, by definition, cannot be a generic concept of divine intention. The incarnation as a theological commitment demands that God know and experience the entire spectrum of what it means to be human.

The second theological theme reiterated in these individual encounters of the resurrected Jesus is that the revelation of God in Jesus means a simultaneous response to the revelation. As the story of Nicodemus exemplified, encountering God in Jesus is a moment of crisis. It is a moment of decision, of response, of recognition. God does not come into the world as Jesus for the sake of being human as some sort of theological experiment. God comes into the world as Jesus for the sake of relationship, and relationship necessitates reciprocity. As a result, the response of each of these individuals in the resurrection appearances should take a central focus. What they say and to what they are giving witness is indicative of the kind of reaction that a preacher would develop in the sermon.

John 20:1–18
Jesus and Mary:
The First Resurrection Appearance

The first appearance of the resurrected Jesus is to Mary Magdalene, yet the initial acknowledgment of the resurrection is not that Jesus has been raised but that the stone has been rolled away from the tomb. Mary comes to the tomb when it is still dark. The reference to the time of day again reinforces one of the major theological themes we have noted in the Gospel, light and darkness. That it is dark at the tomb indicates that full recognition and belief are yet to come; and, as for other encounters with Jesus in the Gospel, the woman at the well, the man blind from birth, there will be a progression of sight throughout this first resurrection story. Mary's conclusion to what she finds is peculiar. The text does not say that she ever actually looked into the tomb but only that she saw that the stone had been rolled away. She goes to Peter and the Beloved Disciple with the first announcement about the resurrection: not the claim of having seen the empty tomb but that the stone had been moved. Mary's inaccurate assumption, "They have taken the Lord out of the tomb, and we do not know where they have laid him" (20:2) succeeds in delaying the real truth that lies behind the stone having been rolled away. We should ask why Mary assumes a missing body. An emphasis on the location of or concern for Jesus' body also highlights the incarnation and the actual body of Jesus. Why not say to the disciples, the stone has been rolled away? Her report, however, succeeds in getting Peter and the disciple whom Jesus loved to the tomb. Preaching on this portion of the first resurrection appearance might explore our assumptions about resurrection and new life. How does what we see, or what we are willing to see, determine what we believe? What does the stone represent?

Like other passages in the Gospel such as the foot washing and the anointing of Jesus, this first discovery in the garden is narrated in real time, creating a sense of wonder and suspense. The disciples sound like two eager and excited little boys, racing to see who arrives first to the playground at recess. Verses 3–8 could easily be condensed into a brief summary of what they found. Instead, the experience is described step by step to delay the discovery but also to give witness to the very real and embodied sense of what this event would be like. The fourth evangelist is creating the same experience for the reader as that of Peter and the beloved disciple. The details about the linen wrappings recall the raising of Lazarus, but there is yet to be a connection between what happened to Lazarus and now what has happened to Jesus. They saw and believed but the fullness of that is not possible, in part because they have yet to offer testimony to what they have witnessed. In many respects, this episode foreshadows Thomas's and even Peter's individual encounters with Jesus. To believe in who Jesus is also requires acting on that belief, particularly in the form of being a witness. Peter and the Beloved Disciple return to their homes after the event at the tomb without saying a thing about what they saw. To be a true believer, a disciple, a follower of Jesus in the Fourth Gospel is to give witness to what you have experienced in encountering Jesus, not only for the sake of making it true for yourself but also for the sake of those who would hear and then have their own encounter with Jesus and believe (20:30-31).

As a result, the story returns to Mary, for we have yet to hear how she will respond. We find her back at the tomb, presumably having returned there after reporting to the disciples what she had seen. She is weeping. While not the same verb as that used for Jesus in 11:35, there is certainly a connection to the death of Lazarus. As discussed in chapter 7 on the raising of Lazarus, there are numerous parallels between the deaths of Lazarus and Jesus. Now here again, there is weeping over the loss of a friend. That Mary cries, weeping in her grief, also draws attention to the deep and intense manifestations of humanity that permeate this Gospel. For the incarnation to be taken seriously, being human must be taken seriously. When a friend dies, we cry. Mary's weeping is mentioned no fewer than four times in these four verses. The repetition has the function of emphasizing this important expression of the human response to death and also validates her reaction. Of course Mary should cry. The scene would suffer a strange and awkward void if her emotions were not given voice. Preaching this scene in the story would acknowledge and explore the levels of grief that would accompany this kind experience. We are painfully aware of our own stages of grief when it comes to loss in death. Mary has certainly mourned Jesus' death already. What do her tears represent now outside an empty tomb?

That Mary decides at this moment to look in the tomb and not before is interesting (20:11). What does she hope to see? What does she expect to see? The angels call attention to her weeping, asking her why she is doing so (20:13). Her answer for the angels is the same as her announcement to Peter and the Beloved Disciple, but with one striking difference, the switch from a first person plural confession to a first person singular testimony, "and I do not know where they have laid him (20:13). "*I* do not know!" The resurrected Jesus appears for the first time, to Mary. The witnesses to Jesus' central moments of revelation in the Gospel of John, the incarnation, the crucifixion, and the resurrection are women. Jesus' first absolute "I AM" is for the Samaritan woman at the well. At the moment of Jesus' death on the cross, there is Jesus' mother. Jesus' first revelation as having been raised from the dead is to Mary. The only witness to the ascension will be the Father.

Jesus asks Mary the same question that the angels inquired of her but now with an additional query, "Whom are you looking for?" This is the third time this question has appeared in the Gospel, every time asked by Jesus. They are his first words to the first disciples, with the only difference being "what" instead of "whom" (1:38). To ask this question of Mary here takes the reader back to the calling of the disciples and implies that Mary, too, is considered a disciple. Jesus poses the same question to the Roman soldiers and the Jewish police who come to arrest Jesus at the garden (18:4, 7). We are then reminded of the setting of this first resurrection appearance, that it is in a garden (19:42-43). Mary assumes that Jesus is the gardener because this is taking place in a garden. This setting is unique to John. As such, Jesus' arrest, crucifixion, burial, and resurrection all take place in a garden. All of what the garden has symbolized up to this point in the narrative should be brought to bear in this encounter, particularly its intimation of life. Preaching this first resurrection appearance to Mary should tend this setting carefully and deliberately.

To locate the crucifixion and burial of Jesus in a garden and the first resurrection appearance in a garden brings this Gospel full circle from its start. "In the beginning" situates this story of Jesus first outside the temporal constraints of the incarnation and at the same time alludes to the theological premises of the creation story in Genesis. Themes of creation, new creation, surround the presentation of abundant life in the Gospel of John. To preach the meaning of the resurrection against the background of the first chapters of Genesis extends our sense of what the resurrection can mean beyond eternal life or some heavenly reality beyond our death. Resurrection is nothing short of re-creation. We should ask in what sense this encounter with the resurrected Jesus will be a rebirth for Mary. That the burial and resurrection of Jesus take place in a garden underscores the Fourth Gospel's unrelenting commitment to holding the divine and the human together. Death is the reality of life, but resurrection points to the reality of abundant life. Furthermore, the sub-theme of the importance of relationship is intimated by this image of the garden. We are back in the Garden of Eden.

It is not until Jesus calls Mary by name that her recognition comes. Two passages in the Gospel must be brought to bear if one chooses to preach on this moment in this first resurrection appearance. The first is the Shepherd discourse (9:40—10:18), Jesus' interpretation of the healing of the blind man. As discussed in chapter 6, the image of Jesus as the Good Shepherd in John 10 is meant to explain or reiterate the significance of the restoration of sight to the man born blind. The blind man's first reaction to Jesus is hearing and not sight. The sheep know and recognize the voice of the shepherd and he calls them by name. Now here, in the garden, Jesus calls Mary by name and that is the precise instance of recognition. Mary is the first person to whom Jesus appears, and she is the first person to realize that it is him, the Good Shepherd, her shepherd.

The second episode that hovers in the background of this moment of Mary's recognition is the raising of Lazarus. Lazarus exits the tomb, and can only do so, when he is called by name, "Lazarus, come out." Responding to his name being called, Lazarus is brought to new and resurrected life with Jesus. The same is most certainly true for Mary. Her life will be made new, once again, in the presence and power of the resurrected Christ. Preaching would explore the specificity of the resurrection for Mary. What does it mean for her that is different from Lazarus? All too often our preaching on the resurrection stops short of particularity in favor of claims, and usually safe and uninteresting ones, about the resurrection in general. In Mary's resurrection moment, how might she begin to understand what it means *for her*? One clue to the importance of the resurrection for her is her response to Jesus. She calls him "Rabbouni," meaning teacher, the very same title given to Jesus by the first disciples (1:39). That she recognizes Jesus as teacher is simultaneously an acknowledgment about who Jesus is and a confirmation of her own identity. She is a follower, a disciple, with Jesus as her teacher. Once again, we are reminded of the fact that there are no set categories for who can be a disciple in this story of Jesus. The juxtaposition of the male disciples, Peter and the Beloved Disciple, with Mary, like Nicodemus with the Samaritan woman at the well, confirms that it will not be the usual suspects taking part in this ministry of Jesus. Furthermore, the balancing of male and female potential disciples offers testimony to the theology of incarnation. The characters themselves give witness to what could otherwise be an improbability or fancy. It is another means by which the narrative itself and how it is told underscores its theological assumptions at work.

Verse 17 has always been a puzzling text for interpreters and preachers of John. Why was Mary holding on to him? Is this a literal or figurative holding? Given the previous tendencies of this Gospel toward misunderstanding and ambiguity, it is likely both. Yet, why provide this detail in the first place? What is Jesus meaning by asking this question? What is Mary holding on to, besides, perhaps, him? The incarnation? What are we? Of what are we being asked to let go? A theological answer to these questions would focus on the certainty that that which becomes flesh must eventually go away. One of the striking aspects of this Gospel, typically overlooked because of the assumption of its "high Christology" is the certitude that the revelation of God in Jesus must end. This unique expression of God, this one and only period of history in which God entered our world as a human being, by definition cannot be forever. This may seem obvious, but is apt to be ignored when it comes to things about God. When Jesus says "Do not hold on to me," he is stating this truth, that the human condition deals every day with death. Jesus' words to Mary indicate that he knows exactly what this truth feels like. He knows what we know—the heartbreak of letting go; that moment when the one you loved is placed in the grave, never to be touched again; that anticipated anguish when you really will have to let go. We may forget that this is the second time Mary has had to say good bye. No wonder she wants to hold on to Jesus for dear life. "Please, Jesus, do not leave me again. I can't take it. I really can't."

It is important to note that Jesus' words of comfort that follow his command do not lie in the promise of the resurrection but in the future of the ascension. It is the ascension that is presented as that in which we can have hope. Yes, the resurrection means release from the grave, but it is the ascension that assures the promise of an abiding relationship with the Father. This abiding relationship with the Father, promised in 1:18 for all believers, is then affirmed by Jesus in his commission to Mary. Jesus does not tell Mary to share the fact that he has been raised from the dead, but rather that he is ascending "to my Father and your Father, to my God and your God." This is the promise. Jesus confirms that all of what he has shared about his relationship with the Father, which 1:18 said would happen, will be for every believer in his ascension. The incarnation will come full circle in Jesus' return to the Father.

Mary's announcement to the disciples of what she experienced in the garden has great significance for this Gospel and for preaching. She does not offer the disciples a third-person, impersonal, doctrinal statement about Jesus' resurrection, much like our liturgical responses at Easter, "Christ is risen! He is risen indeed! Alleluia!" Rather, it is a first-person testimony, a witness to what she has experienced. She gives voice again to that which is so critical for this Gospel, one's own experience and encounter with Jesus so as to recognize who Jesus is. Mary's proclamation is not only a witness to her encounter with the resurrected Jesus but also an interpretation of it. She realizes that for Jesus to be raised from the dead is also an assertion about her own resurrection, her own future. The first-person statement is simultaneously an announcement about what she saw and a statement of belief in her promise of future life with Jesus and with God.

We can also imagine this first witness to the resurrection as an invitation to what preaching can and should be, especially when it comes to preaching the Gospel of John. We stand at the back of the church when the service is over, greeting our people, shaking hands, and say "thank you" to the typical comments we receive about our sermons, "nice sermon, pastor" or "good sermon, pastor." What if our preaching was such that the reaction of the listeners was as Mary's, "pastor, I saw the Lord!" This is exactly what the Gospel of John imagines when it comes to sermons on its story of Jesus. Anything less would not take the incarnation seriously. The incarnation is not just a theological principle, but the very theological premise that undergirds the interpretation and proclamation of this Gospel. As discussed in the Introduction, John invites the preaching of this Gospel to create moments of direct encounter with Jesus so that one cannot help but react with a tangible, personal, and embodied experience of the Jesus who has been "reincarnated" in the sermon.

CONNECTIONS TO THE LECTIONARY

In all three lectionary years, John 20:1-18 is offered as an alternative to the Synoptic resurrection stories (Matt. 28:1-10; Mark 16:1-8; Luke 24:1-12). The challenge for the preacher, of course, is when to choose to preach on John, given that all three years are adequately covered by Matthew, Mark, and Luke. There could be a number of options for the preacher. The preacher might simply choose to preach John on occasion. Another route could be putting John in conversation with the accounts offered by the Synoptics. A third choice would encourage the preacher to infuse John's story of Jesus' revelation to Mary into other preaching on this Gospel. Mary Magdalene's encounter in the garden with the resurrected Jesus is too important to relegate it to an alternative option when it comes to the meaning of the resurrection for John

John 20:19-23
Jesus and the Disciples:
The Second Resurrection Appearance

Whereas most commentaries locate these verses in the larger pericope of 20:19-31, typically entitled "Doubting Thomas," it is helpful for preaching to separate Jesus' appearance to the disciples absent Thomas from his appearance with Thomas present (20:24-31) as two separate resurrection events. Since Mary, the time of day has changed "evening on that day, the first day of the week," nighttime on Sunday. We should anticipate by now that "it is evening" is not simply indicating the time of day. The disciples are in darkness, having yet to believe or understand the events of the last three days. Jesus' appearance is not only his physical presence but yet another instance of the light shining in the darkness. In this setting, the astonishment at Jesus' arrival is heightened, as if entering a room when the doors are locked was not enough. Most English translations insert a particular place for the location of the disciples, either a room or a house, but the Greek text gives no such reference to a specific site. A translation that more accurately depicts what is described here would be something like, "the doors being shut where the disciples were." While this may seem like an insignificant translation issue, the occurrence of the term *door* here is meant to recall specifically chapter 10, where Jesus says, "I AM the door." The commentary on chapter 10 argued that the image of Jesus as door is every bit an image of life as that of Jesus as shepherd. Jesus will once again be both "door" and "shepherd" at his arrest in chapter 18, standing between the disciples and the soldiers who have come to take him away, at the entrance to the garden. He is the Good Shepherd by first laying down his life, giving himself up in that moment for the sake of the sheep. He is the door by protecting his sheep. Both images are critical for how Jesus is presented and what Jesus provides in chapter 10, at his arrest in chapter 18, and now here at the resurrection appearance to the gathered disciples.

The absence of a specific place or location for the disciples calls attention to the locked doors. Because Jesus is the door, he can enter this unspecified space. The promises Jesus reveals as the door of the sheep in chapter 10 should be brought forward to this moment. It is first in connection with himself as the door that Jesus announced the promise of abundant life (10:10). Abundant life has just entered the "room." Moreover, it will be in this moment that Jesus will bestow on the disciples abundant life now in the gift of the Holy Spirit.

As argued previously in this commentary, it is important to translate and understand the fear of the disciples as directed to the Jewish leaders and not the Jewish people. The disciples, like the parents of the man born blind, have every right to be afraid of the Jewish leaders at this point. The disciples have been associated with Jesus—in the case of Peter, his discipleship questioned—and at the very least they could be the targets of the same fate as the blind man, being thrown out of the synagogue or, worse, the same fate as Jesus.

For all intents and purposes, this is John's Great Commission (Matthew 28). Jesus' first words to the disciples are "Peace be with you." Clearly, the presence of peace would calm the disciples in their moment of fear, but the promise of peace also recalls Jesus' words from the Farewell Discourse, "Peace I leave with you; my peace I give to you. I do not give to you as the world gives. Do not let your hearts be troubled, and do not let them be afraid" (14:27). Peace has already been associated with or connected to the work of the Spirit, thereby foreshadowing the giving of the Spirit in the very next verse. The invitation to peace here in the midst of the troubled emotions of the disciples following Jesus' death mirrors Jesus' gift of peace as he begins to describe his departure in the Farewell Discourse. This underscores one of the primary functions or activities of the Spirit, as Comforter, another way to translate *paraklētos*. The Holy Spirit is not merely described *as* the Comforter but is present to *give* comfort during the most intense periods of distress in the lives of the disciples. "But because I have said these things to you, sorrow has filled your hearts" (16:6). The link between this resurrection appearance and the Farewell Discourse suggests that the entirety of Jesus' words of comfort expressed throughout those chapters in which he says good-bye are also applicable in this instant.

This resurrection appearance to the disciples narrates a crucial moment in John, the giving of the Holy Spirit, the *paraklētos* described most completely in the Farewell Discourse. Verse 22 reports the actual giving of the Holy Spirit, John's Pentecost. Only in Year A, however, is this text offered as a preaching option for Pentecost Sunday (20:19-23). Years B and C suggest readings from the Farewell Discourse that describe the activity of the Holy Spirit according to John (15:26-27; 16:4b-15, Year B; 14:8-17, (25-27), Year C). As discussed in chapter 8 on the Farewell Discourse, John offers a portrait of the Holy Spirit that is very different from that of Acts 2, and the giving of the Spirit is equally distinctive in the Fourth Gospel. In contrast to the excitement and verbosity of Luke's Pentecost, John's is quiet, intimate, and personal, much like the nature of the Holy Spirit in the Gospel of John. The actual giving of the Holy Spirit matches the character of its role and work according to John.

There is a critical translation issue in verse 22. Whereas most translations say, "Jesus breathed *on* them" the verb used here, *emphysaō*, should be translated, "Jesus breathed *into* them." English speakers will realize the etymological connection between this Greek verb and the word "emphysema," for example.

This is the same word that is used in the Septuagint in Genesis 2:7, "Then the Lord God formed man from the dust of the ground, and breathed into his nostrils the breath of life; and the man became a living being." It is also the verb used in Ezekiel 37:9, "Then he said to me, 'Prophesy to the breath, prophesy, mortal, and say to the breath: Thus says the Lord GOD: Come from the four winds, O breath, and breathe upon these slain, that they may live.'" (Ezek 37:9) The connection between the creation of the first human being, that the earth creature became a living being because of God's very breath, and the giving of the Spirit to the disciples cannot be overstated. This resurrection appearance is a moment of re-creation, of new birth, of abundant life, of becoming children of God (1:12-13). It further emphasizes the multiple allusions throughout the Gospel to Genesis and the beginning, creation, humanity, relationship, and the creative activity of both God and the Word. That the Holy Spirit is both called alongside us and breathed into us also heightens the intimacy between God, Jesus, and the believer. The mutual abiding (15:4) is both an intimate existing in the presence of each other and, we now realize, God's very breath inside of us. It does not get more intimate than that.

In this moment, Jesus' many words in the Farewell Discourse begin to make sense. It is worthwhile to reread the entire Farewell Discourse again with verse 22 as a lens. How is it possible that the disciples will do greater works than these? (14:12). Because they will be possessed with and empowered by the very Spirit of God. How will believers keep the commandments of Jesus? (14:15). How will the disciples bear much fruit? (15:8). How will I lay down my life for my friends? (15:13). How will we continue to testify to the Word made flesh? (15:27). Looking forward, how will it be possible to be the Good Shepherd when Jesus returns to the Father (21:15-19), to feed and tend Jesus' lambs not yet of this fold? (10:16). All of these activities of discipleship, especially looking toward the future departure of Jesus to the Father, are thinkable and doable only with the breath of God. Furthermore, it is because of the inbreathing of the Spirit that it is possible to be sent. A marked contrast to the Synoptic Gospels, Jesus' disciples are never sent out anywhere in the story until now. Sending can only happen with the security of the Spirit. Or, that Jesus is fully aware of the temporariness of his time on earth, cannot bear to be apart from the disciples he loves. In either case, Jesus cannot be alone, nor can the disciples, when it comes to being in the world.

Verse 23 is one of the more puzzling texts in John's Gospel, primarily because of how the concept of "sin" has been understood and presented. As discussed above, for the fourth evangelist sin is not a category of morality but a category of relationship, depicting a lack of relationship with God or unbelief in Jesus as the Word made flesh. This wider context makes "sins" in the plural bewildering to interpret, yet given that the Gospel has already laid out a case for how sin should be viewed, Jesus' command here should be located in the larger argument for sin in the Gospel. With this in mind, Jesus' words are a charge to the disciples that a significant act of discipleship will be tending the belief of others. This tending will first include forgiving those who do not believe. This is a poignant request, in view of the reality of the Johannine community and its assumed existence outside of its known community. To what extent is Jesus asking them to forgive their former community, not only for not believing in Jesus but also for the excommunication of those who believe? The retentions of sins, therefore, would have to do with preventing belief, discouraging belief, or not nurturing belief in the other. It is helpful to ground this claim in the themes of friendship and loving one another. There is no reason to think that the mutual abiding and intimacy between God and Jesus and believers should not exist between believers.

CONNECTIONS TO THE LECTIONARY

John 20:19-23 is one of two Johannine texts (7:37-39) suggested for the celebration of Pentecost in Year A. Of course, it is up against a selection of texts that offer equally compelling views of the Holy Spirit. The preacher is forced to make a choice of who the Spirit needs to be and what the Spirit needs to do on this Sunday, at this time and space, for the sake of a specific community of faith. John's pneumatological vision may very well not be the most pressing image on a given Pentecost Sunday. The preacher must decide, for the sake of the hearers, which function of the Spirit means the most in this moment of a congregation's life. It may not be John's presentation of the Spirit, but to attend to John's particular portrait of the Spirit suggests that somewhere down the road the preacher will be able to draw on this understanding of who the Holy Spirit is and will be able to minister in congregational life with a renewed specificity of the meaning of the Paraclete.

JOHN 20:24-31
JESUS AND THOMAS:
THE THIRD RESURRECTION APPEARANCE

We do not find out until verse 24 that Thomas was not present when the risen Jesus appeared to the disciples huddled behind locked doors. This detail, of course, informs us of Thomas's absence, which then signals the next resurrection appearance in the story. More importantly, however, it intimates once again the essentiality of having one's own experience of the risen Christ, which the first resurrection appearance to Mary has already indicated. Mary's confession, "I have seen the Lord," foreshadows the episode with Thomas. Verse 24 transitions the story from the disciples to Thomas himself. This transition is significant because it again moves to the individual encounter with Jesus and gives the disciples the opportunity to offer their own testimony, using the same words as Mary, "we have seen the Lord!" Mary's words are a template for response to one's encounter with the resurrected Jesus. The disciples' witness is not an all-purpose statement of Christ being raised from the dead but is personalized. With this in mind, the response of Thomas makes complete sense. He must have his own experience of the risen Jesus. He states the truth of this Gospel, that in order to be in a relationship with Jesus, to know Jesus, one must experience a one-on-one encounter. Thomas's stipulations are not criteria for believing in the resurrection. They are utterances of what is absolutely necessary for a relationship with an incarnated God. That Thomas wants to touch Jesus, to place his finger in the mark of the nails and in Jesus' side where he was pierced underscores the incarnation and looks ahead to Thomas's confession in 20:28. What needs to be revealed in these resurrection appearances cannot only be Jesus' divinity, but also Jesus' humanity.

Thomas gets to say what we all want to say, the truth of what we do not want to admit, how difficult it is to believe in Jesus whom we have never encountered for ourselves. This Gospel realizes this problem (20:30-31) and has included an exemplary story that acknowledges this challenge. A preacher might begin with the conclusion of the Thomas story, (20:30-31) so as to call attention to this primary theme—that Thomas is for all of those, us included, who will not see Jesus but are invited to believe or encouraged to continue to believe. The scene with the disciples is then repeated for the sake of Thomas, with the same setting and even the same words from Jesus. This identical setting and saying underscore Thomas's desire. Thomas needs what the disciples themselves experienced. Anything less would call into question the importance of a personal encounter with Jesus and would discredit Thomas's request.

Verse 27 is remarkably ambiguous. Did Thomas do as Jesus asked? Or, was seeing Jesus in the flesh enough for his confession? The narrative is not clear and invites an individuality of encounter for every believer. What each believer, each disciple, will require for recognition of Jesus' identity will differ. Is seeing enough? Hearing? Touching? What do you need to believe? Once again, the particularity and specificity of the incarnation are honored and upheld, for God and for believers. To take the incarnation seriously means that a "cookie-cutter" belief will not suffice. Most people in the pews will know this story, at least by its colloquial and mainstream title of "Doubting Thomas." This story has taken on a life of its own, much like that of the Good Samaritan (Luke 10) and the Prodigal Son (Luke 15). These parables, along with this story of our dear friend Thomas, have entered into our daily life and dialogue with little knowledge of their literary context. "Don't be a Doubting Thomas" will certainly be floating around in the minds of many without any sense of the origins or meaning of the saying. This is the preacher's opportunity to locate this popular expression in its rightful narrative and theological contexts, inviting both a reevaluation of the words we use and, more importantly, a reexamination of this story and its primary character on its own terms.

At the heart of Thomas's plight is an issue of translation. Most English Bibles render Jesus' words to Thomas as "do not doubt but believe." The actual word used here is *apistos*, literally "unbelieving." To translate *apistos* as "doubt" brings with it connotations that are not at all present or implied in what it means to be unbelieving in the Gospel of John. Our discussion up to this point has repeatedly emphasized the meaning of belief in the Fourth Gospel, that it is a category of relationship. The primary definition of the term *doubt*, however, has to do with uncertainty. Uncertainty, as a category of belief, does not really exist in the Fourth Gospel. One is either certain or not certain; in the light or in the dark. Jesus invites Thomas to move from darkness to light, from a lack of relationship to intimacy. There is no middle ground when it comes to believing in Jesus.

Preaching this text necessitates admitting that this Gospel does not deal with doubt. This is not the same as saying faith does not include doubt. The stakes, however, for John are such that intimacy is too important, whether that of the former community of which you were a part or the present one in Jesus. To be in between is to be alone, on your own, without the presence of others, neither in one place or the other. This void is not only not desirable; it is not even possible if we truly understand what it means to be human. To be human necessitates relationship. This extreme dichotomy for John of either/or is not a matter of exclusion but a radical claim about inclusion. John is naming the truth about the incarnation, that to be incarnated demands relationship. As a result, you are either in one community or another, but you cannot be *not* in community. Life, especially abundant life, is dependent on the reality of multiple expressions of connectivity and belonging, whether that be one-on-one or in various sizes of communities.

That life cannot be imagined outside of intimacy is at the heart of this Gospel, stated clearly in 1:1. Even God was not alone in the beginning, because the Word was with God. Even God cannot be without being in relationship. To interpret the apparent individualism in this Gospel as a personal assent to the teachings and preachings of Jesus would be a theological affront. The God of John has no concept of individuality and can be expressed only by radical intimacy and connectivity. This is the claim of 1:1 and does not let go, given further dimension and depth by the understanding and presentation of the purpose and function of the Holy Spirit.

The testimony of Thomas in verse 28 is the ultimate witness to who Jesus is according to the Fourth Gospel. Jesus is both Lord, emphasizing his humanity, his role as Rabbi, and his earthly ministry, and God. To assert Jesus as Lord *and* God is to hold together what was maintained in the Prologue, the humanity and divinity of Jesus. It is another way to express this primary juxtaposition and dichotomy. What is also important to note in the confession of Thomas is the use of the possessive pronoun "my." The personalization of one's realization of and belief in Jesus is not intended to support an individualized theology but rather accentuates the intimacy that this Gospel imagines between the believer and Jesus. Intimacy happens on many levels, but most concretely and visibly one-on-one. While this may be understood as an over-personalized believer–savior relationship and could be preached in such a way as to suggest that one's relationship with Jesus is not sufficient without claiming Jesus as your personal Lord and Savior, to do so would be preaching antithetically to the communal impulse of the Fourth Gospel. To give witness to a personal relationship with Jesus is immediately to enter into a community of intimacy, between Jesus, God, the Paraclete, and the believer and between the believer and the new community, the flock, that Jesus as the Word made flesh has made possible for the world. Thomas's confession is simultaneously an affirmation of his own recognition of the origin and identity of Jesus and an understanding of his membership in the community of believers. Thomas's confession also testifies to the interconnectedness of the origin, relationship with, and identity of Jesus set out in the Prologue. Thomas is now "with them" (20:24). Once again, a seemingly straightforward confession or witness demands multiple expressions, approaches, and possibilities of meaning. "My Lord and my God" is true at its literal level but invites manifold manifestations of possibility as complex as the human being itself.

Verse 29 is frequently interpreted and preached as a scolding by Jesus directed to Thomas for his inability to believe without seeing. The above discussion was meant to counteract such impulsive and compliant reactions. The verse holds together the magnitude of Thomas's decision. Thomas is on his own, to know and experience Jesus so as to come to believe, but Jesus also directs his response to persons beyond Thomas, to those who have not seen and yet might believe. The reader of this Gospel, the communities that are reading or hearing this Gospel, should immediately imagine that Jesus' comments are directed to them, to us. This is the understated power of this Gospel, that it imagines at every turn speaking to its contemporary audience and its future listeners, that is, its present hearers. This Gospel has to imagine a community beyond its own on the basis of one of its central verses, "For God so loved *the world*" (3:16). That community is us, its present-day readers, further clarified in 20:30-31.

John 20:30-31 has long been described as the "real" conclusion to the Gospel, with the result that chapter 21 has been relegated to an epilogue having little connection to the rest of the narrative. The commentary on chapter 21 will show that this fourth and final resurrection appearance is critical to the story and has multiple themes in common with the entirety of the Gospel. As a result, 20:30-31 is best understood as the conclusion to the resurrection appearances of chapter 20 and not the conclusion to the entire Gospel. The primary reason for thinking that these verses end the Gospel tends to be verse 30, "Now Jesus did many other signs in the presence of his disciples, which are not written in this book."

With that in mind, Verses 30-31 reinterpret the entirety of chapter 20, particularly Mary's resurrection confession. Mary's witness to the resurrected Jesus, "I have seen the Lord," is her own experience but does not preclude others, such as present-day readers, from believing though not having literally seen the Lord. Mary's experience upsets any emphasis on seeing alone, because her first recognition of the resurrected Jesus was located in hearing and not seeing. Essentially, verses 30-31 affirm that readers of this Gospel may not have their own experience with the resurrected Jesus and that is the primary reason why this Gospel is written. Even without a direct encounter with Jesus, the hearing of this narrative is meant to create the experience of the Word made flesh, so real, so close, so present, that one is then placed in the same position as those who experienced the incarnated Jesus. That Jesus performed many other signs that the author of John's Gospel did not record in his story of Jesus is another indication or example of abundance. The seven signs included in the narrative are but seven out of many more, intimating that Jesus' revelation was not only located in these seven signs. Jesus is capable of more miracles than the ones that John decided to include.

As discussed previously, verses 30-31 function as the central purpose and function of the Fourth Gospel. There is an important textual variant in verse 31 that will be noticed in any translation comparison. Translations will render the verse either as "in order that you may come to believe" or "in order that you may continue to believe." The question at hand is the tense of the verb *pisteuō*, "to believe." The verb occurs in a *hina* clause, which means that the mood of the verb is automatically subjunctive. The issue is whether it is an aorist subjunctive, "come to believe," or a present subjunctive, "continue to believe." There is equal external manuscript evidence to argue for either. An argument from internal evidence also yields the same result. At the same time, from the perspective of internal evidence, there is a both/and possibility when imagining how to interpret this variant for preaching these verses. If we recall the perceived audience of this Gospel, a community that has been excommunicated from its synagogue for believing in and following Jesus, then the present tense rendering would be critical. This community would need to hear that this Gospel was written for the purpose of their encouragement, to nurture and sustain them in their faith. To hear this story of Jesus would provide comfort and hope in the midst of loss and uncertainty. The purpose of this Gospel to sustain and nurture faith also mirrors its primary presentation of God as the one who provides everything we need for life. All that is needed for sustenance, for life, God gives. The Gospel's purpose, therefore, underscores one of its primary theological claims.

At the same time, an aorist reading of *pisteuō* can equally be supported internally. The theme of and invitation to witness, by definition a public proclamation of belief, is very much present throughout the Gospel, perhaps most explicitly stated in 3:16, "for God so loved the world." The first overt words that express the centrality of witness for discipleship were Jesus' words to the disciples after his conversation with the Samaritan woman at the well, "see how the fields are ripe for harvesting" (4:35-38). In the Farewell Discourse, Jesus shared that a major role of discipleship is to be sent into this world God loves. A central focus of the resurrection appearances has been Jesus' commission to the disciples, "As the Father has sent me, so I send you" (20:21).

This sending, this mission into the world, is for the sake of invitation to belief, that by hearing these words and the witness of the disciples, others will then "come to believe," thereby having a relationship with the Good Shepherd because there are other sheep that are not of this fold (10:16). This Gospel holds out both of these possibilities in its purpose, the possibility of sustenance and nurture of faith as well as the potential for faith. Preaching on this text means that these same purposes are kept in mind and re-created in the sermon.

As noted above, the power and strength of these words have led many scholars to conclude that this is the true ending of the Gospel, with chapter 21 being a kind of epilogue. There are two problems with this interpretation. First, to designate these final verses of chapter 20 as the ending of the Gospel as a whole ignores their important function as the conclusion to the resurrection appearances narrated in chapter 20. The emphasis on believing throughout these resurrection appearances is summarized in 20:31. Second, there is no external manuscript evidence that the Gospel of John ever circulated without chapter 21. That is, it does not appear that chapter 21 was tacked on at some later point of editing; it was always integral to the entirety of the narrative. As a result, it should be interpreted as part of the larger whole and as the true final chapter to the Gospel. To that we now turn.

CONNECTIONS TO THE LECTIONARY

John 20:19-31 is always the Gospel lesson for the Second Sunday of Easter in all three lectionary years. This consistency is both a blessing and a curse in that the preacher is asked to engage this text each and every year and always the Sunday after Easter. That is, it is a gift to be able to return to a text year after year, anticipating its return, and wondering how you might respond for the sake of the place, people, and purpose in which you are called to preach. At the same time, that return elicits a sense of dread in most preachers. What, if anything, is there new to say about this well-known and oft-quoted story? Perhaps its repetition and its consistent placement as the Gospel lesson for the Sunday after Easter are a lectionary blessing. It forces preachers to approach the text with a renewed sense of discovery. Once again, the entirety of the text need not be preached. The commentary above was meant to bracket out its sections so as to focus its themes for preaching. As this is the text for every Sunday after Easter, the preacher might catalogue the breadth and depth of the text so as to imagine not one but manifold sermons on this story. Even "doubting" Thomas is a multifaceted character who embodies multiple responses to Jesus' revelation.

JOHN 21
JESUS AND PETER:
THE FOURTH RESURRECTION APPEARANCE

Jesus' appearance to the disciples on the shores of the Sea of Tiberius, another name for the Sea of Galilee, in the last chapter of the Gospel of John contains multiple resonances with themes throughout the entire narrative. The disciples have returned to their day job, fishing. It is into the ordinariness of life that Jesus reveals himself once again. We are provided with a list of names of the disciples present, including Nathanael of Cana in Galilee. The only other time Nathanael is mentioned in the Gospel of John is in his relatively prominent role in the calling of the first disciples (1:45-49). Nathanael's reappearance here in the last chapter of the Gospel anticipates that the story that follows will be about discipleship. The reference to Cana calls to mind the location of Jesus' first sign, turning water into wine. As a result, we are meant to interpret what will happen in this chapter with Cana in view. There will be another sign of abundance, an abundance of fish in this case, and now here a miracle of grace upon grace from the *resurrected* Jesus.

Peter's declaration is humorous in its matter-of-fact tone. "Well then. I guess I will go fishing." The other disciples decide to join him and they board the boats, heading out into the sea. The comedy in this opening scene of the chapter is worth attention because it communicates a theological claim that will become more clear in the conversation between Peter and Jesus. Peter and the disciples want to go back to being "regular" disciples, but the ascension of Jesus will necessitate a reevaluation of what discipleship means. We are familiar with the calling of the disciples in the Synoptic Gospels as they are fishing (cf. Matt. 4:18-22; Mark 1:16-20; Luke 5:1-11). The calling of the disciples in John is different, as discussed in chapter 2. Yet we might understand this episode of the resurrected Jesus appearing to the disciples when they are fishing as a new call to discipleship. The resurrected Jesus will elevate discipleship to a new height. What the disciples thought about discipleship before needs a rebirth.

The disciples go out into the boats and catch nothing. It is not an accident that their fishing expedition occurs at night. As we have noted throughout this commentary, night or darkness symbolizes the realm of unbelief, and day or light the realm of belief. The detail that Jesus stands on the shore at daybreak points to the possibility of what now might be seen, realized, and believed. Jesus is still the light and it will be in light that the moment of recognition will happen. Jesus states the obvious, "You didn't catch anything, did you?," with the disciples equally obvious response, "You got that right." This brief interaction postpones the moment of realization and reminds us of the critical role that conversation and dialogue have in coming to believe in who Jesus is. Jesus again states what should be painfully evident. "Did you try the other side of the boat?" There is an honesty and openness here for which the disciples have long asked, a desire for plain speech. Now, they catch an abundance of fish. When the Beloved Disciple says, "It is the Lord!," we realize that it is in Jesus' demonstration of abundance, a sign of grace upon grace, that the moment of recognizing Jesus happens. This provides a powerful preaching moment. The resurrected Christ will be seen in displays of abundance. The ascended Christ will be known when his disciples establish opportunities to experience abundant grace. Peter's eager response also contributes to the humor of the scene and at the same time creates a potent juxtaposition to the poignancy that will be Jesus' questioning of Peter only verses later.

The details of the charcoal fire recall the narration of Peter's denial in the trial narrative, the only other time the mention of a charcoal fire occurs in the Gospel (18:18). As a result, these two episodes need to be interpreted side by side. Peter once again will be questioned as to whether or not he is a disciple. As noted in chapter 9, there is a significant difference between the trial of Peter in John and in the Synoptic Gospels. Whereas in the Synoptic Gospels, Peter is asked if he knows Jesus, in the Gospel of John it is Peter's discipleship that is questioned. "Aren't you one of his disciples? No, I am not." Here again, Peter's discipleship will be put on trial, this time by Jesus, because the meaning of discipleship is redirected and reimagined in light of the death and resurrection of Jesus.

In verse 11 we are reminded of the abundance of fish that the disciples caught in their nets. The details are meant to underscore the fact that this is yet another revelation of the abundance that God provides. Peter has to "haul" (21:6) the net ashore, "dragging" and "drawing" emphasizing the size of the catch (cf. 6:44; 12:32; 18:10). The five details of abundance are reminiscent of the wedding at Cana, where there were six jars, twenty to thirty gallons, filled to the brim, of the best wine—and at the end of the wedding feast, not the beginning, when you least expect it. In chapter 21, the net has to be hauled to the shore, it is full of large fish, 153 of them, and, though there were so many, the net was not torn. The layers of details make certain that we not overlook that Jesus' provision in the midst of resurrection and ascension will be the same as that which he provided in his incarnated life. At the same time, there is something remarkably ordinary about this story. Jesus invites them to have breakfast, "come and eat," recalling the same words he first said to the disciples, "come and see." It is again an emphasis on the fully embodied reality of grace. Grace tastes like an abundance of wine and an abundance of fish. The fourth evangelist brackets the Gospel with miracles of abundance that illustrate grace upon grace by taste.

Verse 13 suggests that this last meal of Jesus and his disciples on the shores of the Sea of Galilee should also call to mind the feeding of the five thousand with five loaves of bread and two fish. The important point about the feeding of the five thousand in the Gospel of John is not only the miraculous event of feeding that many people but that it is Jesus himself who does the feeding, not the disciples. Moreover, as Jesus explains in the discourse that follows the sign, he himself is the bread of life. This revelation and truth are thus carried forward to this last meal, where Jesus hosts his disciples for breakfast, giving them the bread and the fish. The promise is certain that what Jesus has provided during his earthly ministry he will also provide after the incarnation is over. Once again, there is an unending quality to Jesus' ministry that points to the theme of abundance. The abundance, the grace upon grace, manifested throughout Jesus' ministry is not located during the time frame of the incarnation alone, but is promised and possible even beyond the event of the ascension because it is a primary characteristic of God for the fourth evangelist. That the God of the Gospel of John is a God of provision and sustenance is glimpsed here and now in the presence of Jesus and will be known more in our own abiding with the Father.

The threefold question and answer dialogue between Peter and Jesus is critical for understanding what discipleship means for the fourth evangelist (21:15-19). The connection between this post-resurrection affirmation and the pre-crucifixion denial highlights the magnitude of what Jesus is asking of Peter. Chapter 9 discussed the important difference in Peter's denial in John compared to the Synoptic Gospels. In John, Peter does not deny Jesus or knowing Jesus, but he denies his discipleship. Jesus will now reveal to Peter what discipleship demands.

Interpretations of this passage in John tend to reduce the interaction to Jesus' forgiveness of Peter, Peter's reinstatement as a disciple, or Peter's rehabilitation after a failure of loyalty. None of these summaries adequately recognizes the significance of Jesus' request of Peter. Peter is not simply restored to his role as disciple, but he will have to imagine discipleship in an entirely different way.

The language present in this dialogue pulls in multiple moments in the Gospel. The question "Do you love me?" recalls how Jesus expresses what love means in the Farewell Discourse by using two available terms for "love," *agapaō* and *phileō.* "There is no greater love than to lay down one's life for one's friends." This is the only other time outside of chapter 10 that the image of shepherd and sheep is used in the Gospel. Jesus essentially asks Peter to be the good shepherd for the sake of God's love for the world when Jesus cannot be. Jesus will ascend to the Father, from where he came, so the demands of discipleship take on a more acute and critical role. In other words, Jesus is asking Peter to be the "I AM" in the world. He is revealing to Peter that discipleship will demand the same price that he paid, alluding to Peter's death (20:19).

To be the "I AM" in the world may seem initially like an overstatement, even blasphemous. God is the one and only "I AM" and Jesus was the "I AM" because the Word was God. In part, this is true, because only God can be God and only God can be God's presence in the world. Yet, for the Gospel of John, discipleship has to be more that modeling Jesus or thinking "what would Jesus do?" The understanding of discipleship presented in the Fourth Gospel relies on the theological promise of the incarnation. It takes the incarnation seriously so much so that the combination of our humanity and the inbreathing of the Spirit of God means that we do indeed embody the presence of God in the absence of Jesus. This does not mean that we are God. It means that God relies on us, on disciples, to witness in the world God loves, with the entirety of our beings. This concept of discipleship underscores the oneness and unity of which Jesus' spoke in the Farewell Discourse.

John 14:12, "you will do greater works than these," also serves as the backdrop of Jesus' commands for Peter. That promise of Jesus made to the disciples sounds unbelievable and impossible. The response to Jesus' projection is something like that of Nicodemus's to Jesus, "How can these things be?" The fulfillment of this promise lies in this embodied sense of God's ongoing presence in the world. That we, as disciples, might achieve greater works than what Jesus did in his ministry is yet another way of underscoring God's abundance, which carries over after the end of the incarnation. On an outer wall of the Primacy of Peter chapel on the shores of the Sea of Galilee that marks this event in Jesus' life is a plaque that summarizes John 14:12, "The deeds and miracles of Jesus are not actions of the past. Jesus is waiting for those who are still prepared to take risks at His word because they trust His power utterly." Indeed, Jesus' acts of his ministry cannot be relegated to the incarnation. The acts of God in the world count on the witness of our incarnated lives. This is Peter's call to risk, but risk is only remotely possible when there is some semblance of safety.

Commentators generally understand 21:18-19 as referring to Peter's martyrdom. This seems little in doubt, especially given the direct reference in verse 18. Yet the verse is not merely about the death of Peter but is laden with multiple themes and issues related to discipleship. Perhaps the most striking image portrayed in these two short verses is that the means by which Peter will die seems to be like that of Jesus, crucifixion. Regardless of the method, however, the expectation of death draws on Jesus' words to the disciples in the Farewell Discourse, "no greater love than to lay down one's life for one's friends" (15:13). Here, Jesus confirms this aspect of discipleship as no euphemism but every bit true.

There is a certain honesty and directness in Jesus' words here for which the disciples have longed and asked. The speeches of Jesus throughout the Gospel have been less than clear at times or have moved from ambiguity and misunderstanding to more clarity in the course of the conversation. Jesus' forthrightness with Peter at this moment should invite interpretation, particularly its location here and now in the story. Why is Jesus more comprehensible in this final resurrection appearance compared to the rest of the Gospel? It is a touching moment, a tangible vulnerability in naming the plight of the human condition—death. It is a moment of truth-telling from Truth itself. But it is also a candor that is told by the crucified and resurrected Jesus. The disciples can only hear that they will go where they do not wish on this side of the cross and from the promise of the resurrection.

Verse 19 connects Peter's death to having the same result as Jesus' death did, the glorification of God. That this final resurrection appearance of Jesus seeks to connect to what discipleship means is then affirmed by Jesus' next words to Peter, "Follow me." To follow Jesus will be to follow in the death of Jesus. This is not unlike the command to "take up your cross and follow me" that we see in the Synoptic Gospels. Yet, given the trajectory of the revelation of Jesus, "follow me" will not end on the cross. It will be to the resurrection, and particularly for this Gospel, to the ascension, and to abiding with the Father.

Verse 20 reminds us one last time of the disciple whom Jesus loved. The fourth evangelist makes certain we remember that he was the one who reclined on the bosom of Jesus (13:23). In addition, the concept of betrayal is once again raised. Why here and why now? This close to the end of the Gospel, it has the effect of reinforcing what is at stake for the Fourth Gospel. As discussed previously in this commentary, to betray Jesus is not to hand him over but not to believe. The focus on betrayal at this point serves to underscore that not to follow Jesus is to betray Jesus. That the Beloved Disciple comes on the scene at this moment also intimates that at this point, the hearer, the reader imagines her- or himself as being directly addressed. The discussion of the identity and interpretation of the Beloved Disciple in chapter 8 argued that the Beloved Disciple represents the reader or in the case of the first audience, the hearer. The disciple whom Jesus loved is each and every one of us. It is curious that Peter seems to be worried about the fate of his fellow disciple, specifically if he will meet the same end as Peter. This odd interchange functions as a way to highlight that it is one's own relationship with Jesus about which to be concerned. However, the theme of the individual believer's encounter and relationship with Jesus has been central to this Gospel and necessitates one final reminder before the story comes to its close.

The introduction to this commentary discussed the question of authorship of the Fourth Gospel and noted the case for the Beloved Disciple as the author. The primary internal evidence for this reading is 21:24. However, 21:24 can be interpreted on its own merit and not just as proof of Johannine authorship, both on the basis of its location in the narrative and the overall Johannine themes reiterated. There are two important aspects of this verse that at this juncture in the story function as key prompts as the Gospel ends. First, the theme of testimony, so prevalent throughout the narrative, returns. We discover that the entire Gospel itself is witness, is testimony, to Jesus' ministry, to the Word made flesh. In this sense, even the Gospel's genre is called into question. What exactly is the nature of this story of Jesus? As it turns out, for the fourth evangelist, perhaps the "Gospel" according to John is not the most accurate description of how he imagines what his story of Jesus has been. Whereas Mark is clear from the beginning about what his account of Jesus' ministry is: "The beginning of the good news of Jesus Christ, the Son of God" (Mark 1:1), the idea of good news, *euangelion*, is not a prevalent feature in the Fourth Gospel as it seeks both to understand who Jesus is and to present what Jesus means. Perhaps, the Fourth Gospel is better entitled, "the Testimony about Jesus According to John." Second, the emphasis on testimony here carries this theme to the very end of the Gospel and invites a rereading of the Gospel through the lens of this understanding of what this story is. It encourages a reevaluation of the function of this story and of its intended effect. That the concept of truth is connected to witness or testimony here has little to do with factual evaluation or the veracity of the witness in terms of historical proof or truth. That the disciple's witness is true must be interpreted against the background of how truth has been presented throughout the Gospel. That Jesus himself is the truth (14:6) suggests that the disciple's witness is true because it is giving testimony about the Truth. That is, to know Jesus as the Truth is to be in relationship with Jesus.

The final verse of the Gospel of John ends in abundance. There are so many other things Jesus did that not even the whole world would be able to contain the books that could be written. This Gospel began with abundant grace, the grace upon grace (1:16) that is given in the words and actions of Jesus, through the signs but, more importantly, through the abiding relationship with Jesus and God the Father. This emphasis on relationship is highlighted by the first person singular pronoun named as the witness (21:25). The personal relationship, the personal encounter with God in the flesh, is once again underscored by this personal confession. As the narrative comes to a close, we discover that this abundance of grace cannot be contained, neither by the end of this Gospel nor by the end of the incarnation. By definition, abundant grace cannot be drawn to a close or wrapped up in a tidy, literary, narrative conclusion. God's grace extends beyond the confines of this story and even beyond the limitations of the Word made flesh. If God can become human, then there are really no restraints or restrictions, no boundaries or borders that can in any way curb or control the extent of God's love . . . for God so loved the world.

CONNECTIONS TO THE LECTIONARY

The last chapter of John occurs only one time in the lectionary, Easter 3, Year C, and concludes the pericope at verse 19. At the same time, the preacher should allow this final resurrection appearance to shape interpretation of and preaching on the other resurrection appearances. This culminating scene between Jesus and his disciples, particularly Peter, lends a perspective on the entirety of what discipleship means in the Gospel of John. It may appear only once in the lectionary, but this story's effect on the whole should be ever present in preaching this Gospel. The final verses of John will not be heard by our congregations unless added onto the determined lections or brought into the preaching of other Johannine texts. Certainly, the last words of this narrative should be repeated at every utterance of abundance when it comes to this Gospel. Never to acknowledge, point to, reference, or quote these verses will truncate the Gospel's primary impulse, that God loves the world. Preaching the Gospel of John will always have in mind the Gospel's final words, lest the preacher think that the sermon is the final say or that the possibilities of this story have been exhausted. John's closing words are wise ones to the preachers charged with reincarnating the words of this Gospel. They are also words of promise so that every preacher of this story realizes that abundance lies beyond the sermon preached because it is entrusted to the grace upon grace of God.

Suggestions for Further Reading

Brown, Raymond E. *An Introduction to the Gospel of John*. Edited by Francis J. Moloney, S.D.B. Anchor Bible Reference Library. New York: Doubleday, 2003.

———. *The Gospel According to John: Introduction, Translation, and Notes*. 2 volumes. Anchor Bible 29, 29A. Garden City, NY: Doubleday, 1966.

Culpepper, R. Alan. *Anatomy of the Fourth Gospel: A Study in Literary Design*. Philadelphia: Fortress Press, 1983.

Fleer, David and Bland, Dave, eds. Preaching John's Gospel: The World It Imagines. St. Louis: Chalice Press, 2008

Koester, Craig R. *The Word of Life: A Theology of John's Gospel*. Grand Rapids: Eerdmans, 2008.

Kysar, Robert. *John*. Augsburg Commentary on the New Testament. Minneapolis: Augsburg Press, 1986.

———. *Preaching John*. Fortress Resources for Preaching. Minneapolis. Fortress Press, 2002.

Moloney, Francis J., SDB. *Love in the Gospel of John: An Exegetical, Theological, and Literary Study*. Grand Rapids: Baker Academic, 2013

O'Day, Gail. "The Gospel of John." In *The New Interpreter's Bible*, volume 9. Nashville: Abingdon, 1995.

Reinhartz, Adele. *Befriending the Beloved Disciple: A Jewish Reading of the Gospel of John*. New York and London: Continuum, 2003.

Schneiders, Sandra. *Written That You May Believe: Encountering Jesus in the Fourth Gospel*. New York: Crossroad, 1999.

Smith, Dwight Moody. *John*. Abingdon New Testament Commentaries. Nashville: Abingdon, 1999.

Thompson, Marianne Meye. *The God of the Gospel of John*. Grand Rapids: Eerdmans, 2001.

Williamson, Lamar, Jr. Preaching the Gospel of John. Louisville: Westminster/ John Knox Press, 2004.